BAPTISTS IN EUROPE:
History & Confessions of Faith

G. KEITH PARKER

BROADMAN PRESS
Nashville, Tennessee

© Copyright 1982 • BROADMAN PRESS
All rights reserved.
4265-64

ISBN: 0-8054-6564-2
Dewey Decimal Classification: 286.14
Subject Heading: BAPTISTS—EUROPE—HISTORY

Library of Congress Catalog Card Number: 81-65820
Printed in the United States of America

BAPTISTS IN EUROPE
History and Confessions of Faith

TO

Those Baptist-Christians of the past, present, and future in all European countries, whose names will never appear in any earthly book, but whose existence is grounded in the love of God and who make up the very core of his church

CONTENTS

Foreword .... Penrose St. Amant 11
Preface 14
European Baptists and Their Confessions 18

British Isles

England (Baptist Union of Great Britain and Ireland) 31
    Declaration of Principle
Scotland (Baptist Union of Scotland) 37
    A Confession of Faith
Wales (Baptist Union of Wales) .... T. M. Bassett 41
Ireland (Baptist Union of Ireland) 48
    The Basis of Doctrine of the Baptist Union of Ireland

Central Europe

Germany, Democratic Republic (Union of Evangelical Free Churches in the GDR), Germany, Federal Republic (Union of Evangelical Free Churches in the FRG) 53
    Confession of Faith
Switzerland (Union of Baptist Churches in Switzerland) 77
Austria (Baptist Union of Austria) 79
Netherlands (Union of Baptist Churches in the Netherlands) 81
    Confession of Faith of the Dutch Baptist Churches
    Jannes Reiling

Scandinavia

Denmark (Baptist Union of Denmark) 93
Norway (Norwegian Baptist Union) 95
    A Declaration of the Baptist Faith and Order (Organization)
Sweden (The Baptist Union of Sweden) 99
    Swedish Baptist Confession of Faith
Sweden (The Örebro Mission) .... Sigfrid Deminger 103
Finland (Finnish Baptist Union, Finnish-Speaking) 105
    The Confession of the Finnish Baptist Union

Finland (Swedish-Speaking Baptist Union of Finland) 108
    Confession of Faith for the Swedish-Speaking
    Baptist Union of Finland

Latin and Southern Europe

Italy (Baptist Evangelical Christian Union of Italy) 115
Spain (Baptist Evangelical Union of Spain) 118
Portugal (Portuguese Baptist Convention) 120
France (Federation of Baptist Evangelical Churches) 122
    Christian Covenant
    Confession of Faith of the Federation of
    French Baptist Churches
Belgium (The Union of Evangelical Baptist Churches) 134
Evangelical Association of French-Speaking Baptist Churches 135
    Confession of Faith and Ecclesiastical Principles
    of the Evangelical Association of French-Speaking
    Baptist Churches
Greece 145

Eastern Europe

The Union of Soviet Socialist Republics (All-Union Council of
Evangelical Christians-Baptists)...................................... 149
    Confession of Faith of the Evangelical Christians-Baptists
The Union of Soviet Socialist Republics (The Union of Churches
of Evangelical Christians-Baptists, Dissident Baptists).................. 168
Poland (The Polish Baptist Christian Union) 171
    Confession of Faith of the Baptist Churches in Poland
Hungary (The Baptist Union of Hungary) ....Johann Macher 185
    Confession of Faith of the Hungarian Baptist Church
Czechoslovakia (The Baptist Union in Czechoslovakia) 200
Yugoslavia (The Baptist Union of Yugoslavia) 202
    Confession of Faith of the Yugoslavian Baptist Churches

Romania (The Baptist Union of the Republic of Socialist Romania) 216
   Confession of Faith of the Romanian Baptist Churches
Bulgaria (The Union of Baptist Churches in Bulgaria) 231
                        Europe—English-Speaking
Europe (The European Baptist Convention—EBC, English Language) 235
                               Appendixes
Appendix 1: The Apostolic Creed 239
Appendix 2: The Nicene Creed 241
Appendix 3: *The Baptist Faith and Message* (Used by Baptists
   in Spain, Portugal, Greece, and the EBC) 243
Appendix 4: A Norwegian Postscript 256
Appendix 5: Statutes of the UCECB (Dissident) Baptists 258
Appendix 6: The Lausanne Covenant 267
Appendix 7: 1980 Statistics, European Baptists 278
Appendix 8: Declaratory Statement, Adopted by the Baptist Union
   Assembly, 23 April 1888 (Great Britain) 280
Bibliography 282
Indexes 284

Foreword

The story of the major Baptist confessions of faith in current use in Europe has been told heretofore only in fragments found here and there in the various languages of the European Baptist bodies. In this book, G. Keith Parker, an American who has been a member of the faculty of the Baptist Theological Seminary in Rüschlikon, Switzerland, for more than a decade, has brought together in English translation, when required, the bits and pieces of the story and put them in their historical contexts.

This book is the culmination of many years of patient research, correspondence, and travel by the author. The rich mine of material yielded in this project has been organized and interpreted by a historian sensitive to the requirements of his craft and to the subtle nuances of Baptist life and thought.

Baptists belong to what Professor George Williams has aptly described as the Radical Reformation. They were "radical" in the context of the state church systems of Europe, which required infant baptism and creedal subscriptions. They were radical in the challenge posed to the widely held idea that the state church was the cement which held civil society together. Belief in the separation of church and state, religious liberty, believers' baptism, the gathered church, and the Bible as the final authority for faith and practice led them to reject both the Roman Catholic and the magisterial Protestant interpretations of Christianity.

Baptists reject the conception of a coercive Christianity which in the past characterized the European state churches, two components of which were infant baptism and normative creeds. This condition explains the resistance of Baptists to formulating theological statements that are normative and, therefore, their insistence that such statements should be called *confessions,* which are not normative. Confessions of faith, in some instances, were forged in order to secure recognition or toleration of Baptists by states requiring such identification. In other instances, confessions of faith were framed for use in eliciting unity among Baptists and to facilitate evangelistic efforts. Since the state churches are rarely the threat to Baptists today that they were in earlier years, recently formulated confessions are oriented less toward the church-state issue and more toward the problem of the pervasive secularism of contemporary society.

No confession of faith can be an object of faith or a law demanding certain beliefs. Baptists believe that doctrinal questions should be decided in the light of the Scriptures under the guidance of the Holy Spirit. Confessions are useful because they provide theological guidelines adopted by Baptist bodies in relation to specific historical contexts and periods and are, therefore, indexes to the unity and diversity, the similarities and dissimilarities, in Baptist belief and practice.

Until recently, historians tended to neglect the Baptist story in favor of what was considered the mainstream of Christianity. This has changed as a result of the objectivity with which much church history is written today. As a consequence, Baptist history is seen as a significant strand in the story of the church. This book contributes to that end. What is offered in these pages is of interest not only to Baptists who seek a larger grasp of their history but also to others interested in the Christian movement as a whole. This book also provides a handy source for those who wish to glean specific information about aspects of the life and thought of Baptists in Europe.

Nowhere else is there to be found in a single book what is

FOREWORD

available in this treatise. It fills a neglected gap for those with purely historical interests and at the same time offers an account of the Baptist heritage in Europe that is both informative and inspiring.

PENROSE ST. AMANT
The Southern Baptist Theological Seminary
Louisville, Kentucky

Preface

Baptists first began as an identifiable group in Europe, expanded eventually to 140 countries on every continent, and have become a worldwide family of about thirty-three million members. Noted for their unity and diversity, they have also been a people prone to writing confessions of faith and, at the same time, resisting creeds, claiming the Bible itself as their "sole creed." There have been at least two notable collections of Baptist confessions of faith in this century: W. J. McGlothlin's *Baptist Confessions of Faith,* published by Judson Press in 1911, and William L. Lumpkin's *Baptist Confessions of Faith* first published by the Judson Press in 1959 and revised in 1969. Lumpkin's work was far more comprehensive, taking into account the discovery of several seventeenth-century Baptist documents, the knowledge of more English Separatist and Anabaptist documents, as well as the development of twentieth-century Baptist confessions, especially in North America.

In 1854, Edward B. Underhill also gathered and published with the Hanserd Knollys Society a collection of confessions, primarily seventeenth-century English ones. This current work is indebted to the former works in this century but will not overlap significantly with them. In fact it seeks to supplement and complement the work of Lumpkin which is limited in its representation of modern European Baptist confessions. For serious consideration of Anabaptist confessions, early English Baptist confessions, and American Baptist confessions, the reader is encouraged to study Lumpkin's excellent work.

The purpose of this book is to present the major current

PREFACE

Baptist confessions of faith in their historical context. Every major country in Europe is represented, except Albania where there are no known Baptist groups. An English translation is preceded by a brief historical overview. An introductory essay gives a broader perspective of the European context and the confessions. The appendixes provide additional documents that are mentioned in the text, to which the average reader might not have access. The bibliography indicates major works consulted, but is in no sense comprehensive. Copies of the confessions in their original languages may be found in the library of the Baptist Theological Seminary, Rüschlikon, Switzerland.

A few stylistic notes need to be made for clarification and to assist the reader. Efforts have been made to keep all scriptural references near the appropriate article since those reference points were very important to the original compilers. For stylistic reasons most of them have been placed in the margin beside each article, although they may have been in the text or, in some cases, written out in full. The reader should also be aware that, due to structural differences between languages, some Bible verses in another language may not exactly match the verses in English. Some inconsistency in capitalization will be seen, but this usually reflects a particular theological emphasis that was important to a compiler. Likewise, occasionally the reading is uneven, particularly when several phrases are connected by commas, but the translation priority in such cases was more theological than stylistic. The generic use of *man* was chosen, however, for stylistic smoothness in translating such terms as *Menschen*.

In some cases colloquial names for countries have been used and may not always be historically or politically accurate since political boundaries have changed so much in Europe. It is my hope that the use of such terms will not offend any cultural, linguistic, or political group. Also, the reader is cautioned not to weigh the relative length of the sections too heavily in that they do not reflect the importance, value, or even size of one group more than the other. Each section is intended to be very brief as a rule. A few exceptions were made in order to give a little more exposure to a situation not usually well known to the English-speaking reader or to illustrate the role confessions played in an area.

A great many people assisted in this project. Those who wrote sections are noted at the end of each section. Those who served as major resource persons, either in personal direct contribution or through their writing, are noted at the end in brackets. Translators are cited by *TR*. Some asked not to be cited for personal reasons. Scores of others gave suggestions, corrections, feedback, and support. I cannot begin to list them all but wish to offer my deepest thanks to each. Appreciation is given also to the many who provided documents in many languages and did the final corrections in each Baptist union, guiding in matters of accuracy and taste. Both credit and thanks are given to the Baptist Union in Moscow for the pictures on pages 163-167 and to Günter Balders and Oncken Press for those found on pages 159-162, originally published in *Theurer Bruder Oncken, Das Leben Johann Gerhard Oncken in Bildern und Dokumenten* (Oncken Verlag, 1978). Other publishing credits are noted where material is used.

I would underline my particular appreciation to past and present colleagues on the faculty at the Baptist Theological Seminary, Rüschlikon, who have provided suggestions and information at several points. Special thanks go to friend and former president Dr. Penrose St. Amant, who encouraged me in the project for several years; to Dr. Denton Lotz, whose practical help and friendship sustained me, and to Dr. Wayne Pipkin, who provided both guidance and support. My gratitude goes also to generations of Rüschlikon students from many European cultures—Christians of the present and future—whose dialogue, challenge and enthusiasm have been additional forces. Many typists have helped during the years of research; I thank them warmly.

My special gratitude goes to Mrs. Elizabeth Castellina who

has carried the greatest burden in the final stages of completion both in typing and index work and to Dr. John Truesdail for "fatherly" proof-reading in the final stages. I thank also Dr. J. D. Hughey, Area Director for Europe, Foreign Mission Board of the Southern Baptist Convention, for his support, his writings on European Baptists, and his involvement in the life of Baptists in Europe. My appreciation goes to Dr. Erik Ruden of Sweden and the Board of International Ministries of the American Baptist Churches for gracious permission to lean heavily upon the work done with the late Dr. Gordon Lahrson entitled "An Outline of Baptist Life on the European Continent" (mimeographed, 1963). Three other friends in the Baptist World Alliance and European Baptist Federation leadership have warmly supported the project: Dr. Gerhard Claas, Dr. David Russell, and Dr. Ronald Goulding.

Most of all I recognize my great indebtedness to my loving, caring family—my wife, Jonlyn, our son, Paul and our daughters, Leslie and Kim—for their long-term patience and support.

G. KEITH PARKER
Rüschlikon, Switzerland
Spring, 1981

European Baptists and Their Confessions

The Baptist World Alliance held its first congress in London on July 5, 1905, and heard an address by Dr. Alexander McLaren, president of the congress and one of the foremost preachers of the day. He stated:

I should like that there should be no misunderstanding on the part of the English public, or the American public either—before whom we are taking a prominent position, for a day at any rate, as to where we stand in the continuity of the historic Church. And I should like the first act of this Congress to be the audible and unanimous acknowledgment of our Faith. So I have suggested that, given your consent, it would be an impressive and a right thing, and would clear away a good many misunderstandings and stop the mouth of a good deal of slander—if we here and now, in the face of the world, not as a piece of coercion or discipline, but as a simple acknowledgment of where we stand and what we believe, would rise to our feet and following the lead of your President, would repeat the Apostles' Creed. Will you?[1]

The congress participants stood and repeated after their leader the Apostles' Creed, an unusual act for Baptists. Yet, at this inaugural of their first worldwide organization, this was rather symbolic, for Baptists around the world have had a long history of writing confessions. The statements of the president indicated the positive and negative purposes for making a statement. It may be significant that he chose the ancient Apostles' Creed as there was no truly common confession of faith for Baptists then, nor is there now.

From their birth in the context of sixteenth-century English Separatism (see "England," p. 31) and throughout their history, particularly in times of crisis, many Baptist churches, associations, and eventually, national unions have sought to express this faith in some form of confession. The early influence of continental Anabaptists and the Reformed or Calvinist tradition is clear in the earlier confessions. They have been used for apologetic, polemical, and educational purposes. They have been instrumental in forming associations on common doctrinal bases and helped unify individuals or groups of Baptists when a common threat appeared. They have played a role in winning converts and in helping Baptists find their identity. Lumpkin has noted that the seventeenth century confessions not only showed Baptist distinctions that differentiated them from other faiths but also showed points at which they are to be identified with other Christian groups.[2] In some cases, they were also used for discipline or to deal with heresy.

The use of modern Baptist confessions of faith in Europe would include these purposes but some, particularly the continental Baptists, have a different heritage and a shorter history than the Anglo-American Baptists and thus, have some additional reasons for having confessions. Continental Baptists basically arose in the nineteenth century, a time of great social, political, and economic changes as well as religious movements, such as Pietism and revivalism. The pietistic impulses were stronger in central and northern Europe, whereas the great awakenings associated with revivalism had a greater impact on the Anglo-American scene. Although they had some influence, particularly in the lives of individuals such as J. G. Oncken and ministries of the Haldane brothers, the revivalists did not have the deep impact of Pietism with its more individual, private approach to religion.

Perhaps more important was the fact that continental Baptists arose mostly in countries with state churches, in the very countries from which their spiritual ancestors had fled in the face of persecution. Almost without exception, European Baptists have faced many problems and much persecution from both state authorities and the official church (Roman Catholic, Lutheran, Reformed, and Orthodox). This has affected both the reason for, and contents of, their confessions. Until the present day, Baptists in some cases were recognized or tolerated only when they produced a confession of faith and statement of purpose. Freedom of religion is a fairly recent phenomenon in continental Europe. Although freedom of religion varies greatly, it does affect some of the confessions.

On the other hand, in some countries, the confession seems to play little or no role; it appears to be outdated and unnecessary, if they have one at all. Few church members would know if one existed. This seems to be the case in the Netherlands and Sweden, who have older ones, and in Italy. In the latter case, however, an unofficial confession is used for evangelization and for explaining who the Baptists are over against the Roman Catholics.

There is also a general resistance to a creedal understanding of confessions in Europe. This can be appreciated in light of so many cases of large state-church domination and a history of persecution under a creedal definition of who a Christian is and what one is entitled to believe. Due to either painful experiences or a unique history, some unions refuse to have a confession for fear it may be abused, as creeds were. For example, England has the longest, richest history of Baptist confessions and yet today has only a general "Statement of Principles."

The fear of legalistic application could not be too strongly stated as a generality and became most apparent during the recent rewriting of some central European confessions. Before acceptance by the national bodies, a preamble was often necessary. For example, the new German Baptist confession in Austria, Switzerland, the Federal Republic of Germany, and the German Democratic Republic states at the beginning: "This confession of faith is an expression of and a witness to the churches' agreement in belief. Thus it cannot itself be an object of faith or a compulsory law for faith."

That is not unlike the obvious intention behind the five points in the preamble to "The Baptist Faith and Message" of the Southern Baptist Convention (1963). Some Baptists have cautiously approached the matter, underlining the absolute primacy of Scripture itself, with the confession serving as a guide or as a given interpretation for that particular time and place. As the German confession states, such "remains open to the future discussions of further truth." This spirit of cautious appreciation for confessions that resists their possible misuse is reflected in the oft-cited statement of McGlothlin:

No Baptist individual, church, Association, or larger body has ever felt permanently bound by any Confession of Faith in its original, historical, or any other form. . . . This is no doubt due to their insistence upon a converted church-membership, the authority of the Scriptures, and the right and duty of every individual Christian to decide doctrinal questions for himself by a study of the Scriptures under the guidance of the Holy Spirit.[3]

This call to a primacy of the Scriptures is the main thrust of all Baptists, with or without a confession. Since it is so hard to define what is meant in such a broad, diverse book as the Bible, and since the state churches also appeal to the Scriptures, most groups sought to set out some guidelines for their day and age. These guidelines reflected not what all Baptists everywhere must believe but rather what kind of doctrinal consensus they shared at that time in history. This dynamic understanding of both the church in the world and of the self-understanding of a faith reflects the unity-in-diversity identity of Baptists.

Some Baptists in Europe, especially in Eastern Europe where masses of Anabaptists fled during the Reformation, make closer historical connection with that early radical movement in Zürich in the sixteenth century than do most Anglo-American historians. Their point is that those refugees made a long-lasting impact upon society and spirituality in their lands, a fact that cannot be denied. Although admitting no clear historical continuity between Anabaptists and the nineteenth-century Baptist movement in their lands, some Baptists note the deep identification with their forefathers and the context of modern Anabaptist descendants, such as the Brethren and the Mennonites. In some cases, Baptists, Brethren, and Mennonites are members of the same local church, underlying this historical feeling.

Basically, however, the greatest growth of Baptists in continental Europe came with the revolutionary events of the nineteenth century. Although affected somewhat by the English and American scene, a much broader and deeper internal struggle saw the last of ancient European culture and tradition being shaken. Social, political, intellectual, and religious events underlined the turmoil of the times. As the Industrial Revolution brought as many social problems as new solutions, political rivalry reigned in Europe. Rationalism was being challenged by Romanticism. Political theories such as socialism arose. Discoveries in geology, biology, and astronomy gave birth to the controversial evolutionary theory. German scholarship began to introduce historical and biblical criticism. But in the midst of such revolutionary times came also a so-called Second Great Awakening with a general spiritual renewal in Europe. Although admittedly influenced somewhat by great English and Scottish preachers, such as Spurgeon and the Haldane brothers, the greatest impact within continental Europe was probably made by the pietistic movement. German Pietism emphasized a more personal, devotional, Bible-centered religious life and did not have the same impact as the larger revivalistic movement did on the Anglo-American scene. In order to understand the nineteenth-century roots of European Baptists, one must see this general, very broad and, very often, spontaneous spawning of Bible-study or prayer groups which were discovered or gathered together by traveling Baptists. These spontaneous Bible-study groups were spread widely over all of Europe and many came to their own conviction about repentance, conversion, and believers' baptism. There were great pioneers and preacher-missionaries such as J. G. Oncken, but European Baptist history is not to be written only in the light of such persons. Other individuals, Bible societies, and missionary organizations also guided, supported, and directed. But the greater history is probably the unwritten story of those untold thousands who moved and acted on the basis of their own experience with God and his Word, as they perceived it. "Every Baptist a missionary" was more than a phrase coined by Oncken; it was a practice among many who were joined together in groups, touched by the great religious awakening, but who might not yet be named *Baptist*.

These multiple sources of nineteenth-century Baptist "re-beginnings" underline their continuing diversity. It is reflected in Baptist confessions and church polity. Yet they enjoy much unity, not through rigid orthodoxy but rather through common heritage and considerable cross-cultural fellowship. Throughout their history, this sharing and belonging dimension has played a crucial role in mutual support in times of difficulty and joy.

The Confessions

The modern confessions of European Baptists would basically substantiate the words of McGlothlin over three-quarters of a century ago:

Being congregational and democratic in church government, Baptists have naturally been very free in making, changing, and using Confessions. There has never been among them any ecclesiastical authority which could impose a Confession upon their churches or other bodies. Their Confessions are, strictly speaking, statements of what a certain group of Baptists, large or small, did believe at a given time, rather than a creed which any Baptist must believe at all times in order to hold ecclesiastical position or to be considered a Baptist. In the latter sense there has been no Baptist creed.[4]

There appears to be a trend toward more general forms of confessions, although most still maintain the traditional divisions under theological and ecclesiastical categories. The "traditionalists" include those in the Netherlands, Sweden, Finland, France, the French-Speaking Association, Poland, Hungary, Romania, Yugoslavia, and the Soviet Union, as well as those who use the "Baptist Faith and Message" (Spain, Portugal, Greece, and the European Baptist Convention). A more modern form is seen in the new common German confession (used by Baptists in Switzerland, Austria, Czechoslovakia, the Federal Republic of Germany and, in a modified form, the German Democratic Republic. This confession brings together more comprehensive theological concepts under the major divisions "The Establishment of God's Rule," "Life under God's Rule," and "The Consummation of God's Rule." Although put into a narrative style, the confession contains all of the traditional topics.

A third format of confessions is seen in the general statements of British, Scottish, Norwegian, and Swedish-Speaking Finnish Baptists. These are notable for their brevity and very general nature. In many ways these statements reflect a graphic contrast to the older, traditional confessions which give much more detail, as well as the modern confessions with comprehensive theological concepts. But two of these, the Scottish and Norwegian confessions, were modified recently to define their theological stances more clearly in the light of criticism. British Baptists resisted such in the midst of a recent Christological debate. The Finnish confession is the newest in Europe, having been recently submitted to the government as part of a necessary recognition procedure. The confession of Irish Baptists presents a unique listing of terms, reflecting theological controversies at the turn of the century.

Most of the confessions start either with a consideration of God (The Father, Son, and Holy Spirit) or the Scriptures. Generally, man and the Fall, or sin, follow, with subsequent consideration of Satan, salvation, Lord's Supper, baptism, the last days, and other topics. Some integrate matters of church practice and polity; others have it in an additional document.

Theologically the confessions show traditional Baptist diversity and unity, and their availability should provide opportunity for scholars to evaluate them comparatively and in context. A few generalizations could be noted. Clearly the singular authority remains the Bible. Worded in different ways and with varying detail, the main point stands that Baptists consider the Holy Scriptures as final. Such a strong conviction and declaration must be seen in the different contexts, where often tradition, liturgy, or hierarchy appeared to minimize the authority of the Scriptures. In some cases, the books of the Bible are listed or the Apocrypha is excluded, in reference to prevailing local custom.

Calvinistic traditions and formulations do prevail in some areas, particularly in southern Europe and where the Anglo-American influence is felt or revivalism carried the message. But Arminian theological trends are definitely seen, perhaps more in the northern areas. In some of the confessions, due credit must be given to both traditions. Responsibility of the individual before God is taken rather seriously in most confessions, with clearly defined guidelines for the Christian life and with a call to the community of the church. In fact, the ecclesiology might be one of the more distinguishing factors that would differentiate Baptists' confessions from other contemporary groups in Europe. Having been a small and often persecuted minority in the world of powerful state churches, most of these Baptist groups survived in their common hope and common fellowship primarily through prayer, Bible study, and worship. They expressed this in their confessions. With the radical changes in the last years, however, the state church is rarely the threat, but rather overwhelming secularism. Thus, the modern confessions bring newer expressions or formulations for their common hope.

The theological formulations about the Christian's response to the authorities are carefully worded and must always be read not only in the context of their times and setting but also in the total context of that confession. Many of these were written to obtain permission for approval for worship or even for existence (both East and West) and were worded to obtain such permission. The confessions reflect attempts to present consistent theology of final allegiance to God with appropriate obedience to authorities. There can be no doubt that a high Christology prevails in most Baptist groups, although some are more cautious in their pneumatology. Notable exceptions are seen, however, where the Holy Spirit is integrated into many of the other articles in addition to a statement on the Trinity. Baptism and the Lord's Supper are important theological and practical concepts, spelled out in varying detail. The call to and belief in Christian discipleship and evangelism (or missions) are also seen to be part of the self-understanding of Baptists: the belief that God has not only given grace but has also sent them to call others to repentance and faith in him.

Generalities are not always accurate and imply exceptions; such is the case in Europe. The reader will notice the difference and that Baptists in Europe wear a coat of many colors. Not all groups are even listed. There are a few other, smaller Baptist bodies or groups that exist in a few countries. All members of the Baptist World Alliance and The European Baptist Federation are represented, along with several significant other groups so that the reader will have a fair representation.

The interest in confessions in some parts of Europe is very high, reflected by the recent rewriting of several and current study by other groups. That interest in Baptist confessions, their unique ecclesiology and understanding of religious freedom, is as international and cross-cultural as Baptists are. It is hoped that this volume will contribute to the dialogue between Baptists and other Christians around the globe, as well as to the study of Baptists, their history, and beliefs.

Notes

1. *Report of the First Baptist World Congress* (1905), 20. Cited also by W. M. S. West, "Foundation Documents of the Faith," *The Expository Times*, May, 1980, 91:278.

2. William L. Lumpkin, *Baptist Confessions of Faith* (Valley Forge: Judson Press, 1959), pp. 16-17.
3. W. J. McGlothlin, *Baptist Confessions of Faith* (Valley Forge: Judson Press, 1911), p. xii, Introduction.
4. Ibid., p. xi, Introduction.

I
British Isles

BRITISH ISLES

England
The Baptist Union of Great Britain and Ireland

Baptist beginnings can be traced to the seventeenth-century Separatist movement in England. In the midst of the general religious awakening of the day, many sought to purify the church in England; others separated themselves from the official church, seeking a simpler church form based on biblical principles.

Two key figures led in the first move: John Smyth, a former clergyman of the Church of England; and Thomas Helwys, a member of a Separatist congregation in Gainsborough. The two led a group of believers to Amsterdam, Holland, to escape persecution and to be able to practice their beliefs.

In Holland, Smyth became further convinced that baptism was for true believers and thus that all members of a church should be baptized on the basis of that belief. A brief dialogue with the Mennonites indicated not only several similarities in theology and practice but also many dissimilarities. In 1609, Smyth baptized himself and then about forty others, founding the first Baptist church on Dutch soil.

Helwys and part of the group eventually returned to England; Smyth and the others joined the Mennonites in 1615, remaining in Holland. In 1642, the Helwys group started a Baptist church in Spitalfields, at the edge of London. Helwys was imprisoned in 1612 by an angry King James I for writing his book *A Short Declaration of the Mystery of Iniquity,* a strong plea for freedom of conscience and the first cry for total freedom in worship in the English language. Helwys insisted that the king was only a mortal man and that the government should not be involved in spiritual matters.

This group presents the start of the General Baptist tradition, one with emphasis on general atonement (that is, all people can be saved who believe in Christ).

This theological perspective was essentially Arminian; General Baptist church practice was similar to the Presbyterians. The other major early tradition was Calvinistic in theological orientation, "independent" in church order. They were called Particular Baptists because of their emphasis on the effectiveness of the atonement being reserved for the elect (or "particular"). They derived from the Independent (congregational) movement and, particularly, from one congregation that was gathered in Southwark, London, and assumed names of three key pastors: Jacob, Lathrop, and Jessey. In the 1630s, a clear Baptist identity emerged in those who insisted that only believers should be baptized.

Since the primary thrust of both General and Particular Baptists was a regenerate church membership expressed in believers' baptism, the content was the first main issue. Later, in the 1640s, both groups turned to immersion as the *means* of baptism, replacing pouring or sprinkling in an attempt to renew the symbol of death and resurrection.

Although the General and Particular Baptists had several theological differences, they had certain basic Baptist principles in common which drew them together over the years: belief in the personal and voluntary nature of true religion, the baptism of believers, a church made up of such baptized believers, and a democratic church polity.

A third, more evangelical stream came out of the General Baptist tradition during the Methodist revival of the late 1700s: The "New Connection" Baptists. By 1891, all these groups had joined to the Baptist Union of Great Britain and Ireland, which had been begun earlier, in 1813, by the Particular Baptists.

British Baptist history is characterized by variety: heavy religious persecution and, at other times, freedom, growth, decline, problems, and prosperity. The greatest period of growth was in the mid- to late nineteenth century, during the so-called Second Great Awakening. This same movement affected Baptist beginnings on the Continent. There were many great men, such as Robert Hall (1764-1831); Alexander Maclaren (1826-1910); Charles H. Spurgeon (1834-1892); Andrew Fuller (1754-1815); John Clifford (1836-1923); and William Carey (1761-1834), father of the modern missionary movement.

British Baptists have been active in ecumenical organizations, such as the Free Church Council and World Council of Churches. The British Council of Churches was begun in the Baptist Church House in 1942.

In the early years, many confessions of faith reflected not only the particular needs of the day but also the current theological issues at stake. They reveal appeals for freedom of conscience and the separation of church and state, theological correctives, apologetics, and matters of ecclesiology that were radical for their day.[1] The most modern one is entitled a "Declaration of Principle" and is closely tied to the development of the Baptist Union in the late nineteenth century. The blending of at least three major theologically diverse traditions of Baptists into one was long and not without difficulty. In addition, many churches were closely related to Congregational churches; in some cases, Baptists and Congregationalists were in a united church membership.

In 1813, a society or general union was begun with Baptist pastors and churches with clear Calvinist theology and a congregational church polity. In 1815, it named itself "The General Meeting of the Particular (or Calvinist) Baptist Denomination" and focused on cooperation but sought to preserve the autonomy of the local church. With a long history of associations of churches and the example of the Congregational Church Union, they began to grow.

This general meeting was redefined several times, usually to be able to include others that were not strictly Calvinist. In 1832, for example, it was to include those "who agree in the sentiments usually denominated evangelical" (that is, the New Connection Baptists). As E. A. Payne noted, this shows that the older Calvinistic-Arminian issues were now not as crucial as the "catholic" Tractarian movement within the Church of England and the rationalism which had led several churches into Unitarianism.[2] It also reflected a growing distrust of creedal statements, in spite of the long history and use of confessions of faith.

In 1873, the word *evangelical* seemed to be limiting to some who felt that intellectual freedom was at stake and that the right of individual interpretation was more important. Payne noted that the autonomy and independence of local churches was more important than doctrine. In that year, as the "Baptist Union" was designated as the title, it was also decided that all they should have as a basis for union was a general statement of principle that "in this Union it is fully recognized that every separate church has liberty to interpret and administer the laws of Christ, and that the immersion of believers is the only Christian baptism." Several were unhappy with the statement, including the famous pastor Charles Haddon Spurgeon, who called for a clearer doctrinal statement, perhaps like the one adopted by the Evangelical Alliance, an interconfessional movement of that time.

The "Downgrade" controversy between Spurgeon's party and the Baptist Union ensued over the next years; a split was avoided in 1888, as attempts were made to show that Baptists were still evangelical and yet gave intellectual freedom. A "Declaratory Statement" was made to that end and included "doctrine." (See Appendix 8.) No changes were made in 1891, when the New Connection Baptists joined; but the debate continued until 1904, when the 1873 Declaration was enlarged:

1. That the Lord Jesus Christ is the sole and absolute authority in all matters pertaining to faith and practice, as revealed in the Holy Scriptures, and that each Church has liberty to interpret and administer His laws.

2. That Christian Baptism is the immersion in water into the Name of the Father, the Son and the Holy Ghost, of those who have professed repentance towards God and faith in our Lord Jesus Christ who died for our sins according to the Scriptures; was buried, and rose again the third day.

3. That it is the duty of every disciple to bear personal witness to the Gospel of Jesus Christ, and to take part in the evangelization of the world.

The discussions continued, reflecting the issues of each day. In 1906, "Our God and Saviour" was added in the first article to avoid a Unitarian interpretation of Christ. In 1938, "God manifest in the flesh" replaced "our God and Saviour" and the phrase "under the guidance of the Holy Spirit" was added after the word *liberty*.

Payne underlined the contrast to earlier, more comprehensive statements of faith and traditional Christian creeds but noted the changes in the basis of the Baptist Union itself, its history and great diversity.

Some Baptist churches do not belong to the Union; some have their own confession of faith.

It should be noted also that the Baptist Union is not only an organization of churches and individuals cooperating on a national level but also a structure that includes formerly independent societies, funds, and other institutions. These institutions maintain an autonomous status in relationship to the Union, in somewhat the same way as local churches. The title "The Baptist Union of Great Britain and Ireland" is ambiguous since the Union no longer has work in Ireland. Scotland and Wales have their own Unions; in Wales some churches are dually aligned; a few belong only to the British Union.

The Declaration of Principles below is still held by the Baptist Union. Each Baptist minister is expected to ascribe before being accepted on the accredited list of ministers. In the 1970s in a controversy which arose over Christology, the Declaration played a role in settling the matter. Although some interest arose in developing a more detailed confession or formula, English Baptists chose to keep the more general, inclusive statement.

Declaration of Principle

The Baptist Union of Great Britain and Ireland

The basis of this Union is:—

1. That our Lord and Saviour Jesus Christ, God manifest in the flesh, is the sole and absolute authority in all matters pertaining to faith and practice, as revealed in the Holy Scriptures, and that each Church has liberty, under the guidance of the Holy Spirit, to interpret and administer His laws.

2. That Christian Baptism is the immersion in water into the name of the Father, the Son, and the Holy Ghost, of those who have professed repentance towards God and faith in our Lord Jesus Christ who "died for our sins according to the Scriptures; was buried, and rose again the third day."

3. That it is the duty of every disciple to bear personal witness to the Gospel of Jesus Christ, and to take part in the evangelization of the world.

Notes

1. See William L. Lumpkin, Baptist Confessions of Faith (Valley Forge: Judson Press, 1959).
2. E. A. Payne, *The Baptist Union,* 1949.

Scotland
The Baptist Union of Scotland

Although the first Baptists in Scotland probably came in the 1650s with Cromwell's soldiers, their work did not become implanted among the native Scots. The earliest indigenous church is the Kiess Church, founded in 1750 by Sir William Sinclair who had been baptized in England. The eventual development of Scottish Baptists came from two indigenous streams, both of which were affected by the eighteenth- and nineteenth-century religious and political movements.

First, there were the Dissenters who broke away from the Church of Scotland: the Glasites, the Bereans, the Old Scots Independents, and others. Many became Baptists after studying the New Testament and after considering the Baptist doctrine of the church, baptism, and relation of the church to the state.

The second stream is seen in the extensive evangelistic ministry of Robert and James Haldane and their associates. The so-called "Wesley brothers of Scotland" these prominent men started the Society for the Propagation of the Gospel in 1798 and in 1808 became Baptists. The Haldanes' men started churches not only in the remote Highlands and islands but also abroad.

Two conflicting models of church polity appeared and created tension for some years. The Glasite understanding of the "plurality of elders" to lead the church was at odds with the so-called "English church" model where the pastor was the leader. Eventually the latter became the norm. But the years of struggle, accompanied by rugged local independence, vivid theological debates over degrees of Calvinism, and open or closed communion, delayed unity until the mid 1800s. The urgent need for cooperation in facing common tasks such as evangelism, missions, publications, and education, along with the results of religious awakening in the nineteenth century helped to set the stage for the constitution of the Scottish Baptist Union in 1869. For many years associational work had been done at a smaller level and even a short-lived union established in 1835.

The 1869 constitution brought together those who held "evangelical doctrines as distinguished from Rationalism and Socinianism on the one hand and from Ritualism and Romanism on the other, and gave assurance that every local church had power to exercise its own discipline, rule and government." The specified tasks of the new union focused on missions, church aid, ministerial education, and church cooperation. These functions have continued and have been amplified to include Youth work, Sunday School work, evangelism, publishing, temperance work, and men's work.

That constitution was revised and broadened in 1908 to include the declaration of Principle of the Baptist Union of Great Britain and Ireland, as amended in 1906. Although maintaining their own identity apart from the British Union, Scottish Baptists did "affiliate" with them both to cooperate and to resolve problems related to ministerial lists, education, and so on. The brief Declaration of Principle is the closest thing the Baptist Union has to a confession of faith or doctrine, although some unsuccessful attempts have been made to introduce the latter. A number of churches, however, have in their constitution or title of deeds a clear doctrinal confession. Great variety exists in these. A more Calvinistic one states:

Members must be baptized believers who hold, profess and maintain the doctrines of the fall of man, the entire corruption of human nature, the personal eternal election of believers to salvation, justification by faith in the obedience to death of Jesus Christ, God manifest in the flesh, and the inseparable connection between justifying faith and the fruits of practical holiness.

The Declaration of Principle seemed to be the major reference point through periods of difficulty. A long debate ensued over the World Council of Churches and Scottish Baptists' relationship to it. This debate resulted in an "Amplification of the Declaration of Principles," accepted in the 1967 assembly, and reproduced as follows.

(Andrew MacRae)
(Derek Murray)

A Confession of Faith

The Baptist Union of Scotland, in its Declaration of Principle, adopted in 1908, affirms:

1 That the Lord Jesus Christ our God and Saviour is the sole and absolute authority in all matters pertaining to faith and practice, as revealed in the Holy Scriptures, and that each Church has liberty to interpret and administer His laws.
2 That Christian Baptism is the immersion in water into the name of the Father, the Son and the Holy Spirit, of those who have professed repentance toward God and faith in the Lord Jesus Christ, who "died for our sins according to the Scriptures, was buried, and rose again the third day."
3 That it is the duty of every disciple to bear personal witness to the Gospel of Jesus Christ, and to take part in the evangelisation of the world.

Following from this Declaration of Principle, and in amplification of it, Scottish Baptists hold to:
1 A Biblical Christology. At the very heart of the Christian faith, as Scottish Baptists understand it, is the person and work of Christ, as the historic, incarnate, revelation of God, fully God and fully man, the only redeemer of the world. We recognise, clearly and unequivocally, the historicity of the saving acts of God in Christ and of His Lordship as revealed in Holy Scripture. Without the incarnation, atonement and resurrection of Christ, there can be no valid Christian faith or Church.

2 A Biblical Doctrine of the Church. In the New Testament the Church appears as a gathered community of believers, consisting of those who believe in one God, the Father, the Son and the Holy Spirit and are committed to personal faith in Christ as Saviour and Lord. The basis of participation in the Body of Christ is two-fold: the grace of God in Jesus Christ, and the response of repentance and faith on the part of the believer.

3 Christian Baptism. Baptism is a sacrament of divine grace, a sign of the death and resurrection of Christ, with which the believer is consciously identified. It is the recognition and seal of the work of the Holy Spirit and denotes the incorporation of the baptised into the fellowship and witness of the Church.

4 Christian Commitment. This involves personal commitment of the Church member to the Lordship of Christ and to the task of spreading His reconciling word in the world. Basic to our understanding of the Church is the New Testament's insistence on the responsibility of each Christian to be committed to Christ and to participate in the evangelisation of the world through witness to Christ.

5 Christian Unity. Scottish Baptists accept the concern of our Lord for the unity of His people and are eager to manifest that unity. They do so in practical terms as they welcome believers of all backgrounds to share in the Lord's Supper and in their worship. Christian unity depends on the spiritual oneness of those who are committed to Christ.

Wales
The Baptist Union of Wales

Baptist witness had made little impression on Wales before the Great Civil War and progress remained slow even after the defeat of Charles I. General Baptists, spreading in from the English Midlands, gained a foothold in the old shires of Radnor and Montgomery about 1646. Particular Baptists were among the members of the mixed churches gathered in the same area by the Independent Vavasor Powell. Further south, Thomas Evans had gathered an open communion but closed membership church of Particular Baptists. There was a similar church widely scattered in Monmouthshire under the ministry of William Thomas, a former Independent.

The continuous history of the Baptists in Wales commences, however, with the gathering of a church at Ilston, near Swansea, by John Miles in 1649. He established four other churches which, with the Ilston church, formed the first Welsh association. Miles and his followers were familiar with the London Confession of 1646 but the nearest approach to a confession by the group itself is "An Antidote Against the Infection of the Times" authorized for publication by the association in 1656. It was a moderate Calvinist document colored by its immediate purpose which was to summon back erring brethren, especially such as had been seduced by Quaker propaganda. So, while emphasizing the Fall, Christ's atonement, justification by Christ alone, and an effectual calling, it repeatedly returns to the need for repentance. The association had its internal conflicts, especially over accepting financial support from public sources (that is, tithe for the ministry), but the return of the monarchy in 1660 ended the conflicts and the life of the association.

The savage persecution which followed failed to eradicate Baptist witness. Four of the Miles churches survived. In 1668, at the height of the persecution, they threw out a new shoot at Rhydwilyn. The revolution of 1688 saw the dawn of better days. Worship was allowed but at the price of severe civil discrimination. Several Welsh ministers were at the London meeting of 1689 which validated the confession of faith drawn up in that year, and some of them signed the document.

A new Welsh association was formed in 1700, and the confession was translated into Welsh by Rees David in 1721 and again by Joshua Thomas in 1791. Rees David, almost certainly with the concurrence of the association, had added a clause making imposition of hands after baptism an obligatory ordinance. The clause was dropped by Joshua Thomas, as it had become optional after 1768. It is still the practice in some Welsh churches. Neither David nor Thomas had amended the original confession in its reference to the Lord's Supper. It allowed for open or closed communion, but it is clear that the Welsh association had rapidly adopted closed communion.

Throughout the eighteenth century, the association letter either makes a brief reference to the confession as its standard of faith or includes a synopsis of its major doctrines in a preamble, invariably including references to the three undivided persons of the Trinity, the Fall of man, Christ's atonement, personal election, an effectual calling together with justification of God's grace, adoption, and sanctification.

The denomination during this period was still limited geographically to South Wales; the churches, for the most part, kept a low profile. There is little evidence of theological inquiry, but the doctrine of the eternal filiation of the Son of man raised doubts in some minds about 1727 while there was contemporary discussion respecting the validity of preaching to sinners. But the denomination was on the verge of a transformation. In 1776, it embarked on a mission to North Wales. By 1800, the bare remnant of the early years of the century had become nine thousand. Powerful forces, both religious and secular, contributed to this change. In the more immediate religious context, Wales experienced the dramatic awakening of the Welsh Methodist Revival. Its powerful preaching, emotional hymn-singing, and general enthusiasm were regarded with some suspicion initially by many Baptists. Others were deeply affected, and soon the "strange fire" preaching began to kindle on Baptist hearths.

Equally stimulating were the demands for liberty emanating in the American colonies and France and disseminated in Wales by William Richards of Lynn and Morgan John Rhys. Some of the thinking behind this eighteenth-century demand for reform was based on an appeal to an age, postulated by the reformers, when the masses were free, before being constrained by kings and prelates. In the religious sphere, looking to the past meant looking to the Scriptures. This explains the contemporary efforts to provide better versions of the Gospels, the enthusiasm behind the early Sunday School movement, and the motivation of Archibald McLean in his effort to recapture the "pure" pattern of the New Testament community. Many Baptists in Wales were aware of those tendencies, and some were acquainted with the more sophisticated arguments of Robert Robinson in favor of toleration and against human confessions.

From 1779 on, therefore, the orthodox Trinitarianism of the 1689 confession and its uncompromising Calvinism came under increasing attack. The crunch came when the trustees of the Particular Baptist Fund, who assisted some of the poorer Welsh ministers financially, demanded from them and their churches a clear declaration that they adhered to the confession. Some ministers could not do so with a clear conscience while others, orthodox enough in their faith, rejected the right of the trustees or of anyone else to demand such a confession. Orthodoxy triumphed. The two southern associations (the one association of 1700 had been divided into three in 1790) proclaimed that they no longer wished to have fellowship with those who refused to accede. In the northern association there was a contemporary crisis concerned with church organization and ordinances rather than with doctrine.

In North Wales, the growth of the denomination was permanently slowed down; elsewhere the disputes had little numerical effect. The real effects were intangible. The dispute, although its immediate causes were doctrinal, is best understood as a battle for freedom of conscience. The reformers had no wish to compel the orthodox to change their views, indeed, they would willingly have granted them the freedom which they demanded for themselves. Considerable bitterness was generated in the heat of the controversy, and the same unpleasant spirit prevailed when the more moderate views of Andrew Fuller were canvassed in the eighteen-twenties. The first half of the nineteenth century was a period of unceasing bickering. The confession was once more printed in 1846. Many churches built at the time, and indeed much later, insisted on a resumé of the confession in their trust deeds and a Sunday School catechism by Titus Lewis. This catechism, first published in 1804, is little more than a question and answer version of the confession and ran into twelve editions between then and 1903.

From mid-century on, theological discussion subsided. The theologically minded still gravely discussed the weighty problems of election and an effectual calling. However, their discussions seemed to have little relevance to the broad mass of chapel goers who busied themselves in the Sunday School, in the church choir, in the temperance movement and its children's branch the Band of Hope, sometimes with chapel-based adult education classes. The people were involved with home and foreign mission activity and never-ending fund raising for chapel building which had become an obsession in Wales. By 1850, there were some forty thousand Baptists in Wales. The end of the century arrived with the denomination topping the hundred thousand mark, the chapels full, and the leadership in full cry against the

Tory Education Act of 1902 with its provision for public financial support for sectarian education. A powerful religious revival in 1904-1905 tended to confirm the prevailing view that all was well and the overwhelming victory of the Liberal party at the polls in 1906 seemed to indicate that the final battle with the Anglican Church was about to be won and its disestablishment and disendowment imminent.

The more discerning had already seen the danger signals ahead. The economic growth of the third quarter of the century was slowing down, accompanied by industrial strife and the slow spread of socialist ideas. Educated in grammar schools and colleges which Nonconformity had done so much to foster, a younger generation was coming into contact with modern science, younger ministers with the thinking of theologians who sought to reconcile their theology with the newer scientific concepts, and with scholars busily engaged in applying the yardstick of secular criticism to biblical texts.

Welsh Baptists were not isolated from these developments. An elitist theology adopted in the days of a persecuted minority was hard to reconcile with a denomination obsessed by growth. The individualistic Puritan ethos to which they subscribed required modifying to meet the challenge of massive industrial decline. The younger generation would not be restrained from inquiry by reaffirming traditionalist orthodoxies. All these problems drew a reasoned and positive response from a number of prominent young Baptists who sought to lead the denomination in an inquiring and open manner.

Battle lines were redrawn and old issues recontested. There was a bitter struggle in the powerful East Glamorgan association in 1909 when the old Calvinist preamble to the letter came up for review. The West Glamorgan association, another of the stronger associations, continued to include an orthodox preamble to its letter down to World War I. While the Baptists of Wales were still fighting old battles, they were engulfed by World War I with the savage economic and social upheavals which both accompanied and followed it, while the disasters which affected the Liberal party after the war left the leadership of the denomination politically inarticulate. By the late twenties, the process of erosion had already started. World War II hastened the erosion, which continues at an alarming rate.

Meanwhile certain trends seem to be developing. There is a readily discernible trend toward a stricter, more authoritarian Calvinism which would take us back in the direction of the confession of 1689. Although lying dormant at times, the denomination has never really been without this fundamental approach. Now, in a society becoming increasingly and demonstrably less Christian, a return to an elitist theology might be expected. There is also the appeal of ecumenism at two levels: the idealist, which wishes to close the ranks and present a united Christian front in an increasingly non-Christian society; and at a more local and practical level, the view which is concerned with keeping Christian witness alive in areas where separate denominational causes are no longer viable in the traditional sense of a chapel with regular services.

The Baptist Union of Wales is at present in the process of validating a new constitution. A declaration of principle, adopted from the constitution of the Baptist Union of Great Britain and Ireland, lays down the basis of the Union:

1. That our Lord and Saviour Jesus Christ, God manifest in the flesh is the sole and absolute authority in all matters pertaining to faith and practice, as revealed in the Holy Scriptures, and that each church has liberty, under the guidance of the Holy Spirit, to interpret and administer His Laws.
2. That Christian Baptism is the immersion in water into the name of the Father, the Son and the Holy Ghost, of those who have professed repentance towards God and faith in our Lord Jesus Christ who "died for our sins according to the Scriptures; was buried, and rose again the third day."
3. That it is the duty of every disciple to bear personal witness to the

Gospel of Jesus Christ, and to take part in the evangelization of the world.

The constitution then goes on to define membership, stating that the Union shall consist of "Churches which are in membership with one of the Associations which belong to the Union and which accept the Declaration of Principle." The Baptist Union of Wales meets in an English-speaking and Welsh-speaking assembly. The English-speaking assembly accepted the above definition of membership, but it was rejected by the Welsh-speaking assembly who adopted this modified form: "Churches which are in membership with one of the associations and which practise Believers' Baptism by immersion, and which receive their members into the fellowship and privileges of the church on profession of their faith in Christ through baptism."

This restrictive revised version has still to be accepted by the English assembly and the final outcome is uncertain. Yet, even while the Union legislators are closing the door, individual churches are relaxing their closed membership rules and there are even one or two examples of interdenominational ministries. One hopes that this seeming impasse may be resolved in a spirit of goodwill.

T. M. Bassett

Ireland
The Baptist Union of Ireland

Baptists in Ireland date back to the time of the Commonwealth occupation in 1649, if not earlier. When Baptists in Cromwell's army came to Dublin, they may have found a church already there. In any case, at least eleven churches were begun between 1652 and 1654 with about 120 members in the Dublin church, including Cromwell's son-in-law, the governor general. These evangelists, pastors, and workers were essentially "imports" from England and little lasting effect was seen after the Commonwealth was overthrown. A few churches became indigenous and survived. In 1813, the Dublin church became the Baptist Society for Propagating the Gospel in Ireland, which eventually merged with an English society.

During the nineteenth century, English Baptists (especially Andrew Fuller) took an increasing interest in the needs in Ireland. The great Haldane revival that swept Scotland reached into Northern Ireland in the nineteenth century, a number of churches being founded on a Scottish model. One key pastor was the former Presbyterian Alexander Carson. At great personal sacrifice, Carson preached in open spaces and barns until a chapel was built in 1814 in Tubbermore where he labored for thirty years, helping build a congregation up to five hundred members. His scholarly works on baptism reflected his university education and knowledge of Greek. As time passed, however, the strength of Baptists tended toward the north rather than the south.

The northern churches, however, felt the impact of the Brethren (Darbyite) movement as well as dispensationalism.

BRITISH ISLES

Until 1888, mutual work continued with the heavier role played by the English. The transfer of management was made to the Irish (with only some continued help for paying missionaries' salaries for one more year). This was the beginning of the Irish Baptist Home Mission, managed by a committee set up by the Irish Baptist Association. That association was renamed in Belfast in 1895 as the Baptist Union of Ireland (legally registered in 1902 as the Baptist Union of Ireland Corporation Ltd.). Political changes in the 1920s necessitated the formation of a separate corporation for Northern Ireland.

In recent years, Irish Baptists have shown steady growth and maintain a number of organizations including a home missions program; a foreign mission outreach with work in Peru, France, Belgium, and Spain; an orphan society; an annuity fund; a monthly magazine; and a theological college.

Irish Baptists are Separatists and have few official outside links, except with the Fellowship of Evangelical Baptists in Europe (made up of Irish Baptists, some English strict Baptists, some Baptists in France, Belgium, and Spain). They are not members of the European Baptist Federation or the Baptist World Alliance.

The "Basis of Doctrine of the Baptist Union of Ireland" outlines the Irish Baptists' position and must be accepted by all churches and pastors seeking admission to the Union. It is used with young people, new converts, and those seeking church membership. Its own history is interesting, having been accepted, in part, in the association meeting in 1888. The original resolution said simply:

That we, the members of the Irish Baptist Association, having regard to statements made that the following doctrines were denied among Baptists, namely, the inspiration and all-sufficiency of the Holy Scriptures, the Trinity in Unity of the Godhead, the Deity of our Lord and Saviour Jesus Christ and the eternal punishment of those who die impenitent, we as an Association do hereby record collectively and individually our thorough repudiation of the errors imputed to us. We rejoice that such unscriptural and dangerous teaching has no place amongst us or sympathy from us. We take this opportunity of affirming our undivided loyalty to every utterance of our Lord and Saviour Jesus Christ.

When, in 1895, the "Association" became the "Union," the statement was reviewed. The following year these words were added,

the justification of the sinner through faith in the Lord Jesus, the personality of the devil, immortality of the soul, and the second coming of our Lord Jesus Christ, and the responsibility of all saved souls to live soberly, righteously and godly in this present age.

The original, more general statement thus evolved into a list of key words and phrases, most of which were highly volatile issues in the "Downgrade Controversy" that was raging in England at that time. The following "Basis of Doctrine" is the one in current use.

The Basis of Doctrine of the Baptist Union of Ireland

The verbal inspiration, and the all and sole sufficiency of the Holy Scriptures of the Old and New Testaments as originally given, the Trinity in Unity of the Godhead, the essential deity and perfect humanity of our Lord Jesus Christ, the personality of the Holy Spirit, the depraved and fallen state of man, the substitutionary sacrifice of our Lord Jesus Christ, the justification of the sinner through faith in the Lord Jesus, the personality of the devil, the natural immortality of the soul, the second coming of our Lord Jesus Christ, the resurrection of the body, the eternal security of the believer, the conscious eternal punishment of those who die impenitent, the binding character of the ordinances of the Lord's Supper and the immersion of believers as the only Christian baptism, and the responsibility of all saved souls to live soberly, righteously, and godly in this present age.

II
Central Europe

Germany
The Union of Evangelical Free Churches in the German Democratic Republic
The Union of Evangelical Free Churches in the Federal Republic of Germany

The foundations of modern Baptist history in Germany are so closely tied to the work of one man, Johann Gerhard Oncken, the so-called "Father of Continental Baptists," that his biography could almost serve as an early history. Oncken (1800-1884) was born in Varel (Oldenburg) and, after a poverty-stricken childhood, went to Scotland as the servant of a Scottish merchant. In Scotland and England, young Oncken came under the religious influence of Presbyterian, Methodist, and Independent churches. Converted in a Methodist church in London, he later joined the Continental Society upon the recommendation of the Scottish Baptist revivalist Robert Haldane and went to Hamburg to distribute Bibles and religious tracts. His teaching, preaching, and work in "the new English faith" brought many problems with the authorities since he was not a member of the state church.

Over the years, Oncken worked for several Bible societies from both England and the United States. He became increasingly disturbed about infant baptism and wanted adult baptism, writing Haldane for advice. The suggestion was to baptize himself, but he preferred rather to wait for a "Philip" who later arrived in the person of Professor Barnas Sears of Hamilton Literary and Theological Institution, a Baptist school in America. He had heard of Oncken's work through a sea captain. On April 22, 1834, Oncken, his wife, and five others were baptized by Sears in the Elbe River. On the following day, the first German "church of baptized Christians" was constituted. The Baptist Triennial Convention in America appointed him as its worker in 1835 and, along with British Baptists, continued to support the work. Such support was crucial during times of heavy persecution and included official state appeals on behalf of the Baptists.

Among the early church members were Julius Wilhelm Köbner, the son of a Danish Jewish rabbi, and Gottfried Wilhelm Lehmann, a colleague from Oncken's time with the Edinburgh Bible Society. These became the triumvirate of German Baptists for decades, leading in almost every aspect of teaching, preaching, organization, and mission outreach into many other European countries.

Heavy persecution came at the hand of the authorities; the Hamburg senate forbade meetings at one point; from Denmark to Bavaria leaders were imprisoned. Nevertheless the movement continued to spread. Only in the Hamburg fire of 1842 did official attitudes toward Baptists in Hamburg begin to change. Most of the city was destroyed, leaving thousands homeless; the Baptists provided rooms and food for many in a warehouse they had acquired. Also, in the months of rebuilding, many foreigners came to work for money but returned to their homes with a newfound faith as well. The 1848 revolution helped in the Baptist struggle for religious freedom for each individual, but only in the years after 1866 did the slow separation of church and state become a reality and allow Baptists to build their own chapels. The "Union of Baptist Churches in Germany and Denmark" was founded in 1849 with Oncken as chairman and with "organizing brethren" as a directing board. This Union, however, included Baptists from many other countries such as Switzerland, the Netherlands, and several Eastern countries, reflecting the widespread religious awakening over most of Europe that is exemplified in the Baptist movement.

Although Oncken played a key role, the early German Baptist history is far more than his life history. The early expansion of German Baptists is equally indebted to the able leadership of many other persons. The preachers' seminary was begun in 1880 under the influence of Joseph Lehmann, the son of G. W. Lehmann, and Alfred Scheve, among others. Gifts came from outside Germany to assist in building the seminary, especially from the United States. In the early days, the pastors trained at the seminary included a broad international group from different parts of Russia, Poland, Bohemia, Bulgaria, Hungary, Holland, in fact, from most of Europe.

Not only did much financial support from the United States continue but also personal support, even in the form of some reimmigration to Germany. Philip Bickel returned to his homeland in 1878 to take over the publishing ministry that Oncken had utilized so effectively. Under Bickel's leadership, and that of his son, Karl, the "Oncken Verlag" eventually developed into an extensive and vital operation for not only evangelistic and mission outreach in Europe but also for internal cohesiveness and growth. Sunday School materials, tracts, and Bibles gave a broad basis of self-identity. Although some translations were used, such as the popular sermons of Charles Haddon Spurgeon, many German writers, such as Joseph Lehmann, helped provide materials.

One of the first Baptist missionaries from Germany was Emma Rausenbusch who married an American doctor, John Clough. Together they worked very effectively in India, but that work stopped during World War I. The most active long-term involvement in foreign missions has been in the Cameroons, a work the Cloughs shared with the Basel Mission and inherited from the British Baptists. The great driving force behind this was Edward Scheve. In 1891 their first missionary couple, who was residing in the United States, was sent out.

Edward Scheve was also instrumental in encouraging the Union to move into social ministries. In 1887 "Haus Bethel" was begun in Berlin as a center for deaconesses. Over the next years many such programs were to develop with nursing, social work, orphanage work, homes for the aged, and other ministries.

The period surrounding World War II was a very difficult one for the German Baptists for many reasons. Not only did the many tragedies of loss of life and limb, of homes and churches prove to be difficult, but also the ambiguous political situation during and after the war. At the end of the war, Germany was divided. By 1959, Baptists in the German Democratic Republic formed their own seminary and other organizations in Buckow. About 1970, they formalized their own Baptist union. During the war years, Baptists were joined together with a group from the Brethren tradition (Union of Free Church Christians) and Elim Fellowship (a Pentecostal movement), and founded the Union of Evangelical Free Church Congregations in Germany *(Bund der Evangelisch-Freikirchlichen Gemeinden in Deutschland)*. The "Baptists" *(Baptisten)* is often put in parentheses after the name.

The first German Baptist Confession of Faith was drawn up by Oncken and Köbner in 1837 to present to Hamburg authorities. It reflected the Calvinistic tradition of Oncken but was modified by Lehmann for his church in Berlin. Finally, in 1845 a compromise confession was worked out by all three men, printed, and accepted by all German Baptist churches in 1847. It remained basically the same through several revisions until the new Federation when, in 1943-1944, Erich Sauer (for the Brethren) and Hans Luckey (for the Baptists) made a total revision, dropping the article on "Election to Salvation" and abbreviating the articles on the "Word of God."[1]

From 1974 to 1977, a joint effort was made by Baptists from the Federal Republic of Germany, the German Democratic Republic, Austria, and Switzerland to draw up a new confession of faith for all German-speaking Baptists. After intensive discussions and several versions, the following statement was accepted in Switzerland, Austria, and the Federal Republic of Germany, and, except for article 3, the German Democratic Republic.

In all countries the preamble "An Account of Our Faith" is used to clarify the intention and purpose of the confession. The two German unions also list the Apostles' Creed in a modern translation underlining its being presupposed as a common confession for Christians. (For the Apostles' Creed, see Appendix 1).

CENTRAL EUROPE

The international commission that prepared the text included: Franz Hacker and August Hirnböck from Austria; Claus Meister and Günter Wagner from Switzerland; Rolf Dammann and Adolf Pohl from the German Democratic Republic; and Gerhard Claas, Manfred Otto, and Eduard Schütz from the Federal Republic of Germany.

Confession of Faith

An Account of Our Faith

This confession of faith is an expression of and a witness to the churches' agreement in belief. Thus it cannot itself be an object of faith or a compulsory law for faith. As a summary interpretation of Holy Scripture it is grounded in and limited by Scripture. It presupposes the Apostles' Creed as a common confession of Christendom and remains open to the future disclosure of further truth.

The ground and content of our confession is the central event of the rule of God. The predominantly narrative style is in harmony with this. As an account of faith this confession is meant to serve for instruction in the churches, for theological reflection, and for giving witness to the faith to the world. As a lively response of the believing community to God's effectual Word, the confession of faith becomes praise of the mighty acts of God.

Part I
The Establishment of God's Rule

I. God's Revelation in Jesus Christ

God has revealed himself in his Son Jesus Christ and in him has established his rule for the salvation of mankind. *(Heb. 1:1 ff.; Gal. 4:4 ff.)*

As the One who came from God, Jesus of Nazareth brought God near to men and men to God: with unique authority he called men back to the living God; he set them free from the bonds of godlessness, forgave their sins, healed the sick, and had fellowship at table with sinners. With his words and *(Mark 1:15; Eph. 2:13; John 8:36; Matt. 9:10-13)* deeds the royal rule of God dawned.

<small>Mark 10:45; 1 Cor. 11:23-25; John 3:16; 1 John 4:16</small>

The work of Jesus who came to earth "to destroy the works of the devil" (1 John 3:8), was brought to completion in his suffering and dying for all men. In Jesus' vicarious death for the guilt of humanity of all ages, God disclosed himself to us as the One who is love.

<small>1 Cor. 15:14-22; Acts 2:36; Rom. 4:25</small>

In the resurrection of Jesus from the dead, God made the work of reconciliation effectual and raised the crucified one to be the present Lord. God has made him, for us, "wisdom, righteousness, sanctification, and redemption" (1 Cor. 1:30). With his resurrection the end of the age has begun. His resurrection gives assurance, to all of us who believe in him, of our resurrection to eternal life.

<small>John 17:4; Phil. 2:5-11</small>

As the resurrected One Jesus is exalted to the glory of the Father from which he came. In this exaltation he is Lord not only over his church, but over the whole world as well. Christ's rule is believed and proclaimed by his church; it will be recognized by all men when he comes as the perfecter of the world.

<small>2 Cor. 5:17-21</small>

God's saving work in Christ reaches its initial aim in the proclamation by his church of the message of reconciliation. In the ministry of reconciliation, which is performed in the power of the Holy Spirit Christ himself is at work, and he places all the world under the claim of its Creator. The church that proclaims him and lives by his power becomes the sign of God's new world.

II. Man's Sin and His Turning to God

<small>Luke 5:8; Rom. 3:22-24</small>

In the encounter with Jesus Christ we are made aware of the evil within us and in the structures of society as sin against God. God's reconciling and judging word lays bare to us the guilt of men as a denial of responsibility before God. Indifference and indolence, fear and self-assurance are expressions of our separation from God.

CENTRAL EUROPE

Always at work in evil is the Evil One, God's Adversary who corrupts God's good creation. At the same time, evil issues from the heart of man, who succumbs to temptation and transgresses God's commandment. The doing of evil brings him under the dominion of the Evil One. Hence man is "dead in trespasses and sins" (Eph. 2:1), and is estranged from the life that is from God. He is abandoned to the powers and forces that are at enmity with God.
Mark 7:20-23; John 8:34

Turning away from God and contempt for his love lead to exploitation, oppression and subjugation of man by men, and also to despairing solitude. The man who wishes to be like God and thinks that he can define good and evil according to his own estimates misses his own destiny. He corrupts God's good creation and threatens its very existence.
Gen. 3:1-17

Rebellion against God's rule appears not only in morally reprehensible words and deed. It can be actualized also in sacrificial commitment to liberty, peace and justice, to religion, truth and beauty. Any good deed can at the same time be, in relation to God, the most highly refined form of self-justification and self-seeking. In light of the love of God, the mystery of evil is disclosed even in men's "good" and "pious" deeds, and precisely in them, so that no one is right before God, and no one can live without grace.
Rom. 10:2-4

Anyone who rejects God's offer of grace and forgiveness remains under the wrath and judgment of God, forfeits eternal life, and imprisons himself in his own willful alienation from God. Unbelief leads to eternal perdition; but whoever accepts God's judgment upon his sins and the offer of grace lays hold upon the eternal life that Christ has secured for us.
Rom. 1:18; 2 Thess. 1:9

God's grace in Christ effects the conversion of man to God. Through faith in Jesus Christ man is made right before God and becomes a child of God. Faith is not a human achievement, but acceptance of
Rom. 3:21-29; Rom. 8:14-18; Col. 1:13; 1 John 1:9

God's grace. The believer experiences the renewing work of the Holy Spirit in forgiveness and liberation. Through the working of the Holy Spirit he is born again to a new life with God.

III. The New Life from the Holy Spirit

John 9:39-41; 1 Cor. 2:14 ff.; Rom. 8:1-4; Gal. 2:20

The gospel brings every man—even the religious man—into crisis. It means judgment and renewal for one who turns to salvation in Christ. The Holy Spirit initiates in the believers a new life, whose ground and center is Jesus Christ himself.

1 Cor. 12:12 ff.; Jas. 1:22-25; Mark 12:29-31

The new life from the Holy Spirit takes its form by placing man in new relationship and by transforming his old relationships. It binds man to God and to his people, the church of Jesus Christ, and transforms all interpersonal relationships. The new life is expressed in our heeding God's word, in prayer and in doing the will of God.

1 Cor. 1:30; 2 Cor. 6:1-10; Ps. 32; Rom. 8:26-28; John 5:39; 1 Thess. 5:16-18; Gal. 5:1; Neh. 8:10

The new life is God's gift, which should be preserved in submission and sanctification. It does not save us from afflictions and temptations, from suffering and oppression, from doubts and desires, but it gives us the strength to endure them and to confirm our faith in Jesus Christ. Even wrong choices and failures, errors and defeats cannot separate us from Christ, who remains faithful to us and forgives us our faults. The Holy Spirit is promised to us as our advocate and helper, and through the world of Holy Scripture God speaks to our lives. Bible reading, mutual brotherly counsel, and prayer offer the guidance to us on our way as disciples of Christ. The Christian is on the way, together with the church of Jesus Christ, towards the consummation of God's rule, and he lives even here and now in the liberty of the children of God to which his Lord has liberated him. Joy in the Lord is his strength.

IV. God's Creation

In our belief in Jesus Christ we acknowledge that God through his word created the world out of nothing. God's original creation is matched by his creative power today, to which the existence of every man bears witness. This world of ours did not come into being of its own accord, but it has its origin and its destiny in the goodness of God, who imparts his life to his handiwork, because he wills not to remain alone, but to have fellowship with men as his creatures. Gen. 1—2; Heb. 11:3; Rom. 4:17; John 1:4; Gen. 1:27

In spite of the sins of men, God preserves the world for its redemption. The Christian community lives in the midst of the yet unredeemed world, as Christ is beginning in her the restoration of fallen creation. As children of God, Christians experience in themselves how God is beginning to lift the fate of death and nothingness that rests upon the world, by bestowing, through the Holy Spirit, liberty and righteousness, peace and joy. Together with the whole creation they yearn for the full and complete redemption that is promised to them. Matt. 5:45; Acts 14:17; Rom. 8:16 ff.; Rom. 14:17

As the Lord of history God is Lord of all men and nations, all ages and generations. He has given to men the charge, "Subdue the earth and rule over it." God's will and world bestow upon man his dignity and make him the holder of inalienable human rights. Acts 17:26; Gen. 1:28; Ps. 8:6

Jesus Christ is Lord even over the fallen world, and he discloses to those who believe in him the overthrow of the world's gods, both manifest and hidden. Through him the world regains its goodness as God's creation. Therefore Christians take seriously their responsibility for the preservation and protection of creation. Matt. 28:18; Col. 2:15; 1 Cor. 8:4; 1 Tim. 4:4 ff.; 1 Cor. 3:21 ff.; Gen. 2:15

The Christian community acknowledges God as Ex. 20:1-17

the Creator and preserver also of the structures of creation, in which we as Christians are called to live. God created man in his shared humanity. In marriage and family, society and state, he provides for man the setting for a life in community.

V. God's Old and New Covenants

Rom. 9—11; Ex. 19:5 ff.; Deut. 7:7 ff.; John 4:22; Gen. 12:1-3

In our belief in Jesus Christ, whom God brought forth from Israel in due time, we recognize Israel as God's chosen people. God has demonstrated in a unique way, in choosing and calling this people, his creative power and his lordship over all peoples. His love for all peoples led to the covenant with this special nation. In them God willed to bless all nations and to set them as a light for the peoples. God's election and calling of Israel have not been nullified by their unfaithfulness and disobedience. In God's preserving the Jewish people down to the present we perceive a sign of his faithfulness and mercy. The secret of this people is and remains their election and deliverance by God.

Rom. 11:26; 2 Cor. 3; Jer. 31:31-34; Heb. 8:6-13; 2 Cor. 1:20; Matt. 28:19 ff.

The new covenant, in which God has established his rule of grace for all men, dissolves the old covenant and at the same time brings it to fulfillment. Jesus Christ is the Savior of the world, as he is the Messiah of Israel. Therefore salvation in Christ is for the Gentiles as well as the Jews, for in Christ all the promises given to Israel are fulfilled in a manner and a measure going far beyond all the prophetic predictions in the Old Testament. In Christ all peoples are included in God's salvation, because from them the church of Jesus Christ as the new people of God is called and gathered.

VI. God's Word – The Bible

Acts 4:12; Rom. 10:13; Rom. 1:16 ff.; 1 Cor. 1:18

Jesus Christ is God's Word in person to us men. In his life and work God has revealed himself comprehensively and definitely for the salvation of men. The resurrected and exalted Christ becomes present reality for us in the power of the Holy Spirit. He makes the proclamation of the gospel, which is accomplished through men, the word of God for us.

In the New Testament we hear the first witnesses to Jesus Christ. The Christian community is grounded in their testimony. That testimony cannot be expanded or superseded by any subsequent Christian proclamation or teaching. Under the guidance of the Holy Spirit the authors of the New Testament have borne witness to God's salvation that has appeared in Christ. This constitutes the authority and the normative character of the New Testament for the life and teaching of the church. It is the written word of God. *[1 John 1:1 ff.; Acts 1:2,8]*

The Old Testament bears witness to us of God's dealings with his people Israel and of God's will for all mankind. The Christian community understands the Old Testament from the perspective of God's revelation in Christ and sees it as pointing toward that revelation; for Christ is the goal and the end of the law. The New Testament bears witness to us of God's saving work in Christ for all mankind and of the outpouring of the Holy Spirit. The gospel of the crucified, risen and coming Lord Jesus Christ is the center of the New Testament and hence of the entirety of the Holy Scripture. *[Ex. 20:1-17; Rom. 10:4; Acts 2; John 5:39]*

The Bible is God's word in human language. Therefore its books bear the signs of the times in which they originated. Their language, their patterns of thought, and their literary forms are bound to the times and places whence they come. Therefore the historical understanding of Holy Scripture is an obligation of the Christian church and its theology, in their listening to the word of God. The historical interpretation of Scripture takes into account the working of the Holy Spirit, both in originating and expounding the Holy Scriptures of the Old and New *[Heb. 1:1; Luke 1:2-4; John 20:31 ff.; 2 Tim. 3:16 ff.; 2 Pet. 1:19-21]*

Testaments. The Bible lives, because God speaks through it.

Part II
Life Under God's Rule

I. The Church of Jesus Christ

1. *The Gathering and the Sending of the Church*

<small>2 Cor. 4:5 ff.; Col. 1:13 ff.; Mark 3:31-35; Rom. 15:7; Matt. 6:12</small>

God, who has revealed himself in his Son Jesus Christ and has established his rule for the salvation of men, calls men to a life under this rule. All who believe on Jesus Christ have been transplanted from the dominion of darkness into the kingdom of Christ. Christ gathers them into his community in a common life, witness and service. The Holy Spirit gives them the will to live in harmony with God's reconciliation. Because Christ first loved us and loves us still, we belong to the family of God as brothers and sisters. As Christ has accepted us, we also accept ourselves and those whom Christ has called, with us, to faith. As Christ has forgiven and still forgives our sins, so we also forgive our neighbors.

<small>2 Cor. 5:19 ff.; Eph. 1:3 ff.; John 15:1-8; 1 Tim. 2:1 ff.; John 20:21; Matt. 28:16-20; 1 Pet. 2:9 ff.</small>

The church of Jesus Christ responds to God's reconciling act in praise and worship. Bowing before God she confesses her guilt and receives from him forgiveness and the authority for her mission. In evangelization and service the Christian community bears witness to God's salvation for all men. She intercedes in prayer and supplication for all men and nations. As God sent his Son into the world, so Jesus Christ today sends his church into the world. All members of the church of Jesus Christ are under the commission of their Lord: "Preach the gospel to the whole creation!" (Mark 16:15).

2. *Proclamation and Instruction*

<small>Mark 16:15 ff.; Deut. 6:7-19,20-25</small>

The sending of the church into the world is focused in the public proclamation of the gospel of

Jesus Christ to all men and in the biblical instruction of her members and their children.

In the gatherings of the Christian community Jesus Christ establishes his rule, by giving his word to his disciples, assuring them of his forgiveness, bestowing his love on them and granting to them his Holy Spirit. In the service of worship Jesus Christ constrains those who are his own to discipleship and obedience, to faith and ministry, to love and hope. In the service of worship Jesus Christ calls men who are not yet Christians to the decision of faith and to the surrender of their lives to God's Lordship. Matt. 18:20; Gal. 3:2; John 20:22 ff.; Acts 4:31; Rom. 12:1 ff.

The task of Christian instruction is the training of the members of the community in the obedience of faith and their equipment for a responsible life. At the center of this instruction are the study of the Bible and the translation of the gospel for our time and our world. The teaching of children and youth is a special task of the Christian church, which bears the responsibility before her Lord that the younger generation shall be encouraged to believe in Jesus Christ and to live as his disciples. Eph. 4:15; Col. 3:1 ff.; Col. 3:20 ff.

3. *Faith and Baptism*

To all who hear the gospel of Jesus Christ, God offers his grace in that gospel. In his word he calls for the response of faith. God's Spirit empowers man to make a mature decision for Jesus Christ. Whoever turns to God in repentance and faith receives forgiveness of his guilt and eternal life. Acts 2:38; 1 Thess. 1:9ff.; John 5:24

Man's conversion to God is expressed in his confession of Christ which he makes in the presence of God and men in baptism, which was instituted by Jesus Christ. Therefore, in accordance with the teaching of the New Testament, we baptize only those persons who on the basis of their personal faith ask for baptism and declare their intention with God's help to lead a life of obedience in discipleship to Acts 8:36-38; 1 Pet. 3:21; Luke 3:10 ff.; Matt. 28:19 ff.; Titus 3:5 ff.; Rom. 6:1-11; Col. 2:9-15; 1 Cor. 12:13; Matt. 6:33; Acts 14:22

Jesus Christ. The baptism that was instituted by Jesus Christ, in the name of the Father, the Son and the Holy Spirit, and is performed by the community with water and by immersion of the person, is a sign of the forgiveness of sins, of God's acceptance of the person, and of the renewal of the person by the Holy Spirit. In baptism one is equipped, by the gift of the Holy Spirit, for a new life of praise to God in discipleship to Jesus Christ. In baptism he is incorporated into the one body of Christ and is received into the fellowship of the church. By means of baptism Christ and his church declare their solidarity with the one who is baptized, who is recruited for struggling and suffering in the kingdom of God.

4. The Lord's Supper

1 Cor. 11:23-29; 1 Cor. 10:16 ff.; Acts 2:47

As the Lord of his church Jesus Christ has established the Lord's Supper as the act in which his people assemble with joy at his table, to share the bread and the cup in his name, and as a sign that he gives himself to his disciples.

Luke 24:30-35; Matt. 26:26-28; Acts 2:42

In the observance of the Supper we experience the saving nearness and fellowship of Jesus Christ, by recalling his suffering and dying for us. We experience anew our acceptance by the crucified and risen Christ. In the Supper we experience fellowship with all our brothers and sisters whom God has called to faith along with us. In worship and with thanksgiving and supplications we celebrate our reconciliation with God and with each other.

Luke 22:16-20

We celebrate the Lord's Supper in joyous anticipation of the return of Jesus Christ and the consummation of his rule, by proclaiming the Lord's death until he returns. We are sent forth from the Lord's table, strengthened and with renewed faith and courage, to a new life in Christ in discipleship, witness and service.

5. Spiritual Gifts, Ministries and Orders

In the experience of the grace of God the members of the community of Jesus Christ are given gifts of grace that serve to build up the body of Christ. The Holy Spirit bestows in the community particularly the gifts of proclamation and teaching, of love and care, of leadership and day-to-day direction. Thus the Spirit of God enables the people, on their way through time, to fulfill their mission. There is no member of the body of Christ without gifts. All gifts of the Spirit are bestowed with the aim of forming our life under God's gracious rule in peace and order, in cooperation and mutual regard. The priesthood of all believers is the basic structure that is given to the Christian church by her Lord. *[1 Cor. 12—14; Rom. 12:1-8; Eph. 4:11-16; 1 Pet. 2:5-10]*

The Christian community calls suitable men and women, whose special endowment by the Holy Spirit and calling by God she recognizes, into special ministries and equips them to perform these ministries. In particular she provides for the ministries of proclamation, instruction, pastoral care, service to the needy, and leadership. Spiritual gifts and offices alike serve the gathering together and the sending-forth of the church of Jesus Christ. *[1 Tim. 3; Acts 20:28; 1 Tim. 5:17-22; 1 Tim. 4:12-16; 2 Tim. 2:2]*

Each local congregation is understood as a manifestation of the one body of Christ and is responsible for ordering its own life and ministry. These local congregations are bound together, not primarily through organizational ties, but by the one Lord and the one Spirit. The congregations strengthen each other through fellowship in the faith, and by learning from each other, through intercession and by mutual aid. Such things as structure of the congregation and denominational organization, administration and finance, institutions and works, are not ends in themselves, but are instruments of the mission of the church in this world. *[1 Cor. 1:2; Eph. 4:3-6; 1 Cor. 16:1-4]*

6. Pastoral Care and Church Discipline

Phil. 2:1 ff.; 1 Pet. 4:10 ff.; Gal. 6:1; Jas. 5:19 ff.; Rom. 12:9 ff.

The pastoral care of the members is entrusted to the entire congregation. The aim of this pastoral care is to encourage and empower all members of the community to live a life of discipleship to Jesus Christ and of submission to God. Rebuke and comfort, confession of sin and promise of forgiveness serve this aim, as do sharing in joys and fears, sufferings and trials, afflictions and distresses of our neighbours. Here the word of Scripture applies: "Bear one another's burdens, and so fulfill the law of Christ" (Gal. 6:2).

Matt. 18:15; 1 Cor. 5:13; 1 Tim. 1:19 ff.; 1 Cor. 5:5

If in a member of the church the belief in Jesus Christ is extinguished, the love of God and neighbour has grown cold, and all pastoral efforts to bring that person back to Christ and his church remain fruitless, the community will exclude him from its fellowship. In the case of conscious and willful offense and sin against God's manifest will and of persistence in that way, the community has no alternative but to use this means of discipline. It will do this in sorrow for not having believed firmly enough and not having loved devotedly enough, and in the hope that the member under discipline will find grace with God anew and will return to the fellowship of the church.

7. The One Body of Christ and the Divided Churches

Eph. 4:3-6; 1 Cor. 10:16 ff.

The Christian experiences the fellowship of the church primarily in the local gathering of believers. There the one baptism upon confession of faith is performed and the one bread, instituted by the one Lord, is broken and shared. Therefore the local congregation is seen to be the manifestation of the one body of Jesus Christ, permeated by the one Spirit and filled with the one hope.

The one Spirit bestows many gifts, which can be exercised in the local congregations but also in the churches that are separated from each other, in a mutually enriching diversity. Jesus Christ is building his community in the various churches and fellowships. Regardless of the diversities, and regardless of error and fault on all sides, it cannot be God's will for denominational barriers to hinder the visible fellowship of all believers and thus their credible testimony to all the world. Therefore we pray, with Christians of the whole earth, for the renewal of all communions and churches, that more mutual recognition may become possible, and that God may lead us to the unity that he wills for us. Even today it is the task not only of the individual Christians from various churches, but also of these churches themselves, to take whatever steps are possible out of their separation toward each other, to eliminate existing prejudices, and conscientiously to formulate and represent objections, to learn from each other, to pray for each other, and together to glorify Christ in witness and service.

1 Cor. 12:1-11; John 17:22 *ff.*; Eph. 4:1-6; Acts 15; Gal. 2

II. Christians in the World

1. *The Responsibility of Faith in the Situation of the Diaspora*

It is the will of God for the Christian church to be the salt of the earth and the light of the world. The church seeks no dominion in society or over society but is called and empowered for worship of God in the everyday life of this world and thus for the development of shared human life by the power of the Holy Spirit. The church as a whole and each of its members are ready for the responsibility of faith. They speak for God and his righteousness, and in their life as brothers and sisters God's gracious rule can be discerned.

Matt. 5:13-16; Rom. 12:1 *ff.*; John 13:1-17; 1 Pet. 3:15; Rom. 3:21-31; Acts 2:42-47

We live as Christians scattered among those who do not believe. In this situation where we are a minority and are on a mission, we know that in our work and our leisure, in the family and in society we are called to serve God in all our fellow men. Because Christians rejoice in being accepted by God and called to be his co-workers, they live their faith in bearing witness to Christ personally, in demonstrating their solidarity with people who are suffering, in acts of personal assistance, and thus in obedience to the commandment that we love our neighbours. To take our stand for the truth of Jesus Christ also includes our readiness to accept disadvantage and even persecution.

[margin: 1 Pet. 1:1-12; 1 Cor. 3:9; Matt. 5:43-48; 1 Pet. 4:12-19]

2. The Call to Reconciliation

Because we have our origin in reconciliation with God, we are called also to serve the cause of reconciliation among men. In this spirit Christians make their contribution to understanding between generations, social and political groups, parties, classes, races and nations. They strive to eliminate any and all discrimination by persons against persons and work for peace in the world. The Christians' calling is to be validated precisely when in substantive issues they must speak a resounding "No." The readiness for reconciliation works for agreement, but it does not mean capitulation in the face of conflict or suppression of real problems.

[margin: Gen. 3:27 ff.; Eph. 2:14; Matt. 5:43-48]

Because we have our origin in God's justification of the ungodly, we are called to serve the cause of justice among men. Since Christians live in the liberty for which Christ has set them free, they oppose every form of dependence that injures human dignity. In the spirit of Jesus they support corresponding efforts to liberate men from economic, social and racial oppression. Accordingly,

[margin: Eph. 6:9; Rom. 14:19; Heb. 12:14]

they contend for the basic freedoms of man, especially for freedom of belief and of conscience.

3. Marriage and Family

Man and woman are called, in accordance with the will of God, to be joined in lifelong marriage and to build their life together in love and fidelity. Marriage offers a fundamental and exemplary portrayal of God's will for the ordering of human life. One person esteems the other more highly than himself and accepts him as Christ has accepted him. *(Gen. 1:27; Gen. 2:18-25; Mark 10:7-9; Eph. 5:25)*

For the person who is reconciled with God, bodily existence and sexuality are good gifts from the hand of the Creator. In love for one's partner one will use these gifts responsibly before God. Man and woman, united in marriage, are privileged by God to share in the creation of new life, to be responsible for their children in love and care, to train them in the sight of God, to develop their gifts, and to lead them to faith in Jesus Christ. *(1 Cor. 6:19 ff.; Mark 10:13-16)*

In the unmarried state the Christian can discover and accept God's guidance and opportunity. Both gifts, marriage and the unmarried state, are given to Christians to mold their shared life in accordance with God's will and to place it at the service of God's rule. Accordingly, Christians will conduct their lives, in keeping with the model of the New Testament, in homes that are open and hospitable, places of a common life in conversation and celebration, work and prayer, caring for and comforting one another. *(1 Cor. 7:7; Gal. 6:2; Heb. 13:1-3; 1 Cor. 6:9 ff.)*

Unrestrained exercise of sexuality is a sign of man's alienation from God, from himself, and from his fellow man. Christians will not abet the deification of sexuality, but will set an example of how the freedom of the children of God takes its form in a new life.

4. Christians in Society and State

Rom. 13:1-7; Jer. 29:7; 1 Tim. 2:1 ff. — In accordance with God's will, shared human life finds its form, in the history of this world, in structures of society and in orders of the state. For the maintenance of these orders there is need of law and of the state's instruments of power, but also of the intercession and thanksgiving of the church. Christians stand ready to accept responsibility for the well-being of their fellow men and to share in the task of shaping social and political orders in accordance with human dignity. Christians and Christian communities will seek in every social and political system to find ways to fulfill their mission.

2 Pet. 3:13; Rev. 13 — Social and political order may not be confused and intermingled with the rule of God and the church of Jesus Christ and can never take the place of these. Therefore we stand for the separation of state and church. Social and political order represents a mandate of God for the world. Its claim is limited: "Give to Caesar what belongs to Caesar and to God what belongs to God" (Matt. 22:21, *by the translator*). It is not in keeping with the will of God for society and state to lay claim to man in his totality and to leave him no room for living under the rule of God and in the Christian church. When conflict arises in this matter, "One must obey God rather than men" (Acts 5:29, *by the translator*).

Over against all social and political theories with their human designs for a manageable future, Christians bear witness to God's promise of a new creation and confess God's rule as the future of the world.

Part III
The Consummation of God's Rule

I. The Future of the Christ Who Has Come

Acts 1:11; 1 Thess. — Jesus Christ, the Lord of his church and of his world, who was crucified, rose from the dead, and was raised to the right hand of God, will appear, on the day that God alone will determine, in glory as the fulfiller of God's kingdom and as judge of all men. The Christ who will return is the future of our world and at the same time he is the unsurpassable limit of the progress of which men are capable as well as the end of the history of human failure. *4:13-18; Acts 1:7; Rev. 18:21-24; Rev. 21:4*

Jesus Christ's appearing in glory will transform the belief and unbelief of men into sight. The same Lord who already rules over the church and world will make his hidden Lordship manifest to all. The return of Christ will bring an end to the time of preaching of the gospel. The last day of our world-epoch will also be the first day of God's new creation. *Matt. 5:8; 1 John 3:2; Rev. 20:11 to 21:8*

In view of this hope we, as the Christian community, confess all the more surely that eternal life is granted to us even now and that the same Spirit who creates new life today will transform our mortal bodies. We confess that no power of death is able to separate us from God's love and that the dying person rests in the sheltering hands of the God who raised our Lord Jesus Christ. *1 Cor. 15:20; Rom. 8:11; John 14:19; Rom. 8:38-39*

The return of Jesus Christ will bring about the downfall of all forces that oppose God and will lead the still believing and waiting, suffering and faltering Christian church out of all its affliction and temptation into the fulfillment of God's rule. The annihilation of evil and of death will unveil to all eyes God's intention for his fallen creation: the ultimate redemption of the people of God and the restoration of the creation to the peace of God. *Matt. 6:12; 1 John 1:8; Rev. 20:14; 21:4; 1 Cor. 15:56; Rom. 8:19-23*

In view of this hope the Christian church confesses its Lord as the future of the world. In the strength of this hope the church works for the renewal of men through the grace of God which is proclaimed in the gospel, and through faith which is active in love. *1 Cor. 15:58; 1 Thess. 1:9 ff.*

II. The Judgment of the Coming Christ

Rom. 2:16; Acts 10:42

With the appearing of Jesus Christ we anticipate the resurrection of the dead as the ultimate demonstration of God's creative and redemptive power. But the resurrection of the dead also signifies that we are set in the presence of our judge, "so that each one receives his reward for what he has done in his lifetime, whether it be good or evil" (2 Cor. 5:10, *by the translator*).

Matt. 10:32 *ff.*; Matt. 18:18; Matt. 25:45 *ff.*; Luke 14:16-24; John 3:36

As judge, Christ implements the gospel. He discloses whether the works of men are wrought by God's power or men's own doing. The faith that has responded to the gospel is recognized by Christ. Whatever is being done now in the authority of the risen Christ and of the Holy Spirit, every pronouncement of forgiveness as well as the binding and remembering of sins, will then be publicly confirmed by Christ as judge. All self-made righteousness and all self-willed detachment of man from God will be brought to light in the judgment, will be excluded from the new creation, and will end in final separation from God. God respects the freedom of his creature, in that he allows to unbelief the reality that it has chosen for itself. Anyone who rejects God's love, him will God reject.

Ezek. 18:23; 1 Tim. 2:4

We extol the love of the God who is free in his grace and mercy, who does not will the death of the sinner but his repentance, whose aim is the redemption and not the rejection of man, whose intention is not the perdition but the salvation of the world.

III. God's New World

Rev. 21:1-5; John 17:24; Rev. 22:3-5

God's aim for the world and for humanity is eternal life in a new creation. God's will is directed toward the new man, who ultimately will attain his destiny to live by God's power and for God, and toward the new people of God, who ultimately will be liberated for true worship of God. God wants to be their God for eternity, and they are to be his people forever.

As surely as this future is promised to the Christian church, it is far from being able properly to grasp and to express the vision of the new heaven and the new earth. The church takes the biblical parables and images of the earthly paradise, of the celestial city, of the Father's house, and of the new banquet as a sign and an earnest of the promised glory in which God's rule will come to fulfillment. God's new creation will be the world of resurrected, transformed and transfigured bodily existence. In that world, death and tears, hunger and pain, injustice and sin, loneliness and godforsakeness will be no more. Instead, there will be joy and peace, righteousness and blessedness, adoration and the vision of God forever. In God's new world the creation will find happiness and fulfillment. The perfect and complete redemption of the created universe will also be the final victory of the honor and glory of God.

Rev. 22:1-2; 21:9-27; John 14:2; Luke 22:16 *ff.*; 1 Cor. 15:42-49; 1 Cor. 15:28

TR: John Steely

(Difference between FRG Baptist confession and the GDR Baptist confession: Part II, Life Under God's Rule, I. The Church of Jesus Christ)

3. Faith and Baptism

To all who hear the gospel of Jesus Christ, God offers his grace in that gospel. In his word he calls for the response of faith. God's spirit empowers man to make a mature decision for Jesus Christ. Whoever turns to God in repentance and faith receives forgiveness of his guilt and eternal life.

Rom. 1:16; 1 Thess. 1:9 *ff.*; John 5:24

Whoever has accepted the Word requests the

Acts 2:41; Acts 8:36

ff.; Matt. 28:19; Rom. 6:3 *ff*.; 1 Pet. 3:21; Acts 2:38; 28:20; 2:44-47

baptism which was instituted by Christ. The community hears her/his testimony and accepts her/him as sister or brother in Christ. They carry out baptism in a worship service by immersion in the name of the Father, the Son and the Holy Spirit. Through baptism the person commits himself in a public and binding way to his faith and to Christ as the ground of his faith. He lays his life without Christ into the grave in order to share the life of Christ in discipleship. To this end he requests the grace of God in baptism. At the same time he subscribes to a learning and serving fellowship with the Christian community which before God declares itself to be in a spiritual and social solidarity with the person.

Baptism belongs in the operating realm of the Holy Spirit for the purpose of building up the Christian community. But as soon as we attempt to conceptualize the spiritual happening in baptism, we come to different assertions.

Some see, according to their understanding of the New Testament, baptism basically as an act of man in response to the Gospel which, however, is not performed from within oneself but as one is filled and carried by the Holy Spirit. God will show his loyalty to him with new evidence of his faithfulness and with the granting of new gifts and tasks. Others see in baptism received through faith not only an act of man but also an act of God. The person is conveyed to his Lord in his baptism, receives participation in the death and the resurrection of Christ and permits himself to become a member of the body of Christ.

Note

1. For the Confession, see William L. Lumpkin, *Baptist Confessions of Faith* (Valley Forge: Judson Press, 1959).

Switzerland
Union of Baptist Churches in Switzerland

Baptists in Switzerland are indebted to the efforts of Johann Gerhard Oncken who, in addition to his work in Germany, made several visits to Switzerland, distributing literature, preaching, and making contacts with already existing Bible study groups. Oncken visited one such house church in Hochwert, in the Toggenburg region, in 1847 and declared it to be a "true Baptist church." His diary reveals many such visits in a "collecting," as well as evangelizing, missionary travel throughout Switzerland. Oncken commissioned Friedrich Maier, his colporteur in southern Germany, to do further missionary work. He was effective in helping establish the church in Zürich in 1849, which quickly became the center of Baptist outreach in Switzerland. By 1870, the Swiss churches joined the ever-broadening German Baptist Union.

Although there was persecution of early Baptists, it did not last long. Growth was slow and often included the gathering together of existing groups. Since the Reformation, the growing Swiss Federation has been basically balanced between Roman Catholics and Protestants (Reformed), divided for many years along state lines. The Federal Constitution of the Swiss Confederation (1848), Article 44, called for religious freedom for the "recognized Christian confessions." Article 49 of the 1874 Revised Constitution, however, guaranteed total "freedom of faith and conscience."

After World War I, Swiss Baptists formed their own administrative structure, which enabled them to develop a union, publication, a deaconess house, mission outreach, and other work.

The Constitution of the Swiss Baptist Union states in Article 1 its purpose and bases first in theological and biblical terms, indicating their call to preaching the gospel, leading into Christian life and service. In addition, it states that they support freedom of faith and conscience and separation of church and state. And, in order to carry out "preaching of the Gospel and service in the world," the Union calls for working with other churches.

Since Switzerland is not only very small but also quite diverse linguistically and culturally, it is natural that Baptists should reflect some of that diversity. French-speaking Baptists in Switzerland never joined the Swiss Baptist Union, but remained a part of the conservative "Evangelical Association of French-Speaking Baptist Churches," which is made up of some churches from France and Belgium, as well as Switzerland. Limited work exists in the Italian-speaking area in Lugano with support from the Swiss Baptist Union. The international Baptist Theological Seminary was established in Rüschlikon, Zürich, Switzerland in 1949 and trains students from all of Europe and some other continents. Supported primarily by the Southern Baptist Foreign Mission Board, as well as by European Baptists and Swiss Baptists, its faculty is international.

Swiss Baptists were actively engaged in preparing the common German-language Confession of Faith with the German and Austrian Baptists. The Convention of Baptist Churches in Switzerland voted in Basel on June 17, 1977, "to recommend the . . . text to the congregations for their use." The Swiss text contains the preamble and the Apostles' Creed. (For the Confession of Faith, see pp. 57-76.)

(Claus Meister)

Austria
The Baptist Union of Austria

Baptist beginnings in Austria are related to the migration of Austrians to work in Hamburg after the great fire of 1842. Five workers were converted under the influence of J. G. Oncken and eventually returned to their native Austria, starting Bible study groups and preaching. On October 28, 1847, some were baptized in Vienna. The following year Oncken himself visited the group. Shortly thereafter civil unrest and direct persecution created many problems for the struggling group. In 1851, the British and Foreign Bible Society sent Edward Millard to Vienna. He gathered Baptists and helped work toward founding their first church. Forced to leave Austria for twelve years, Millard was able to return. After a visit by the aging Oncken, Millard organized the church in 1869. The early history of the church in Vienna, as well as in most of Austria, was filled with great difficulty, heavy persecution, and direct government opposition.

Rigidly Roman Catholic for centuries, the Austrian-Hungarian empire had little toleration for other groups; hardly a century had passed since the ecclesiastical policies of Emperor Joseph II had again strengthened Catholicism in Austria. The Vienna church was the key to early Baptist history and outreach to several stations in (modern) Austria and to Prague and Bohemia, as well as Hungary and Romania. World War I not only took many lives but also resulted in the break-up of the Austrian-Hungarian empire, according to the Treaty of Versailles. The rebuilding work among Baptists came with the long and powerful leadership of Pastor Arnold Koester who, for thirty-one years, unified most work under the Mollardgasse (Vienna) church.

Many unique and risky ministries were carried out during World War II. Koester was often in trouble with occupation authorities. After the war, ministries focused on refugee problems; some dynamic evangelistic work also took place with considerable openness and response among the people. This was lessened, however, with the consolidation of Austrian life.

In spite of outside help from Baptists in the United States, Germany, and Sweden, Baptists in Austria have not gained much numerically and have been weakened by emigration to other countries. Religious freedom is now guaranteed and chapels may be built. In 1953, the Union of Baptist Churches in Austria was created and was composed of the seven churches and mission stations. Austrian Baptists helped write the joint German-speaking Confession of Faith in the 1970s (see pp. 57-76).

(Emmanual Wieser)
(Martin Lange)

Netherlands
The Union of Baptist Churches in the Netherlands

Although Baptists trace their earliest roots both to England and English Baptists in Holland in the seventeenth century, the roots of modern Dutch Baptists are to be found in the nineteenth century. The revivals that swept much of the Western world also affected Holland and many Reformed clergymen, such as Dr. Johannes Elias Feisser.

Feisser had been led to a fuller experience of the life in Christ through personal conversion and attempted to lead his church in the same direction but found very little response. A conflict arose when Feisser refused to baptize the child of a church member who did not take the slightest interest in the church and in the faith. This refusal led to Feisser's suspension and, in the end, removal from his ministry. In the meantime, Feisser's thoughts on baptism developed. He discovered that the only legitimate New Testament baptism was believers' baptism.

Julius Köbner came from Hamburg to Gasselternijveen in order to inquire about Feisser and his views. Köbner informed Feisser about the Baptists, of whom the latter had never heard, and about their congregational life. This led Feisser to the decision to seek baptism. After consultations with his handful of faithful followers, the decision to make a completely new start was made. When Köbner returned to Gasselternijveen in the spring of 1845, seven people were baptized on May 15, including Feisser and Roelof Reiling and his wife. The first Baptist church in the Netherlands had come into being. Soon the church moved to the neighboring village of Stadskanaal in the province of Groningen. For many decades this church has been one of the most vital centers of Baptist life in the northeastern part of the Netherlands. Today there are four churches in the area.

The second place where a Baptist church came into being was the small town of Zutphen on the border of the river Ijssel in the province of Gelderland. A Mennonite minister, Jan de Liefde, turned away from the Socinianism then prevailing in the Mennonite community, to a living and personal faith in Christ who had died for his sins. When he started to preach this newly discovered gospel to his congregation, a severe conflict arose. Contacts with Feisser and Köbner brought de Liefde to the verge of rejecting the baptism by sprinkling which he had received at the age of twenty in the Mennonite church and accepting the other. Due to his millennialist views, he declined to be baptized. In the summer of 1845, however, when de Liefde was away for reasons of health, some of his close friends in Zutphen took the step and were baptized on June 24, 1845. When de Liefde returned, he did not join the new church and soon left Zutphen. The young church went through difficult vicissitudes. After a number of years, it disappeared altogether.

The third Baptist church was formed in the capital, Amsterdam. Around 1840, a small group of friends began to meet regularly to read and study the Bible. Soon they touched upon the subject of baptism and discovered that believers' baptism was the only biblical way of administering and accepting baptism. After visiting in Zutphen, Köbner and Feisser visited Amsterdam in May 1845. Four members of the Bible study group were baptized, and two years later a Baptist church was established. In 1849, none other than de Liefde joined them and was baptized. After a short time, however, he left the church when he started to preach in places outside Amsterdam and to advocate admission into church membership without baptism. The small Baptist church continued to exist but did not attract the attention of the public. For several years it was torn apart by controversy over the teachings of John Nelson Darby. In 1866, it received royal recognition and counted this as the year of its official beginning.

EUROPE 1871-1914

New impulses came into the Baptist movement in the 1860s with the return to Holland of such personalities as Peter Johannes de Neui from Germany and H. Z. Kloekers from China where he had met and joined Baptist missionaries (BMS). De Neui had been a fervent evangelist in the province of Friesland and settled in Franeker, founding churches in the area and becoming pastor of the Franeker church.

In the late sixties and throughout the seventies, several attempts were made to bring the scattered churches together but without lasting success. When in 1880 and 1881 a new attempt was made, Kloekers was one of the leading personalities. This time the attempt was successful and seven churches became charter members of the new union. Franeker and Amsterdam did not join the union, probably because the Calvinistic spirit which prevailed in their constituencies was an obstacle to entry into fellowship with the more Arminian spirit represented by Kloekers (who became the first president of the Union) and the churches which followed him. After ten years, Amsterdam applied for membership of the Union, but Franeker never did.

One of the most far-reaching results of the founding of the Union was the decision to publish a paper, *De Christen (The Christian)*. The first issue appeared on January 15, 1882. Kloekers was one of the editors. This paper, which still exists under the same name, proved to be an important instrument in offering a sense of identity and fellowship among the Dutch Baptists. Yet it occasioned the one really serious doctrinal controversy which the Dutch Baptists had to go through. In 1884, Kloekers wrote an article on Romans 3:25 which he interpreted as a challenge to follow the example set forth by Christ in his suffering. His coeditor, J. Horn, who happened to live near the printer blocked its publication and the ensuing conflict between the two editors was brought before a special assembly of the Union in November 1884. Opinion was strongly divided. In the end, Kloekers resigned as president of the Union; two churches left the Union. The majority of the churches followed Horn, who represented the orthodox view. The two churches returned into the fellowship of the Union in the 1890s.

The remaining years of the century and the first decade of the next were a period of steady growth. In some places, however, the growth was almost spectacular due to the influence of revivals in Great Britain which swept over to the Netherlands, particularly in the early years of the twentieth century. Around the turn of the century, the membership of the churches in the Union was about one thousand. Ten years later it was close to fourteen hundred, and at the beginning of World War I it was seventeen hundred members in twenty-one churches.

World War I did not affect Baptist life beyond the average. The country remained neutral. Apart from shortage of food and fuel, distribution and mobilization, no disaster happened. Baptists did not participate actively in social and political life but concentrated on church growth and evangelism. Membership rose from seventeen hundred in 1914 to twenty-one hundred in 1918, the number of churches from twenty-one to twenty-four. The postwar years witnessed the strongest growth in Baptist history. This was in part due to migration from the Baptist strongholds in the north to other parts of the country, in part also to continued evangelistic work. From 1918 to 1932 membership increased to over four thousand (that is, 91 percent). The number of churches climbed from twenty-four to thirty-one.

The twenties and thirties represented continued, organic growth and the founding of the Baptist Young Peoples' Movement, the Baptist Ministers' Fellowship, a deaconess' house and a building fund as well as the beginnings of the national theological seminary which eventually opened in 1958 as "De Vinkenhof."

World War II did not leave the Netherlands untouched. Soon after the occupation, the Dutch Baptists came to experience what it means to live under oppression. Several ministers were arrested, some even deported. Yet on the whole they did not suffer severe losses. Only one church building was destroyed in 1945. Spiritually, however, the years of the war were tremendously important because many barriers between the Baptists (usually considered a sect) and the historic churches were overcome. This paved the way for an emancipation of the hitherto isolated Baptists.

When the nightmare of World War II was over, the Dutch Baptists recovered remarkably with steady growth, extensive cooperative activities in education, missions, and Youth work.

The years since the end of the war have been, on the whole, a peaceful time. The only serious controversy that occurred was over participation in the ecumenical movement. In 1945, the Union joined the Ecumenical Council of Churches in the Netherlands and, in 1948, the World Council of Churches. In the early sixties, however, a growing number became dissatisfied with both memberships because of the alleged modernism of leading personalities in the WCC. When a few churches threatened to leave the Union if membership were maintained, the General Assembly of 1963 voted to discontinue its connections with the WCC, and the ECC. Only the participation in the Ecumenical Relief Service was continued. In 1968, the Ecumenical Council was replaced by a new body, the Dutch Council of Churches. The aim was to make conditions for membership such that the Roman Catholic Church Province and the Reformed churches could enter. To many friends of the ecumenical movement, this suggested that the Baptist Union could also join the council since it did not require mutual recognition of its members as churches of Christ. But when it was suggested unofficially that membership implied that no member church would do on its own what could be done by two or more churches together, the Baptists shrank back. Though the matter was discussed several times in the General Assembly no decision was made and the subject was dropped in the early seventies.

Church and state are separate in Holland, with guarantees of freedom of religion in the constitutions ot 1815 and 1947. This applies to all denominations, including Baptists.

The confession of faith is found in the second articles of the

Statutes of all Baptist churches in membership with the Union of Baptist Churches in the Netherlands. Many churches have in their Statutes another article to the effect that the second article cannot be altered but has to be kept in its present wording. In the nineteenth century, there were various attempts to draw up a confession of faith binding for all churches in membership with the Union, mostly modeled after German examples. These attempts delayed the formation of the Union, as several churches rejected the idea of a confessional basis for the Union. When the Union was formed in 1881, the article was included which identified the member churches as "the churches which confess and experience that Jesus Christ is the only begotten Son of God and an all-sufficient Saviour of sinners; which maintain the baptism of believers, as distinct from sprinkling." In 1953, this was changed to read:

The churches of which the Union consists exist on the basis of the revelation of God as handed down to them through the Bible, and their members in obedience to the Holy Scripture confess to have accepted as their Saviour and Lord Jesus Christ, the Son of God, the Head of the Church and the Lord of the world, and are baptized on the basis of this confession.

The confession of faith was, in all probability, drawn up in the early decade of this century and was offered to the churches to be used as a model. It was gradually accepted and introduced by the churches then existing and by those that have come into existence later. It never gained binding power over churches or individuals and played seldom, if ever, a role in the life of the churches. It is very little known and is little used, even for study. It bears the marks of orthodox Christology and of evangelical belief in the salvation of sinners; it stresses the necessity of believers' baptism, but contains no regulation for the life of the churches and their members beyond the institution of baptism and the Lord's Supper.

Jannes Reiling

Confession of Faith of the Dutch Baptist Churches

The church accepts as its only foundation the revealed Truth of God as contained in Holy Scriptures or the Bible, the content of which it accepts as the infallible Word of God.
She believes and confesses therefore:

A. That the whole human race by falling away from God is in its nature wholly corrupted and inclined to all evil, and because of the crime of sin is righteously given up to the eternal judgment of death;

B. That God has sent His only begotten Son into the world to seek and save the lost, so that the redemption of the world and the salvation of souls is wrought and granted only through the grace of God in Jesus Christ, who by His incarnation humbled and gave up Himself to fulfil the counsel and will of the Father to the glory of His Father and the salvation of men, to reconcile through His mediating suffering and death on the cross the world with God and to destroy the works and the rule of Satan; who is buried but on the third day rose in person and by that is declared to be the Son of God and the all-trustworthy and all-sufficient Saviour of sinners; who, now ascended to heaven and exalted at the right hand of the Father, is clothed with all power on heaven and on earth; who sent to His Church the Holy Spirit with its distinct gifts and powers in order to sanctify her and to enable her to reveal everywhere in the world through the Gospel, life and incorruptibility; and who shall return according to His promise to gather personally all who belong to Him in His glory and to act as the righteous judge of the world;

C. That men can only share in the salvation which is in Christ through personal faith and conversion and that there is no hereditary or sacramental grace;

D. That all who believe sincerely in Jesus Christ are called and compelled to confess the Lord and by being baptized unite publicly with the Church which is the Body of Christ and the temple of the Holy

Spirit, and to submit herself to all the ordinances which the Head of the Church has ordained; (and)

E. That the two institutions given by the Lord Jesus Christ—Baptism and the Lord's Supper—are for members of the Church of God only and are to be administered according to the original form and order; first Baptism (as distinct from sprinkling), then the Lord's Supper as a meal of communion (as distinct from mere ceremony and sacrificial mass).

TR: Jannes Reiling

III
Scandinavia

SCANDINAVIA

Denmark
The Baptist Union of Denmark

As in the rest of Scandanavia, a stirring of the people, a spontaneous religious awakening was happening in Denmark in the 1800s. Many communities were reacting to the rationalism of the day; groups of believers were forming through the country, many of whom turned to a more personal form of faith. Julius Købner, the converted Danish Jew and Oncken's able associate, traveled to his homeland to evaluate the situation. He was able to preach often and was eventually led to a group of believers in Copenhagen gathered around Peder Christian Mønster, an engraver. A longer correspondence followed that contact. Købner and Oncken returned in 1839 to baptize the eleven, including Mønster. Mønster became pastor of this, the first Baptist church in Scandinavia.

The succeeding months and years brought heavy persecution, including imprisonment for Mønster and his brother. In spite of international petitions, little changed; more baptisms precipitated more persecution. Some Baptist families were transplanted to a remote area with Hugenot descendants. But the law required that children be christened. By 1849, the pressure let up and a new constitution not only declared that Lutheranism was (still) the Danish national church but also that there should be political and religious freedom to all. In practice, this meant that there were two categories of non-Lutheran churches, those "recognized" communities of faith that could perform weddings and maintain their own records and those "tolerated" groups who could do neither. Danish Baptists were recategorized in the former "recognized" status only in 1952, five years after they had hosted the seventh Baptist World Congress in Copenhagen.

Though small in number, Baptists are the largest and most

active Free Church group in Denmark and have made their own impact through publications, kindergartens, education (including theological and the "folk high schools"), temperance movements, scouts, seaman's mission, foreign missions, and so on. In the early, most difficult days, financial assistance was given by the American Baptist Missionary Union. Others, such as Southern Baptists, have joined in more recent projects, such as in building the seminary at Tølløse. Basically, however, Danish Baptists are totally self-supporting.

Danish Baptists have no confession of faith as such. The study of Bent Hylleberg has shown that this was not always the case and that Købner brought the 1837 German confession with him in 1839, having it translated into Danish and accepted by the Danish Baptists in 1849. They were in union also with the German Baptists and readily adopted this as their norm—all except Mønster and his large Copenhagen congregation. Apparently, there were two basic reasons for this opposition: (a) He was in principle against confessions and, when imprisoned in 1842 and pressed to clarify the Baptist standpoint, wrote, "It is a principle in our Baptist Union not to have any written confession, either as an extract of or as based on, the New Testament, which in every part is our norm." (b) Likewise, Mønster was requested by the king in 1842 to comment on the Augustinian Confession which he followed with notable exceptions relating to regeneration by baptism, to the Holy Spirit in the sacraments, the congregation, and gifts. He fully rejected Articles 8-11 and 15. In essence, Mønster's leanings were more Lutheran and in contrast to the more Calvinist tendencies of Købner and the Germans.

Unfortunately, Mønster's congregation was one of many that disintegrated in 1853 under the Mormon movement. In 1888, the Danish Baptists withdrew from the German Baptist Union and, implicitly, from their confession of faith, assuming indirectly the original stance of the dissenter Mønster.

(Bent Hylleberg)

Norway
The Norwegian Baptist Union

Norway experienced the Pietist awakening of the 1800s in many ways, so the soil was well prepared when the first Baptist evangelists began their work. The original trio was made up by two sailors converted and baptized in the United States, Frederik L. Rymker, a Dane, and Gotfred Hübert, a Norwegian, and a Swedish blacksmith, O. B. Hansson, who was a successful evangelist in Northern Norway. Both Rymker and Hübert received support from English Baptists and the Seaman's Mission in New York. The first churches were founded in 1860 at Porsgrunn and Larvik. The first district associational meeting took place in 1872, and the first all-Norwegian Baptist Conference met in 1877, reporting fourteen churches. Foreign support continued (primarily from the American Baptists) but always on a limited scale or for special needs.

In 1910, Norwegian Baptists began the first Free Church theological seminary in Norway at Christiana with the able guidance of O. J. Öie, an American-trained Norwegian. Both American and Southern Baptists helped financially in the purchase of property for a new seminary near Oslo after World War II. Several noteworthy programs were begun, including Sunday School work, a publication, Youth and women's work, an extensive foreign missions enterprise (including a Scandinavian Seaman's Mission in the United States, along with the Danes and Swedes), and home mission work.

The Norwegian constitution of 1814 declared the Evangelical Lutheran Church to be the official state church in Norway. Some further regulations in 1891 opened the doors for freer worship and work. Persecution, however, was not a major problem in Norway as it was in Sweden during this period. All citizens still must pay church tax, but it can be returned to the appropriate denomination. In the early 1960s, a new state law was enacted to broaden freedoms to Free Churches and other religious bodies outside the state church. Each group was to submit a statement on doctrine and practice. Thus, in 1963, the Norwegian Baptist Union accepted the statement at the end of this chapter as their first "official" statement.

It was not the first Norwegian statement, however, because several individual churches had adopted their own during earlier days. In 1860, the first Baptist church in Porsgrunn, at its very start, adopted a confession with fourteen articles. This was essentially the same as the Swedish confession with the addition of Articles 9 and 14 of the New Hampshire Confession. Also, the Tromsø Church adopted a confession at its organization, in 1871, which was based on the German Baptist Confession of 1847 with significant changes.

At the adoption of the 1963 Norwegian Confession, it was made very clear that it was not to be considered a "creed" (that is, as binding for churches and individuals), nor is it to be used in a disciplinary way. It was simply a statement of what Norwegian Baptists at that time found to be representative of their beliefs and practice.

(Peder A. Eidberg)

In 1966, after a widespread public debate between denominations, Norwegian Baptists issued a further statement concerning the authority of the Bible. Although never officially approved in the assembly, it has widespread use. (See Appendix 4.)

A Declaration of the Baptist Faith and Order (Organization)

I. Faith

1. Baptists believe that the Bible is the revealed word of God, and regard it as normative for faith, doctrine and life.
2. Baptists have no written creed other than the Bible, but they affirm the content of the ecumenical symbols (the Nicene and Apostolic creeds).
3. Baptists belong to the evangelical churches which affirm the Reformation principles concerning salvation, expressed in the polemic phrases "grace alone" and "faith alone."
4. Baptists practice baptism based on a personal confession of faith. Baptism takes place at the time of conversion, as in the apostolic times.
5. Baptists regularly celebrate the Lord's Supper. They regard it in principle as a communal meal, but as it takes place in public worship services, the invitation is extended to all those who believe and are baptized.

II. Church Organization

1. Baptists have a congregational church order, with each local church being independent. A church council and a pastor deal with administration. The church leader is usually a full-time pastor, who has the usual pastoral duties and responsibilities.[1]
2. The Norwegian Baptist Union is a cooperative agency for all the Baptist churches in the country. The churches have a close, though voluntary cooperation in matters which are of common interest and beyond the capacity of individual churches to take care of. Such matters are evangelization, educational work, children and youth work, social work and mission. At the annual meeting of the Union elected representatives from the local churches come together to elect Union officials and to deal with financial and work planning.
3. The Norwegian Baptist Union is a member of the European Baptist Federation and the Baptist World Alliance. These organiza-

tions are cooperative bodies at the international level, without any authority over the national Unions.

III. Relationship to Other Denominations
1. Baptists have a tolerant attitude toward other denominations.
2. Baptists cooperate with other evangelical denominations in different areas of common concern, such as mission work, Sunday School work, Youth work, the cause of total abstinence, and ecumenical work.

IV. Church and State
1. Baptists have always proclaimed religious freedom. Their ideal is a free church in a free state, where all churches enjoy equality over against the state.
2. Baptists look positively at the state and its many functions, and they encourage their members to be loyal and responsible citizens.

Note

1. This statement is made with reference to the obligations of a priest in the Lutheran state church.

Sweden
The Baptist Union of Sweden

The vigorous Swedish Baptists date their beginnings to 1848 when the first church was begun near Gothenburg by F. O. Nilsson, a sailor and colporteur. Nilsson was converted in America and brought under the influence of Baptist beliefs by the Swedish sea captain G. W. Schroeder whose own ties were to the Baptist Mariner's Church in New York. Nilsson, who had traveled to Hamburg for baptism and later for ordination by Oncken, was soon arrested, tried, imprisoned, and eventually banished from Sweden for preaching. He stayed in Copenhagen for a while, as well as in the United States, until the king reversed his sentence in 1860 after adverse publicity.

Anders Wiberg, a Lutheran clergyman who resigned to become a Baptist by conviction, was baptized by Nilsson in 1852. After a three year stay in America, Wiberg became pastor of the Stockholm Church which had been organized in 1854 by two furriers, D. Forsell and P. F. Hejdenberg.

Wiberg, through his books on baptism, his travels, journalism, and his evangelistic and organizational talents, led Swedish Baptists into rapid growth in spite of constant difficulties with authorities. Bethel Seminary was the first Baptist seminary on the continent (1866) and was supported greatly by financial help from America, as well as the leadership of K. O. Broady. No other group in Europe experienced such rapid growth in this period, especially in terms of publications, education, evangelism, churches, and missions. Swedish Baptists were organized in 1889 as a missionary society with responsibilities for both home and foreign missionaries who were sent to Spain, Russia, Asia, and Africa.

Although the persecution began to lessen after the 1860s, there were still localized problems, such as children being forced to be baptized. Since the Baptists refused to register as a dissenting group, they were still legally Lutheran state church members by birth. Although the Constitution of 1809 had called for freedom of conscience, it was not until 1952 that the first state law was legislated to guarantee religious freedom and equal rights to Free Churchmen. The actual practice, however, preceded this law by several years.

The first general conference of the Union took place in 1857 in spite of the laws; the second in 1858 included Oncken and Köbner as guests. The third conference took place in Stockholm on June 23-28, 1861, reported 125 churches with 4,930 members and adopted the "Confession of Faith of the Swedish Baptists." The confession was one adopted in 1856 by the Stockholm church and shows the influence of Wiberg. It reveals the sense of self-identity at that time in the context of a rigid Lutheran state church. It was not, however, the one recorded by authorities as representing Baptists since it was not presented to them as a basis for legal recognition. Another drawn up in 1865, and presented by a rural Baptist church, was accepted in 1868 by the authorities. The confessions apparently served their purpose in the early days of Swedish Baptists but now play neither a positive nor a negative role in church life. No one is required to subscribe to them, nor is the average Baptist aware of their contents.

(David Lagergren)

Swedish Baptist Confession of Faith

1. We believe that the Holy Scriptures of both the Old and the New Testament (the commonly so-called Apocryphal books excepted) are

SCANDINAVIA

inspired by God and constitute the one perfect rule for our Christian faith and practice.

2. We believe that there is one only living and true God—who is a Spirit infinite in all perfections; who has revealed Himself in three equal persons, the Father, the Son, and the Holy Ghost.

3. We believe that the first man Adam was created holy, in the image of God, but fell by voluntary transgression of the law of God into a state of sin and death; and that in consequence of his fall all his natural posterity have inherited his corruption, are void of all will to turn to God, and without power perfectly to keep His law, and therefore they are guilty before the wrath of God and condemned to eternal punishment.

4. We believe that our Lord Jesus Christ, in his one person united true Godhead and manhood, that he through his perfect obedience before the law of God and through his atoning death has opened for all a way to redemption and salvation from this lost state, and that every one who from his heart believes in him shall become a partaker of this redemption and salvation without any merit or worthiness of his own.

5. We believe that the gospel—viz. the glad tidings of the salvation which is acquired through Christ—ought to be preached to the whole world; that every one who hears the gospel is under obligation to repent—viz. with a sincere grief before God to confess and abandon his sins, and at the same time to believe in Christ as his only and all-sufficient Saviour, and that whosoever may refuse to do so will incur upon himself a worse condemnation.

6. We believe that saving faith is a gift from God and entirely a fruit of the working of the Holy Spirit through the word; that all who are to be saved have been given by the Father to the Son and were chosen in him for salvation and sonship before the foundation of this world was laid; and that we ought with utmost diligence to seek to obtain assurance of our own election.

7. We believe that the law of God has its end to be: 1) a restraint for the ungodly to restrain them from performing all the evil purpose of their heart; 2) a schoolmaster to bring sinners to Christ, inasmuch as it sets before them the just claims of God and his wrath over sin, shows them their inability to fulfil these claims, and thus awakens in them the need of grace and the forgiveness of sin; 3) a rule for the walk of believers to be followed in the spirit of the new covenant; and that, there-

fore, with these ends in view the law ought to be inculcated in all.

8. We believe that baptism ought to be administered only to such as have personally by a trustworthy confession given evidence of possessing a living faith in Christ; that it is properly administered only through the immersion of the whole person in water; and that it should precede admittance into the fellowship of the church and participation in the Lord's Supper.

9. We believe that a true Christian church is a union of believing and baptized Christians, who have covenanted to strive to keep all that Christ has commanded, to sustain public worship, under the guidance of the Holy Spirit to choose among themselves shepherds or overseers, and deacons, to administer baptism and the Lord's supper, to practice Christian church-discipline, to promote godliness and brotherly love, and to contribute to the general spread of the gospel;—also that every such church is an independent body, free in its relation to other Christian churches and acknowledging Christ only as its head.

10. We believe that as the first day of the week was kept holy by the apostolic churches as the Lord's day, instead of the Jewish Sabbath, and that we especially on this day are together for common worship and to exercise ourselves in godliness.

11. We believe that civil government is ordained by God, and regard it our duty to honour and pray for the king and magistracy and in all things to obey the laws of the land, unless they are plainly in conflict with the law of Christ.

12. We believe that this world is to come to an end, that our Lord Jesus Christ will again appear on the earth on the last day, wake up the dead from their graves, and execute a general judgment in which all wicked men will be irrevocably condemned to eternal punishment, while all believing and righteous men will be solemnly established in their possession of the kingdom which was prepared for them from the beginning of the world.

Erik Rudén
(Originally published in Lumpkin,
Baptist Confessions of Faith, 1969
edition). Used by permission

Sweden
The Örebro Mission

Baptists of Sweden count in their number a major segment called the Örebro Mission which is almost equal in number to the Baptist Union group. There were two critical periods in the relations between the Baptist Union in Stockholm and the Örebro Mission, the first during 1892-1907 when the movement in Örebro started. There were several tensions including women preachers, foreign missions, and the Pentecostal revival. (Örebro supported women preachers, was very expansive in foreign missions, and positive in a moderate way to the revival.) John Ongman, who had been a pastor in America for several years, was the key figure in the development of the mission movement. He was the dynamic, independent, and practically oriented pastor at Örebro and started a school for training pastors, missionaries, and evangelists.

The second critical period came after Ongman's death in 1931 when tensions became even more obvious. At least two major issues were at stake. One was a critical attitude in Örebro toward central organization—a necessary move on the part of the Baptist Union in Stockholm to deal with such rapid growth. The election of a general secretary in 1932 in Stockholm became a crucial issue. The other main reason was a lasting difference in attitudes toward the Pentecostal movement. Other issues included a more restrictive attitude in Örebro toward the ecumenical movement and a suspiciousness towards liberal theology.

None of these differences exist today. It is possible that only slight variations are present in terms of the more practical view of central organization and the role of the local church. Many joint projects take place, especially in education and missions.

Örebro Mission has no confession of faith as such. Their image centers around mission or outreach into the world. In their written history, in the training of workers, and in all church work the emphasis is on such evangelistic activity. They were active participants in the Lausanne World Conference on Evangelism and have subscribed to the Lausanne Declaration. (See Appendix 6.)

The Örebro Seminary has also made a statement on social justice and responsibility which shows the relationship to the "new evangelicals" as well as an orientation toward a more profound responsibility concerning society and the world as a whole, with obvious political dimensions.

Sigfrid Deminger

Finland
The Finnish Baptist Union, Finnish-Speaking

Work among the Finnish-speaking was later than among the Swedish-speaking population in Finland, with contacts first in the 1870s. One zealous sailor had preached briefly at Luvia and baptized Esaias Lundberg who founded the church there in 1870. About that time, a Lutheran pastor, John Hymander, came to doubt child baptism, resigned, went to Stockholm to be baptized, and returned to organize a church in Parikkala. But the connections with the stronger Swedish group were the most important, in spite of the great language gap. The broader, early influence throughout Finland was initiated by Baptist preachers through the Swedish Pohjanmaa (Österbotten, the western coastal region of Finland). Relations between Swedish and Finnish-speaking groups were not uncomplicated however. In 1903, the Finnish Baptist Union was constituted, with about a dozen churches. In the next four years, these increased to about twenty-five. But war, political independence struggles, and strong Pentecostal movements caused a severe setback. A Bible institute was founded at Vasa in 1949; Sunday Schools were started, as well as Youth organizations, foreign mission effort, and evangelistic campaigns. The Baptist paper began in 1896.

Finnish Baptists have felt little of the persecution others in Scandinavia experienced, due perhaps to their late arrival on the scene with certain liberties already granted. It could also be due to their being part of the majority language element of the Finnish population. Finnish Baptists have a confession of faith which was approved by the Russian Czarist Imperial Senate in 1891 when Baptists became an official "dissenter group." In 1922, the

Finnish Baptists became an officially registered "religious community" when the Law of Religious Freedom was passed. Entitled "The Finnish Baptists' Confession of Faith and Church Order," the document includes a number of incidentals such as a statement on the apostolic faith, the Imperial statute of November 11, 1889, details on practical matters, and, finally, certification by the Imperial Senate. The confession was probably based upon the Swedish work of Wiberg, used earlier in Stockholm. Introduced at a time when both language groups worked together, and through the Swedish group, it nevertheless remained a Finnish confession after they no longer were together.

(Annti Marjaren)
(Markku Niskanen)

The Confession of the Finnish Baptist Union

1.

We believe that the Holy Scriptures of the Old Testament as well as the New Testament (except the so-called Apocrypha) are inspired by God or have come to being under the influence of the Holy Spirit, thus forming a source from which we get all our knowledge about God and about the redemption of man through faith in Jesus Christ; and that they are the only directive and guideline of our faith and life.

2.

Gen. 1:1,26; 17:1; Ex. 15:11; Pss. 8:4; 33:6,9; 104:24; 147:5; Isa. 6:3; 9:6; 40:28; 45:5; 46:9; Jer. 10:10; John 4:24; 5:17,21,23; 14:9-11,23; 15:26; Acts 17:24-26

We believe that there is only one living and true God, who is a spirit, infinite in His perfection. He has revealed His being as follows: 1) as the Father in creation, 2) as the Son in the work of redemption and 3) as the Holy Spirit in consecrating people and separating them from the world. The Father, the Son and the Holy Spirit are all self-contained and are working as persons, but they still are one single, infinite personal God.

3.

We believe that our Lord Jesus Christ in his one person united true divinity to true humanity. Through His perfect obedience to God's law and through His atoning death He opened the way of salvation and redemption for all who are under condemnation because of sin and death. We believe that whosoever in his heart believes in Him will share in this salvation and redemption without his own merits.

John 1:1-14; 3:16; Acts 13:29; Rom. 3:21-28; 4:4-8,16; 5:1,17-21; 1 Cor. 1:30; Gal. 3:13; 4:4-5; Eph. 1:7; 2:8-9; Phil. 2:6-11; 1 Tim. 2:5; 3:16; Heb. 2:9-17; 5:9; 9:12-15; 1 John 5:11-12

4.

We believe that a man cannot be born again either by baptism or by any outward deed, but only by faith in Jesus Christ.

John 1:12-13; Gal. 3:26; 1 Pet. 1:3,23; Jas. 1:18; Rom. 5:1; 10:9,11,13,17

5.

We believe that it is not God's will or commandment to baptize infants because this practice has no clear basis in the Holy Scriptures of the Old Testament or the New Testament; but we believe that according to Jesus' own words and because of His atonement and death "the kingdom of heaven belongs to them."

Matt. 19:14; 1 John 2:2; Rom. 5:13,18; Ezek. 18:20

6.

We believe that children must be carefully brought up and taught in school knowledge as well as Christian truths, but the Baptist Union does not allow them to take part in the congregation's holy ceremonies, especially in baptism and communion, before they have enough understanding to discern between evil and good, between sin and grace, and have allowed the Holy Spirit to work in their hearts the repentance toward God and the faith in our Lord Jesus Christ. When this has happened and they confess it, then they can be baptized and in accordance

Eph. 6:4; Acts 20:21; Matt. 28:19-20; Mark 16:16; Acts 8:35-40; 16:25-34; 2:41-46 with Jesus' commandment have the right to take part in the holy communion.

7.

1 Cor. 1:2; Acts 2:40-42; 1 Pet. 1:1; 2 Cor. 11:2; Eph. 1:17-18,22-23; 4:4-5, 15-25; 2:20-22; 1 Tim. 3:15

We believe that our Lord Jesus Christ Himself through His apostles established and appointed on earth the holy church, which is founded on a living faith in Christ and on God's own, everlasting word. The church consists of people called out from the world, people, who have been converted and baptized and have "one Lord, one faith, one baptism, one God and Father of all"; and we confess Christ to be our only Teacher, the Head of the church and the Shepherd of our souls.

8.

Matt. 5:15-16; 6:10; Acts 11:19-24; Matt. 28:19; Mark 16:15-16; John 21:15-17; 1 Cor. 9:16; Ps. 126:5-6; Dan. 12:3; Matt. 25:14-29

We believe that every Christian's duty is to help and further the expansion of Christ's kingdom in the world. Those that believe that the Lord has called them to preach and whose Christian life and conduct are approved by the church are allowed to witness to the Lord publicly and privately, and to preach the gospel of Christ to Jews, Gentiles and nominal Christians. Because the church finds as its absolute duty to spread the gospel of Christ on earth, it wants to establish and regulate a system which in harmony with laws and statutes of the country makes it possible for every church member to do something for spreading the good news either by means of a financial gift or work.

9.

Matt. 28:5-6; John 20:19; Acts 20:7; Rev. 1:10; Rom. 14:4-13; Col. 2:16-17; Heb. 7:12

We believe that the apostolic Christians observed the day of the Lord in the first day of the week instead of keeping the Jewish sabbath. Christ, the fulfilment of prophecy, cancelled the sabbath as well as Jewish feasts. We believe that we are to come to-

SCANDINAVIA

gether on the day mentioned to worship God and exercise our faith.

10.

We also believe that this period of time will soon come to an end, and those believers who then live "shall be transformed in the twinkling of an eye," and "those who have departed this life will rise first in the clouds to meet the Lord in the air." We believe that our Lord Jesus Christ will again reveal Himself on the last day, will raise the dead and hold the judgment. Then all the ungodly will be irrevocably condemned to an ever-lasting punishment, but all the believers and righteous ones will solemnly be given "the kingdom prepared for them from the foundation of the world."

1 Cor. 15:51-52; 1 Thess. 4:16-17; Matt. 16:27; 25:31-46; John 5:28-29; Acts 1:10-12; 24:15; 2 Cor. 5:10; 2 Thess. 1:6-10; 2 Tim. 4:8; Jude 6-7; Rev. 20:11-15

TR: Anneli Kothavnori
TR: Anntti Marjaren

Finland
Swedish-Speaking Baptist Union of Finland

Baptist preaching in Finland began in 1854 with the Swede C. J. Möllersvärd among the Swedish-speaking islanders of Aland. The first church was formed in 1856 and met hard persecution at the hands of local police "in order to prevent proselytism and the speaking of false doctrines." Ideas spread, however, to the mainland and the family of the Lutheran clergyman Henric Heikel became the center of a revival. In 1870 a Baptist church was founded at Jacobstad and from there the movement spread rapidly and widely among Swedish-speaking Finns ("Finländer") and in cities such as Vasa (1881) and Helsinki (1885).

Close ties to Stockholm were maintained and much assistance has come from Sweden in terms of pastors, education, and financial support. Schools, publishing, evangelism, Youth work, temperance work, Sunday School, missions, and other work is supported by the tiny union, which was organized in 1883. Theological education was begun at Vasa and was supported also from Sweden, although more recently a joint effort is being made in Stockholm at the Bethel Seminary to take care of these needs. Swedish-speaking Baptists were tolerated under the so-called "Dissenter Law" of 1889. The 1922 law of Religious Liberty spelled out the meaning of the constitutional guarantee of freedom of religion, with its implications for civil rights. Certain groups, such as the evangelical Lutheran state church (with 95.9 percent of the population) and the Greek Orthodox (2.7), are registered as "religious communities" and provide a list of members (including children) for official registration; pastors may perform wedding ceremonies. The other category is that of an "association" in which a less formal relationship existed. Swedish-speaking Baptists in Finland kept the latter category for many years, while the Finnish-speaking Baptists were an official denomination.

Some individual Swedish-speaking churches did register and present the required confession of faith. In 1979, at the annual meeting and a subsequent organizational meeting the "Swedish-Speaking Baptist Union of Finland" came into being, replacing the "Baptist Mission" and beginning a registered denomination with legal status under the law of 1922.

The brief Confession of Faith which follows was presented for the "new" denomination, along with other articles. The descriptive "Form of the Religious Practice" is included since it contains some points found in some other confessions.

(Leif Olin)
(Tor Smith)

Confession of Faith for the Swedish-Speaking Baptist Union of Finland

Finland's Swedish-Speaking Baptist Union, which confesses the Bible as God's Word and guide for the activities of the Union as well as of the churches and for the way of living of the individual church members, accepts the Apostolic Creed as a comprehensive creed for the Union while the church membership is based upon a personal faith in Christ and consequent baptism, which is made by the whole body's immersion in water.

The Form of the Religious Practice

Finland's Swedish-speaking Baptist Union is a common organ of activities for the individuals and the Baptist churches who have associated themselves as members to the Union. The churches within the Union are as such independent, but they are also working commonly within the Union concerning National and Foreign Missions, pastor's training, children and youth work, study and training activities which aim at the spread of the Kingdom of God. Concerning founding churches, dedication of children, baptismals and the Holy Communion the Union follows the prescriptions which are in the New Testament. The Union seeks to realize the church fellowship according the pattern of the Bible.

IV
Latin and Southern Europe

LATIN AND SOUTHERN EUROPE

Belgium
- Brussels

France
- Douai
- Chauny
- Paris
- Muhlhause
- Lyon
- Marseille

Italy
- Turin
- La Spezia
- Bologna
- Rome
- Naples

(SICILY)

Greece
- Athens

Portugal
- Oporto
- Leiria
- Lisbon

Spain
- Barcelona
- Madrid
- Alicante

Italy
The Baptist Evangelical Christian Union of Italy

Modern Baptist work began in Italy in 1863-1864 when two Englishmen, James Wall and Edward Clark, began work in Bologna and La Spezia. At that time, many radical changes were occurring within Italy which eventually led to the union of the country under the Savoy monarchy, the end of the temporal rule of the Pope in Rome, and the breaking up of the Catholic states. An edict of King Carlo Alberto in 1848 had granted some limited religious freedom for non-Catholics in one small area. In 1871, the Roman Catholic church lost its privileges. The general evangelical awakening in the nineteenth century in Europe was also being felt in Italy, echoing to a limited degree the twelfth-century pre-Reformation movement of the Waldenses. Anglo-Saxon Protestant missionaries who introduced the awakening into Italy stimulated a new missionary endeavor of the ancient Waldensian Church as well.

Wall moved to Rome and received support from the British Missionary Society (B.M.S.), who had heard of his work. In the early 1870s, the Foreign Mission Board of the Southern Baptist Convention sent missionaries, including Dr. George B. Taylor, who spent thirty-four years establishing several churches, institutions, and the Baptist Mission.

W. Kemme Landels, a Scots businessman in Sicily, joined Wall in Rome in 1875 and then moved to Turin. He worked also with the B.M.S.

The first Baptist church was founded in Rome in 1871. Many more were founded throughout Italy over the next thirty years amid great resistance and persecution. A number of outstanding Italian pastors emerged as leaders in the early days: O. Cocorda (translator of the New Testament into modern Italian), E. Paschetto (professor of Hebrew and Semitics, University of Rome), M. Rossi (former Jesuit and Lutheran scholar), L. Paschetto (writer, scholar, and archeologist), and others. In 1923, most Baptist work in Italy was united in response to a recommendation of the Baptist World Alliance. Southern Baptists assumed responsibility for most work, excepting the work of the La Spezia Mission begun by Clark and carried on an independent basis.

In 1939, the Baptist Federation was founded and took over some leadership roles, as the missionaries began to step back from their prominent positions. World War II took a heavy toll in physical, emotional, and spiritual ways, but the work continued. Fascism was very detrimental to Baptist life. A new constitution in a general assembly of churches was ratified in 1956, whereby the Italian Baptist Union, as an independent body from the Baptist Mission, was organized. Thereafter, the Assembly itself (made up of elected representatives from all the churches) would guide the work. The work of the Union was now autonomous, although working in a fraternal relationship with the Southern Baptist Mission. In cooperative endeavors with missionaries, the Italian Baptists have done extensive work in publication, theological education, an orphanage, two old people's homes, a girl's training school, camps and conferences, evangelism, and lately in radio broadcasting, and other projects. They have also played a role in gaining religious liberty in Italy. During the 1960s, Baptist played a fundamental role in the formation of the Federation of Protestant Churches in Italy which includes the Waldenses, Methodists, Lutherans, and the Salvation Army, in addition to the Baptists.

The constitution of 1946 guaranteed equal legal rights and freedom for all religious confessions. Not only could each confess his own faith freely but also he could propagate his faith and worship freely. This meant that assemblies could be held without official permission. For some years, remnants of old concepts and practices remained, as well as different interpretations of the law. In 1956, a supreme court was established which has helped to bring more freedom for Free Churches. The Italian Baptist Union does not have a confession of faith but many feel that there should be some sort of agreed statement about faith and Baptist principles. A theological commission is currently working on the matter.

(Piero Bensi)
(Paulo Spanu)

Spain
The Baptist Evangelical Union of Spain

The close alliance of church and state in historic Spain has had its impact on Baptist roots there. Rigidly Roman Catholic since the Jews and Moors were expelled in the fifteenth and sixteenth centuries, all Spanish citizens were regarded as Catholics. Early Protestants felt the hand of the Inquisition in the sixteenth century. After the revolution in 1868, and brief religious liberty, Baptists appeared for the first time. William Knapp, an independent Baptist missionary who later worked under the Northern Baptists, was the first, baptizing 1,325 people in 7 months. He organized a church in Madrid in 1870 with 30 persons who were baptized in the Manzanares River. Knapp organized a Baptist church in Alicante in 1871, after baptizing a group of people in the Mediterranean Sea. He was forced to leave in 1876 because evangelical activity was forbidden. About 1880, Eric Lund (some writers say that he came to Spain at the beginning of 1880), a Swedish Baptist missionary and talented linguist, began work in publicity and Bible translations, especially in the Barcelona area. Others came from Sweden. Also help came from American Baptists. The 1920 London agreement transferred the mission work to Southern Baptists, who have worked extensively up to the current time.

The Spanish Republic which began in 1931 brought not only freedom but also anticlericalism and indifference. The Franco regime, which took over in 1939, closed many churches. Although religious toleration was granted to Protestants in 1945, it was very limited; in 1948 many churches were again closed under the accusation of being enemies ot Spain (that is, if a non-

Catholic). The 1945 Concordat between the government and the Vatican declared:

> The profession and practice of the Catholic religion, which is that of the Spanish state, shall enjoy official protection. No one shall be disturbed because of his religious beliefs or the private practice of his worship. No other outward ceremonies or demonstrations than those of the Catholic religion shall be permitted. This law expressly forbids public worship outside private houses or chapels which must show no signs on the outside; it also forbids proselytizing through the written or spoken word, which is in itself a public act.

Baptists experienced extensive growth, nevertheless, and almost doubled in the ten years following 1948. The Constitution of 1966 promised religious liberty, and a special law the following year required Protestant churches ("associations") to register with a guarantee of many rights in the process. Since they were required to furnish membership rolls and financial records for government inspection, many churches refused and tension arose for a while. The new Spanish Constitution of 1978 grants full religious freedom and establishes separation between church and state. Many freedoms have been increased. Baptists now sponsor a seminary, mission, and evangelistic work, Youth and women's work, and a publications ministry.

The Confession of Faith of Spanish Baptists is essentially a translation of "The Baptist Faith and Message" of the Southern Baptist Convention and was officially approved in 1970, although it had been used unofficially much earlier. (See Appendix 3)

(José Borras)
(José Garcia)

Portugal
The Portuguese Baptist Convention

The earliest Baptist witness that is known in traditionally Catholic Portugal is that of Joseph Jones, who began to preach and baptize in Oporto in 1888. An English layman, Jones was born in Oporto and baptized by Charles Haddon Spurgeon in London. Other foreigners, such as Reginald and Kate Young, began evangelical work around the turn of the century. The first Portuguese Baptist church in Oporto, after the departure of the Youngs in 1908, chose one of its leading committee members, Teixeira de Sousa, to be pastor of the new congregation. The Brazilian Baptists heard of the work and sent Zachary C. Taylor, a Southern Baptist missionary to Brazil, to investigate the possibilities of mission work in Portugal. These connections with Brazilian Baptists have played a key role in their history. Such men as J. J. de Oliveira and Antonio Mauricio helped maintain the bridges between the two groups and new churches were started in Wisen (1913), Tondela (1914), Leiria (1916), and Lisbon (1922). A small evangelistic newspaper was started and other programs begun. The Portuguese Baptist Convention was formed in 1920 as a cooperative body of churches with its main efforts directed toward publication and theological education.

But amid persecution from both the state and the official church, times were very difficult for the Portuguese Baptists, especially during World War II when the financial and other support from Brazil could not be maintained adequately. After the war much outside help came, this time not only from Brazil but also from the Conservative Baptist Foreign Mission Society in America who now sponsored J. J. de Oliveira (who had returned to Brazil in 1918) and from independent, self-supporting Baptists such as the W. L. Hatchers who helped reopen the oft-closed seminary that was first begun under the sponsorship of the Baptist Missionary Association of Texas in 1922. The Conservative Baptists also helped another seminary in Leiria in 1949, as well as an institute for Christian Education of Girls (1955). Later the Foreign Mission Board of the Southern Baptist Convention also gave assistance, both in education and direct evangelism.

In 1948, the pastor of the Third Baptist Church of Oporto, Eduardo Machado and his wife, founded the Portuguese Evangelical Home, "for all people in need." After the war a number of other organizations were begun, such as alliances, associations, and task-oriented groups, some of which lasted only a few years. "Every Baptist a missionary" became a Portuguese slogan, and missionaries were sent out to Angola and Mozambique. There are still two basic conventions with a total of about twenty-one churches.

Portuguese Baptists have a "Statement of Principles of the Baptist Faith" which was approved by the General Assembly of the convention in September 1975. Prior to that time, they claimed the New Hampshire Confession (1833). The political changes of 1974 appeared to open new doors of freedom to the non-Catholic churches, and a more modern expression of their position was deemed necessary. The task was assigned to the theological seminary and was the primary responsibility of the director, Professor Manuel Alexandre, Jr. He chose to simplify, clarify, and adapt the 1963 Southern Baptist Convention's "The Baptist Faith and Message" to fit the Portuguese setting. The article on education (XII) was omitted, as it was not seen to be essential in a declaration of faith and not so relevant since the government bears all responsibility for education.

(Isabel and Abel Pego)
(Manuel Alexandre, Jr.)

France
The Federation of Baptist Evangelical Churches

Along with political, intellectual, and other great changes, there were also in the early 1800s winds of revival in France. Spontaneous groups formed for Bible study, with one such group gathering in 1810 in the home of a farmer in Northern France. He had discovered an old Bible in the corner of his home. In 1815, just after the Battle of Waterloo, a British occupation soldier came to teach. In 1819, Henri Pyt, a Swiss evangelist and devotee of the Scottish Baptist Robert Haldane, came to lead, to teach, and to baptize them secretly. The American Foreign Mission Society heard about this group and sent a representative, Casimir Rostan. Rostan, a native of Marseilles, served briefly in Paris before dying of cholera. Isaac Willmarth replaced him in 1834, and the first Baptist church was formed in Douai in 1835.

In 1839, Willmarth organized a school for pastors but met many difficulties, as did many pastors and congregations. New churches were founded in Paris (1850), Lyons, Marseilles, and other areas in spite of the many hindrances and persecution from the state. Matters changed with the founding of the French Republic in 1871 and the guarantee of religious freedom. (Since 1905, church and state have been separate; the constitution of 1958 guarantees equal legal status for all regardless of origin, race or religion. All religions are respected and tolerated.) Considerable growth occurred from 1871 to 1895, with noted men from other churches joining Baptist ranks. But the social and theological turmoil at the turn of the century took its toll on

EUROPE 1814/15 (Vienna Congress)

French Baptists. Little unity was preserved in the absence of a common school or organization.

The French Baptist Federation was formed in 1919, bringing together a group from the north which was working in Brittany and Belgium and a group from the south which served the great urban centers, the south, and French Switzerland. Assistance has come in several forms from the United States and England. In addition to outreach to Belgium and Switzerland, French Baptists have done mission work in Africa and among the immigrants inside France. Domestic work also includes homes for the aged and youth, camps, and education. French Baptists have been limited by the heavy impact of two world wars and internal division.

The French Baptist Federation has a confession of faith, drawn up by six French Baptist pastors, led by A. Ramseyer and H. Andru in 1879. It followed two previous attempts, the first being done by the American missionary Erasmus Willard and printed in Douai in 1848. That one was later revised but finally rejected for the 1879 version published at Chauny as an independent effort of French Baptists. Although they did keep the American Covenant as a preface, a second edition in 1895 omitted one section about the congregation. The edition which follows and the covenant are still used today by the French Baptist Federation, although the second part on church order is currently being reworked to update their ecclesiological self-understanding.

Christian Covenant

As a result of the truths that we receive fully and the conviction we have, having been led by divine grace to accept Jesus Christ our Saviour and to give ourselves to Him and to put our trust in His gracious help, we constitute together a solemn alliance and promise:

That we will walk together in brotherly love as is fitting of members of a Christian Church; that we will maintain a loving vigilance over each other, and will at all times advise and urge each other faithfully to charity and good works;

That we will never neglect to meet for our mutual edification, nor fail to pray for ourselves and for others;

That we will always strive to bring up the children in our care according to the ways of our Lord and in knowledge of His teachings, and that we will ever be good examples of pure and agreeable conduct to our relations and friends so that they may come to love the Lord, lead a saintly life and rejoice in life eternal;

That we will rejoice in the happiness of each other and strive with tenderness and sympathy to carry each others' burdens and sorrows:

That we will live warily in this world, renouncing all wickedness and worldly desires, setting a good example and remembering that, as we have been voluntarily buried in baptism and have been resurrected from that symbolic tomb, thus there rests upon us a special obligation to lead a new and holy life;

That we will do all within our power to support a faithful ministry in our midst;

That according to our abilities and circumstances, as worthy stewards of our Lord we will do good to all men, particularly endeavouring to spread the Gospel in all its original strength and purity throughout the inhabited world.

Lastly that, during all our pilgrimage on this earth, through scorn or honour, we will seek humbly and ardently to live for the glory of Him who has called us out of darkness into His marvelous light.

Confession of Faith of the Federation of French Baptist Churches
Doctrine

I. On the True God

We believe there is only one God, Father, Son, and Holy Spirit, creator of all things infinite and eternal, all-powerful, and worthy of the highest degree of confidence, love, obedience, praise and adoration.

Gen. 1:1-2; Deut. 6:4; 2 Sam. 13:2; Job 33:4; Pss. 24:8-10; 45:7-8; Isa. 11:2; 12:2; Dan. 9:24; Matt. 12:28; 28:19; Mark 12:29-33; Luke 2:10-11; John

1:1-14; 10:30; 14:9-10;
Acts 1:16; 3:3-4; Rom.
8:9-11,14; 2 Cor. 13:13;
Eph. 4:4-8; Col. 2:9-10;
Rev. 4:11

II. On the Holy Scripture

Ex. 24:4,12; Deut. 18:18; 2 Sam. 23:2; Ps. 78:5 (cf. Rom. 3:2); Isa. 8:20; Matt. 4:4; John 5:39,46; Acts 1:16;3:21;17:11; Rom. 1:2; 1 Cor. 14:37; Gal. 1:6-12; 2 Tim. 3:16; Rev. 22:18

We believe that the canonical scriptures of the Old and the New Testament are the Word of God and must be the only and infallible rule of faith and Christian life by which we shall be judged, and the only foundation stone from which shall spring all tradition, all doctrine and all religious practice.

III. On the Fall of Man and the Wages of Sin

Gen. 1:27,31; 3:6,24; 5:3; Deut. 24:16; Pss. 51:7; 53:4; Isa. 53:6; Dan. 12:2; Matt. 25:46; Rom. 3:19,22; 4:15; 5:12; 2 Cor. 5:10; 2 Thess. 1:9; 1 John 3:4; Rev. 20:15

We believe that Adam our first father was created innocent and good, but having voluntarily broken the commandment of His Creator, he lost his original state; as a result all his descendants, inheriting his nature, are disposed to sin. We believe also that all who have broken God's rules are justly exposed to eternal death.

IV. On Jesus Christ and His Work

Isa. 53:4-5; Matt. 24:15-42; Luke 1:26-35; John 1:14; Acts 1:1; 3:18-21; 10:42; Rom. 1:4; 3:25; 14:9; 2 Cor. 5:14-15,19; Gal. 4:4; Phil. 2:8; 1 Thess. 3:13; 1 Tim. 2:5; 2 Tim. 4:1; Heb. 1:2-6; 4:15; Rev. 1:7

We believe that Jesus Christ, the Word made flesh, born of a Virgin, conceived by the Almighty, is the Son of God, and after having been tempted in all things as we are, He remained holy, innocent, without stain; that He suffered and died on the cross for the remission of our sins; that He rose and ascended into Heaven where He is the only mediator between God and man and from whence He will come to judge the quick and the dead.

V. On Salvation Through Faith in Jesus Christ

1 Kings 8:47-48; Ps. 51:3-4; Luke 13:3-5;

We believe that, to be saved, a sinner must repent of his sins, accept the work of Jesus and unite himself with Him by faith. From this union comes justification, regeneration and sanctification without which no man will see the Saviour. We also believe that true faith is manifested always through works that are agreeable to God.

John 1:12-13; 3:3,16,36; Acts 20-21; Rom. 5:1-9; 1 Cor. 1:30-31; Eph. 2:8; Heb. 12:12-17; Jas. 2:14,18,25; 1 Pet. 2:1-2,11-12; 1 John 3:4-9; Matt. 7:17-21

VI. On the Work of the Holy Spirit

We believe that it is the Holy Spirit who, carrying out the truths of the Holy Scriptures, produces in those who have been elected through the predestination of God, true Christian life in principles and in action, and enables them to persevere to the end.

1 Sam. 10:6; Ezek. 37:14; Zach. 7:12; John 3:5-6; 16:8; Rom. 5:5;8:9,14,16; 1 Cor. 3:16; Gal. 5:16,18, 22; Eph. 1:13-14; 5:9; 1 Pet. 1:2,22-23

VII. On the Ministry of the Word

We believe that God has instituted a ministry of the Word which is composed originally of the prophets, apostles, evangelists or missionaries, elders, or pastors and doctors, in order to bring sinners to conversion and to guide them in the Christian life. This ministry, from the point of view that it touches our lives in the work of pastors and evangelists must be carried out until the second coming of Christ.

Deut. 4:5; Isa. 58:1; Ezek. 33:7; Amos 7:15; Matt. 28:18-20; Mark 3:13-15; Luke 10:1-20; Acts 6:4; 8:15;13:1; 15:6,22-23,33; 20:17-28; 21:18; 1 Cor. 12:28-29; 14:29-30; Eph. 4:11; 1 Tim. 3:1-7; 4:13-16; 2 Tim. 2:2; 1 Pet. 5:1-5

VIII. On Local Churches

We believe that each local church constituted according to the Word of God is an assembly of baptised believers, independent of all authority other than that of Jesus Christ, the sole Head of the universal church, which is his body.

The members of a local church, associated by free engagement, are governed by the laws of Christ, and carry out in the general interest, the duties that have been given them according to the talents with which they have been endowed.

The Christians who have a special work in the

Matt. 18:17,20; Acts 2:38-41; 6:2-5; 11:24-26; 14:23,27; 15:3,22; 19:9; 20:17-28; 1 Cor. 16:1,3; 2 Cor. 8:19,23-24; Phil. 1:1; 1 Thess. 5:12; 2 Tim. 2:2; Titus 1:5; Heb. 13:17; 1 Pet. 5:1-4

Church are the pastors, the deacons and the deaconesses whose duties are laid down in the New Testament.

IX. On Baptism

<small>Matt. 28:19; Mark 1:5,9-10; 16:16; John 4:1-2; Acts 2:38-41; 8:36-39; 10:47; 16:33; Rom. 6:3-4; Gal. 3:27; Col. 2:12; Titus 3:5; 1 Pet. 3:21</small>

We believe that Baptism is, for Christians who are voluntarily dead to the world and to sin, the dramatic and solemn symbol of the entombment and resurrection with Christ, with whom they are united through faith, to live in Him a new and holy life.

We believe, following Christ's command and His example, and that of the apostles, that immersion of believers must precede their admission into the church and their participation in communion.

X. On Communion

<small>Matt. 26:26-29; Mark 14:22-25; Luke 22:14-20; Acts 2:42; 20:7; 1 Cor. 10:16-17; 11:23-29</small>

We believe that the Last Supper as instituted by our Lord Jesus Christ must be observed in churches until He comes again; that the bread and the wine of which all the members of the church partake, are the symbols of the body and the blood of our Saviour; that through this communion, the members who participate in it profess that they form the same body with Christ and are united one to another in the same understanding.

XI. On the Return of Christ and the Resurrection

<small>Dan. 7:13-14; 12:1-3; Matt. 13:49; 24:30-31; 25:31,46; Mark 8:38; Luke 21:27; John 14:3; Acts 1:11; 24:15; Rom. 2:5; 1 Cor. 15:12,20, 42-58; 1 Thess. 4:14-17; 2 Thess. 1:6-12; 2 Pet. 3:10-13; Rev. 1:7</small>

We believe that our Lord Jesus Christ will come down from heaven as He ascended in accordance with what is written in the Scriptures. We believe in the resurrection of the dead, both the just and the unjust, in the final judgement where an eternal separation will be made between the wicked who will suffer eternal punishment and the good who will obtain everlasting life.

XII. On the Holiness of the Lord's Day

We believe, in accordance with the example set by the apostles and the first Christians, that the first day of the week should be considered as the Lord's Day, in memory of the resurrection of Jesus Christ, and that consequently, Sunday should be used for the moral improvement of our souls by means of church meetings, and works of charity which will prepare us for the rest that awaits all of God's people.

Matt. 28:1; Mark 16:1; Luke 24:1; John 20:1,26; Acts 20:7; 1 Cor. 16:2; Rev. 1:10

XIII. On Civil Government

We believe that civil government is ordained of God in the interests of law and order within the society, and we should pray for the magistrates and the elected authorities, honour and obey them in everything that is not contrary to the teachings of the Scriptures as shown in these words of the Lord: Give unto Caesar the things that are Caesar's and unto God the things that are God's.

Matt. 17:24,27; 22:21; Luke 20:25; Rom. 13:1-7; 1 Tim. 2:1-2; Titus 3:1; 1 Pet. 2:13-17

The Church

I. Formation of Local Churches

The apostles, or their helpers, after having baptised the first believers, united them into local churches to which they communicated the divine laws that they had to follow. The churches of Jerusalem, Antioch, Corinth, Philippi, Ephesus, Rome, Rhodes were founded in this way. Such is the apostolic rule.

Matt. 28:19; John 4:1-2; Acts 2:38,41,47; 5:13-14; 8:12; 9:26; 11:19-26; 13:1-3; 15:3-4,22,30; 16:14-15, 30-33,40; 18:8,10; 19:1-5; Rom. 12:5; 1 Cor. 12:13; Phil. 1:1

To form a new church today the missionary must still start by baptising those who have accepted the evangelical doctrines. Once formed, this association will continue to grow as new members who have been baptised come to join.

Baptism, the doorway to the church, constitutes

a true alliance between the new members and the old with mutual obligations on both sides. The candidate who wishes to be baptised publicly accepts the evangelical doctrines, promises to put them into practice in the same way as those with whom he is uniting himself: the church on the other hand, receives him into its midst as one of its members and allows him to participate in all the spiritual privileges.

II. Nomination to Office in the Church

Acts 1:15-26 6:3-6; 11:30; 14:23; 15:2-4,22-23; 16:4; 20:17,28; 21:18; 2 Cor. 8:18-19; Phil. 1:1; Col. 4:17; 1 Thess. 5:12-14; 1 Tim. 3:1-6; 4:14; 5:17-22; 2 Tim. 1:6; 2:2; Titus 1:5-9

After having founded the first churches themselves, the apostles personally committed the continuation of their work with the Christian congregations to pastors and teachers whom the Scriptures call without distinction bishops and elders or pastors who, with their successors, must build on the foundation that has been laid. They were installed in their offices through prayers and the laying on of hands by the elders.

After the death of the apostles, the choice and the nomination of pastors has always belonged to the churches. We maintain this principle.

III. Pastors and Teachers

Acts 20:17-28; 1 Cor. 3:5-8; 4:1; 9:6; 2 Cor. 1:24; 11:7-10; Phil. 1:1; 2 Thess. 3:9; 1 Tim. 3:1-6; 4:12-16; 5:17-18; Titus 1:5-9; 1 Pet. 5:1-3

In the Scriptures there are no distinctions of hierarchy or of authority between the pastors and the teachers, nor between the bishops or supervisors and the elders or pastors, except for the respect that is accorded to older people. The elders, as chosen supervisors of the church, are responsible for the administration of baptism and the Lord's Supper, for leading the services and church discussions and for carrying out the decisions of the church. They should never dominate God's church but should be models to the rest of the flock, watching over the souls as one who is responsible for them.

LATIN AND SOUTHERN EUROPE

As far as their conduct is concerned, the pastors, like all the other members of the church, remain subject to the discipline of the church keeping in mind at all times 1 Timothy 5:19.

A pastor who is responsible for the management of a church can at the same time carry out secular activities; but it is best that he give himself wholly to his spiritual vocation.

IV. Deacons and Deaconesses

Apart from elders or pastors, the only other officers of the local churches are the deacons and deaconesses. They must be elected by the congregation and invested in their position by the laying on of hands. They should possess the qualities stated in the Scriptures: their job is to aid the pastors in their ministry, to serve the church by using the talents they have been given by God and they should particularly be responsible for all the material needs of the congregation.

Acts 6:1-6; Rom. 16:1-2; Phil. 1:1; 1 Tim. 3:8-13

V. Voting and Admission

Every local church must herself manage her own affairs, independent of all other political or religious authority. As far as accepting candidates for baptism and dealing with questions of business a final vote should be taken. All members, without any distinction of sex or position, hold equal rights in church and a decision is taken as a result of a majority vote.

Matt. 18:17; Acts 1:15-26; 6:5; 9:26-27; 11:2-4,18,22,29; 15:3-4,12,22-23,30,33; 18:27; Rom. 16:1-2; 1 Cor. 5; 16:3; 2 Cor. 2:6-8;8:19,23

The admission of a new member who comes from another believing Baptist Church takes place on presentation of a letter of recommendation from the church from which he comes. When he has no such letter, the alien brother must confess his faith, make known his beliefs and the church makes its own decision.

VI. Church Discipline

Matt. 18:15-20; Rom. 16:17; 1 Cor. 5; 2 Thess. 3:6-15; 1 Tim. 1:19-20; 6:3-5; 2 Tim. 3:1-5; Titus 3:10-11; 2 John 9-11; Rev. 2:14,20

According to the evangelical teachings, the church should exclude from its midst all members whose conduct belies their profession of faith; who knowingly break one of God's commandments and who repudiate all fraternal advice that is addressed to them in an attempt to lead them to repent and renounce their sins.

The dismissed member is excluded from communion and deprived of all his rights in the church, but is not refused admission to the public meetings of the congregation for worship.

VII. Re-Admission

2 Cor. 2:1-11

An excluded member can, on request, be re-admitted into the church if his conduct shows that he has once more become pious and faithful.

VIII. Independence of Churches and the Duties of Members Toward Their Pastors

1 Cor. 9:11-14; Gal. 6:6; Eph. 5:23-29; Phil. 4:14-16; 1 Thess. 5:12-13; 1 Tim. 5:17-18; 1 Pet. 5:5

Following the apostolic principle our churches are separated from the State and receive no salary from it so that it is the duty and privilege of the members to maintain their pastors, to support their efforts and to love, honour and respect them because of the work they do.

The Congregation

I. Those Who Make Up the Larger Congregation

Outside the church, which is made up of baptized believers who take part in communion, there is the congregation of all those who are not members of the church but who bind themselves with the flock and come to the evangelical service or who request visits from the pastor without being converted or baptized. Admitted are all those who declare themselves attached to the evangelical service, who ask to be put on the congregation list and whose conduct does not dishonour the Gospel.

II. Privileges of Members of the Congregation

Those who are considered as members of the congregation have the right to:
   (1) Present or consecrate their children to God through prayer by the Pastor and the church;
   (2) Religious instruction for their children; and for themselves, special instruction for adults;
   (3) Pastoral visits;
   (4) Marriage blessings;
   (5) Religious burial ceremony.

III. Responsibilities of Members of the Congregation

The members of the congregation, as well as the members of the church, should consider it their duty and privilege to contribute, according to their means, towards the general expenses of the service and for evangelical work.

IV. Exclusion

In the following cases cited below, the member is struck off the church register:
   (1) When he has himself asked to be struck off;
   (2) When he stops attending the services;
   (3) When his conduct dishonours the Gospel.

Belgium
The Union of Evangelical Baptist Churches

Baptist life and history in Belgium is tied to that of France. French Baptists from the border town of Denain helped establish churches across the border in Peruwelz and in Bonsecours, in Ougrée, near Leige (1895), and in Mont-sur-Marchienne. Baptist work remains small in Belgium, with practically no work among the Flemish-speaking populations. Support comes from both major Baptist groups in the United States.

Although they are a small union and close ties have existed to the French, the Baptist union of Belgium maintains its own identity. Its confession is entitled "Confession of Faith and Ecclesiastic Principles of the Union of Baptist Churches of the French Language" and is the same as that of the French Baptist Federation (see pp. 125-131).

Evangelical Association
of French-Speaking Baptist Churches

Drawing their numbers from France, Belgium, and Switzerland, the Franco-Association Baptists acknowledge their earlier, common heritage with all French Baptists. After about 1890 two groups emerged; the Franco-Swiss, primarily under the leadership of R. Saillens, and the Franco-Belgian group, under the Vincent family's leadership. A common journal, the *Echo of Truth*, biannual meetings, and common financial help from North America helped bind the groups together. Pastors Arthur Blocher and (the Swiss) Auguste Cross provided liaison for United States aid during and after World War I.

In 1920, the Americans suggested unification of the two groups, promising financial aid and a theological school. Developing doctrinal differences prevented such, and many misunderstandings resulted. With the election of "liberal" leaders to the Baptist union in 1921, the "orthodox" decided to separate amicably in order to remove the tensions. In May 1921, six churches separated. In July, they formed the *Association Evangélique d'Eglises Baptistes de Langue Francaise* (AEEBLF). By 1922, the association was in financial difficulty; they were disappointed that the promised aid from America was not provided for their group. At the official conference in 1923, the statutes were adopted. In 1924, the confession of faith was approved. In spite of many difficulties, the association grew, with eleven churches and eleven hundred members by 1928. There are currently twenty-six churches with two thousand members.

Although Association Baptists consider Georges Guyot (1875-1964) and Robert Dubarry (1875-1970) to be their main pioneers, Dubarry was probably the key individual in formation, leading, training, and guiding over the years. He stressed the united family of the local church on one hand and warned against the work of the devil and various sins on the other.

Prior to World War II all churches were self-supporting. After the ravages of the war, Dubarry helped reunite the churches through publications and meetings (regional, general, and pastoral) and yet underlined the strictly autonomous nature of each church. He remained president of the association from 1921 to 1960. Guyot's primary impact was as long-term editor of the official journal *Lien Fraternel*. This and other publications served as the link between the churches, in seeking to "edify, instruct, and inform." They also make the association known in other Evangelical circles. The assocation provides publishing opportunities for churches outside the association, as long as the materials are "strictly evangelical."

Workers and pastors studied at several different colleges and Bible schools (in Canada, England, Ireland, France, and elsewhere, with supplementary education by Dubarry (until his death in 1970); they also study at a Bible center in Brussels and a Christian culture center in Mulhouse, France.

External links are made with those Baptists of similar persuasion, primarily in French-speaking lands (as in some African contexts) and also with the Strict Baptists in England, Irish Baptists, and a few churches in Germany, Portugal, and Spain. North American contacts are now limited to Canada (the Association of Regular Baptists in Canada), as many former links made by Dubarry have been lost.

The Confession which follows is a modification of the 1979 French one, but it plays a significant role in the life of the churches as a general doctrinal and teaching guideline.

(Association Evangélique d'Eglises Baptistes
de Langue Francaise, 1921-1971: Notice Historique)

                      (J. Hoffman)
                      (F. M. Buhler)
                      TR: Lieven and Angela Schoorens

Confession of Faith and Ecclesiastical Principles of the Evangelical Association of French-Speaking Baptist Churches.

First Part
Doctrines

1. Concerning the True God:

We worship one only God in three persons, Father, Son and Holy Spirit, creator of all things, eternal, infinite, immutable, omnipotent, omniscient, perfectly wise, holy, righteous and good, to whom are due, to the highest degree, obedience, trust, gratitude, love and praise.

Gen. 1:1; 14:1; Ex. 20:11; Lev. 19:2; Deut. 6:4-5; 1 Sam. 2:3; 1 Kings 8:60; Pss. 37:3; 40:7; 62:9; 90:2; 102:25-28; 139:1-12,16; 145:1-13,17; 147:5; Prov. 3:5; Ezra 6:3; Mal. 3:6; Matt. 28:19; Mark 12:30; John 1:1-3; 17:3; Rom. 16:27; 1 Cor. 8:4,6; 2 Cor. 13:13; Col. 1:16; 1 Tim. 1:17; Jas. 1:17; 1 Pet. 1:15-16; 1 John 1:5; 4:8,16; 5:20

2. Concerning the Holy Scriptures:

We believe that the canonical writings of the Old and New Testaments are the Word that God directs towards us and constitute the only and infallible rules of faith and Christian life and the only touchstone by which every doctrine, every tradition and every religious and ecclesiastical system as well as every method of Christian action are to be tested.

Deut. 31:24-26; 2 Sam. 23:2; Matt. 5:18; Luke 24:27,44; John 5:39; Acts 1:16; 3:21; 17:11; Rom. 1:2; 3:2; 15:4; 1 Cor. 10:11; Gal. 1:6-12; 2 Tim. 3:15-17; 1 Pet. 1:10-11; 2 Pet. 1:19-21; 3:15-16

We believe that the Holy Scripture is a providential document and that the Holy Spirit presided in sovereign manner at its origin and at the formation of the biblical collection. We believe that He has Himself assured therein the perfect teaching and the entire historic truth, despite the imperfection of the human instruments who, by His divine inspiration and under His control, have contributed toward communicating to us the divine oracles.

We believe that the Holy Scriptures reveal to us

all that we must know in the spiritual realm. We believe that they need not be modified or completed by any other revelation in the course of the present dispensation.

3. Concerning Man, the Fall and the Consequences of Sin:

Gen. 1:27,31; 3; Deut. 24:16; 30:19; Pss. 51:7; 53:4; Ex. 53:6; Matt. 13:4-23; 15:19; 16:24-27; 25:41; Luke 11:17-20; John 3:18,36; 5:24; Rom. 2:5-11; 2 Cor. 11:3,14; Eph. 2:2; 6:12; 2 Thess. 1:8-9; 2 Pet. 2:4; 1 John 3:6; Jude 6; Rev. 12:9; 20:10-15

We believe that man, who is personally and directly responsible to God, is called to determine himself freely and definitely his eternal destiny down here on earth, by the spiritual position which he shall have taken during his earthly life and in the clearness of the lights that have been accessible to him.

We believe that the fall of man has been provoked and that the rebellion of mankind is being maintained by the intervention of a fallen angel, called Satan, who, having become the adversary of the Eternal long before the creation of man, and having involved in his revolt angels whom he has made his instruments, is destined, together with them, to torments without end through the assured triumph of the Son of God.

We believe that our first parents were created innocent, but having wilfully disobeyed their creator, they lost their primitive estate and incurred the just judgment of God. All their descendants, enveloped in this judgment and inheriting their fallen nature, are inclined towards evil and brought under the subjection of the Prince of this world. We believe that all those who like them shall have consciously transgressed God's laws, are justly exposed to an eternal punishment.

4. Concerning Jesus Christ and His Work:

Deut. 18:15; Ps. 2:7; Ex. 7:14; 9:5; 53:4-5,10; 55:4-5; Matt. 1:23; 5:17; 17:5; 24:30-31;

We believe that Jesus Christ, the Word made flesh, the only mediator between God and men, is from all eternity the unique Son of God.

LATIN AND SOUTHERN EUROPE

We believe that Jesus, conceived by the power of the Holy Spirit and born of a virgin, was just as truly man as he was truly God and after having been tempted in all things like we are, he remained perfectly holy.

We believe that by voluntarily abasing Himself the Son of God manifested in the realm of truth the same perfection as in the realm of goodness and that He never erred, neither in His acts nor in His teachings.

We believe that Jesus Christ of His own free will suffered and that He died on the Cross, suffering there in order to satisfy the divine justice, the penalty which is due to sinners, and presenting to the Father for all whom he has purchased by His blood the merits of His perfect life.

We believe that Jesus Christ rose bodily from the grave and ascended in glory to heaven where He intercedes for His own. We also believe that He will return bodily to take His own with Him and in order to establish His glorious reign. We believe that He will be the judge of the quick and the dead.

26:36-39; Mark 8:38; 16:19; Luke 1:35; 9:35; 22:24; John 1:1-14; 3:16,34; 5:22,27-29; 10:15-16; 14:2-3,6; 17:5-6; 20:25,27; Acts 1:9-11; 2:23-24,32; 10:42; 17:30-31; Rom. 1:3-4; 3:25-26; 5:19; 6:9-10; 8:34; 9:5; 1 Cor. 15:3-4,25; Gal. 4:4; Eph. 5:2; Phil. 2:6-8; Col. 1:19; 2:3,9; 1 Thess. 1:10; 3:13; 4:15-17; 1 Tim. 2:5; 3:16; 2 Tim. 4:1; Heb. 1:2,5-6; 2:9,14,17; 4:15; 7:25-26,28; 9:14,24; 10:10; 12:2; 1 Pet. 1:19-20; 3:18; 1 John 2:1-2; Rev. 1:7-8

5. Concerning the Salvation Through Jesus Christ:

We believe that in order to be saved man must, under the action of the Holy Spirit, repent of his sins, unite himself to Jesus Christ in his death and claim for himself, through faith, the expiatory work of the Redeemer and of His infinite merits. The sinner, thus justified, regenerated and sanctified by grace, has eternal life which involves the entire redemption of spirit, soul and body.

Ps. 32:1-2,5,51; Prov. 28:13; Ezek. 11:19; Joel 2:12-13; Mark 1:15; Luke 13:3,5; John 3:16,36; 6:37,39-40,44,65; 17:2,17; Acts 3:19; 20:20-21; 26:18; Rom. 3:22-30; 4:4-5; 5:1,9,12,17,19; 8:30; 1 Cor. 1:30-31; 2:10,12; 15:42-44; 2 Cor. 5:19,21; Gal. 4:4-6; Eph. 1:7-14,18-19; 2:5,8; 1 Thess. 5:23; 2 Thess. 2:13-14; Titus 3:3-7; 1 John 1:9; 3:2

6. Concerning the Holy Spirit and His Work in Christian Life:

Joel 2:26,29; Luke 24:49; John 14:16-17,26; 15:26; 16:7-8,13-14; Acts 1; 8; Rom. 5:5; 8:9,13-14,16,26-27; 1 Cor. 3:16; 6:11,19; 12:11,13; 2 Cor. 1:22; 5:5; 13:13; Gal. 4:6; 5:5,16,18,22,25; Eph. 1:13-14; 3:16,19; 4:30; 5:18; 6:17-18; 1 Thess. 5:19; 2 Thess. 2:13-14; 1 Pet. 1:2; 1 John 2:20,27; 4:13; Jude 20

We believe that the Holy Spirit, a divine person, works by applying to hearts the truths of Holy Writ with which He could not be in disagreement. He produces in those who are elected according to the purpose of God the Christian life in its principle and its effects. He enables them to make progress in it and persevere until the end.

We believe that the Holy Spirit is given to each child of God as the earnest and seal of his eternal heritage. He reveals and communicates the glorious riches of Christ. Every prayer and every work, in order to be truly Christian, must result from His action. He alone can assure to the believer the communion with his God and with his brethren.

7. Concerning Baptism:

Matt. 28:19-20; Mark 16:15-16; Acts 2:38,41; 8:12,36-39; 10:47-48; 16:33; 19:3-5; 22:16; Rom. 6:3-4; Gal. 3:26-28; Eph. 4:5; Col. 2:12; 1 Pet. 3:21

We believe that immersion is for the generated man the divinely chosen symbol of the purification of his sins, of his burial and resurrection with Christ. We believe that, according to the order of Christ, the immersion of believers is perpetually obligatory and that, according to the apostolic practice, admission to the local church necessarily implies it.

8. Concerning the Lord's Supper:

Matt. 26:26-28; Mark 14:22-24; Luke 22:19-20; Acts 2:42,46; 20:7; 1 Cor. 10:16-17; 11:23-29

We believe that the Supper, instituted by our Lord Jesus Christ, for the commemoration and proclamation of His atoning death on the Cross ought to be observed in and under the control of local churches until He comes again. We believe that bread and wine are symbols of the body and the blood given and shed by our Saviour and by participating in them Christians testify that they are one body with Jesus Christ. We believe that by this participation they likewise proclaim their firm assurance

LATIN AND SOUTHERN EUROPE

of His return in glory of their divine Saviour and Master.

9. Concerning the Resurrection and the Final Judgment:

We believe that all the dead shall be resurrected, both the just and the unjust. We believe in the final judgment. We believe that the rebellious will consciously suffer the eternal punishment that they shall have merited, and by virtue of the grace which they shall have accepted by faith, the redeemed shall enjoy eternal glory.

Job 19:25-27; Dan. 12:2-3; Matt. 7:21-23; 12:36-37; 25:31-46; Luke 13:25-28; John 5:22-29; 6:39; 11:23-25; Acts 4:2; 17:31; 24:15; Rom. 2:2-16; 9:22-23; 14:10,12; 1 Cor. 15:20-25; 2 Cor. 5:10; Phil. 3:24; 1 Thess. 4:14; 2 Thess. 1:5-10; 2 Pet. 2:4-9; Jude 6-7; Rev. 20:4-6,11-15; 21:8

Second Part
Ecclesiastical Principles

1. Concerning the Local Church:

We believe that the local church constituted, according to the Word of God, is an assembly of believers, managing its own affairs, and separated from the state, receiving no subsidy from the latter, and, being completely independent in religious matters from any and every authority save that of Jesus Christ, its Head. We see in the local earthly church the reduced and imperfect image of the heavenly community which, after the nuptials of the Lamb, will bring together in one body the redeemed of all times.

Matt. 16:16-20; 18:17-20; 28:19-20; Acts 2:41-47; 5:13-14; 6:2-7; 7:1,4-5; 9:19,26-31; 16:4-5,18,26-27; 19:9; 20:17,28-31; Rom. 12:4-8; 16:1-2; 1 Cor. 1:2; 5:9-13; 11:16; 12:12-31; 14:5,12,19,26-40; 2 Cor. 8:18-24; Eph. 4:4-7,11-16; Col. 1:18; 1 Tim. 3:14-16; 4:14; Titus 3:8-11; Heb. 10:24-25; 1 Pet. 2:1-10; 3 John 1:5-8

We believe that, conforming to the practice of the apostles, it is indispensable that all those who compose a local church have accepted the evangelical message, that they have manifested their regeneration by a Christian walk of life, and that they have testified to their faith by being buried symbolically.

Attachment to the local church creates among the

newly baptized and its members a union of mutual obligations. By proclaiming through baptism his faith in the evangelical truths, the candidate takes upon himself the obligation to practice these truths in full harmony with the church.

The members of the local church ought, in the common interest, to exercise the gifts which they have received from God.

The admission of new members is declared by the local assembly itself. In the case of candidates coming from other groups of regularly baptized believers the presentation of a letter of recommendation from such a group is sufficient for admission.

We believe that the local church, a pillar and buttress of the truth within the environment wherein its vocation is being realized, has as its mission to accomplish by its witness, through teaching and by the service it shares, all the tasks which the Lord has left in the charge of Christian local fellowships. It is incumbent upon such a local congregation, in responsible manner, to declare the Gospel, maintain sound doctrine, to control the celebration of Christian ordinances, to establish and realize its program of action, to acknowledge the ministries and to exercise discipline.

2. Concerning Ministries:

Acts 6:1-6; 20:17-36; 21:17-18; Rom. 16:1-2; 1 Cor. 3:1-9; 9:7-14; Eph. 4:11-16; Phil. 1:1; Col. 4:17; 1 Thess. 5:12-13; 1 Tim. 1:3-4; 3:1-7; 4:12-16; 5:17-21; 6:3-5,11-14; 2 Tim. 2:2; 4:1-2,5; Titus 1:5-9; Heb. 13:7,17-18; Jas. 3:1; 1 Pet. 5:1-5

We believe that all those who officially fulfill a ministry within the local church ought to have been called by the latter, after it has been established that they possess the qualifications required by the Word of God for their charge, which they must discharge in a spirit of personal disinterest, of wisdom and love.

The Scriptures establish no distinction in rank or authority between bishops (overseers), as pastors and elders. The pastors or elders are particularly charged to watch over the teaching and the spiritual health of the local church. In a general sense, it is their mission to preside over its religious meetings, its public functions and deliberations, whose execution it is incumbent on them to assure. They ought never to dominate over the church of God, but they ought to make themselves examples of the flock by watching over the souls of men as having to give an account of them before God.

In addition to pastors and elders, the local church may have other responsible servants, for example deacons and deaconesses whose role it is to assist the pastors or elders in their ministry, by assuming special responsibility for everything that relates to the material interests of the congregation.

With relation to their attributes and their individual conduct, members entrusted with a ministry are, just like the other members, subject to the control and the discipline of the local church which sovereignly determines the particular charge of each member.

It is the privilege and duty of the members of the congregation to support its servants, to assist them in their ministry, and to manifest love and respect towards them for reasons of the work that they accomplish.

3. Concerning Discipline:

We believe that the local church possesses, conforming to the evangelical teaching, the power to exclude from its bosom, after having solemnly warned them, all those of its members whose profession is belied by their conduct, or who without reasonable cause abandon the holy assemblies, and who persistently show that they have no interest in the different needs of the church or who reject the brotherly exhortations which are addressed to them.

Matt. 18:15-18; 1 Cor. 5:2,6-7,9-13; 2 Cor. 2:1-11; 2 Thess. 3:6,13-15; Heb. 10:24-25; 2 John 1:10-11

The member who has been thus excluded and deprived of all his rights in the church may however continue to benefit of the good will and spiritual solicitude of those who have had the pain of separating themselves from him. He may, moreover, at his own request, be admitted to the local church, if his testimony and his conduct demonstrate that he has again become pious and faithful.

(TR: Lieven and Angela Schoorens)

Greece

Greece is one of the more recent European countries to experience Baptist beginnings. The one indigenious Greek church was begun in Athens by Marcus Bousios whose mother had been converted in Patras, just after the turn of the century, under the influence of a man from Switzerland. She encouraged her son to be a Baptist although the name Baptist was not highly thought of in rigidly Orthodox Greece. Visiting independent Baptists from North America encouraged him to start the church and ordained him in 1969.

Although there is no union of Baptists in Greece, there is an official confession which was submitted to the government in 1972 in order to obtain official recognition. The recognized name is the "Evangelical Baptist Church of Greece," and the confession is a Greek translation of the 1963 Southern Baptist confession.

(Norman Burns)

V
Eastern Europe

The Union of Soviet Socialist Republics
All-Union Council of Evangelical Christians-Baptists

Baptists began in czarist Russia in the nineteenth century, deep in the largest Eastern Orthodox county where church and state were one. Moscow was seen by many Russians as the "third Rome," the successor to Rome and Constantinople as both religious and political leader of the world. Intolerance and heavy persecution awaited not just Baptists but all who dared to differ from the established belief of the day.

There are many roots to Baptist beginnings in Russia, just as there are many peoples and traditions. A number of spontaneous groups sprung up all over Russia during the periods of nineteenth-century religious awakenings, some of which had older, deeper traditions dating back to the seventeenth or sixteenth centuries. Two groups arose at the same time in southern Russia, both among simple, working folk. Serious Bible study led some members of the native Russian sect of Molokans to reconsider baptism. A merchant, Nikita Issajewitsch Voronin, met a Baptist believer from Lithuania, M. K. Kalweit, and was baptized by him after dark on August 20, 1867, in a mill creek near the Kura River. Voronin, in turn, baptized other Molokans who began to call themselves Baptists because they had been baptized on their conscious profession of faith. From that group three key leaders later developed: (1) Vasilii Gurevich Pavlov, the virtual patriarch of the movement; (2) Vasilii Vasil'evich Ivanov-Klyshnikov, who started the second congregation in the Caucasus and led in the awakening there; and (3) Johann Kargel, a German who joined the group and later carried the message to the capital of the empire, becoming not only a reconciler but also theologian for the growing Baptist movement.

Another source of pietistic and Baptist ideas is seen in the *Stunden* movement. Religious German immigrants, mostly Mennonites, practiced their "hours" (*Student*) of prayer and Bible study. Many Russians were influenced and sought not only meaning but also Bibles. The ideas of J. G. Oncken and adult believers' baptism entered through the *Stundists*, but it was difficult to find Germans courageous enough to baptize the Slavic orthodox. The translation of the Bible into Russian and brought in by colporteurs played a key role as well. Russian Baptists note the almost automatic result of peasants reading the Bible in their desire to imitate primitive Christianity and develop a sober lifestyle. Efim Tsymbal led the *Stundists* into water baptism and considerable problems with orthodoxy and officials. Persecution and imprisonment in the 1870s and 1880s seemed to assist the cause. Believers in the Ukraine numbered in the thousands, while the Tiflis congregation in the Caucasus grew slowly.

The Tiflis church sent Vasilii Pavlov to Germany to study with Oncken. Pavlov was ordained and commissioned as a Baptist missionary in Russia. On his way back, he made contact with the *Stundists* of whom he had heard in Germany. He then evangelized broadly, organizing small groups and giving direction. He also introduced the confession of faith drawn up by Oncken in Germany as a guide.

Meanwhile, Iakov Deliakov, the colporteur who had introduced Voronin to Kalweit, preached very effectively among the New Molokans (who called themselves Evangelical Christians). Baptists in the Caucasus made contact with the "Evangelical Christians." By 1879, Pavlov was trying to form a union of Baptists but the meeting in Tiflis did not provide one. One of the Molokan converts, I. I. Zhidkov, became an extremely effective evangelist, baptizing over fifteen hundred converts.

The third notable source of Baptists in Russia is seen in the so-called "drawing-room *Stundists*" among the nobility of Saint

Petersburg. In 1874, they invited a lay preacher from England, G. A. W. Waldgrave (Lord Radstock), to lead a series of evangelistic meetings among the aristocracy. A member of the Plymouth Brethren, Waldgrave saw several converts, the key one being Vasilii Aleksandrovich Pashkov. Pashkov was an army officer who became so active in evangelistic work that the descriptive name *Pashkovism* emerged. Pashkov's literature was the basis of contact with other groups of a similar mind. He gave financial support to other groups and helped establish a colony of Baptists. He also visited Christians in the Ukraine and Caucasia. His attempt to bring believers together in 1884 drew several different groups but was stopped by the czarist authorities, a forewarning of persecutions that would follow. These reached great intensity under the organized efforts of the procurator of the Holy Synod, Konstantin Petrovitsch Pobjedonoszev, who sought to stamp out Baptist, *Stundist*, and Pashkov "heresies." Children were removed from homes; practically all civil rights were lost. Only in 1905 did persecution let up some. When Czar Nicholas II proclaimed at Act of Toleration and Manifest, Russian Baptists began to obtain some freedom of conscience, to meet and speak. Amnesty came for those who had been imprisoned or exiled for "religious crimes."

The Baltic countries of Estonia, Latvia, and Lithuania, because of their history, had close ties to Germany and felt the direct impact of Oncken's work. The first church was begun in Memel in 1841. Estonia was reached by Swedish missionaries in the 1870s, and the island of Hiiumaa experienced the first strong awakening. The Haapsalu church reached out broadly and began work in Tallinn in 1884. The conversion and work of Baron Woldemar Reinhold Alexander van Üxküll, a wealthy landlord, greatly strengthened and expanded the work not only in Tallinn but also throughout Estonia. Expanding to eighty churches and fifteen thousand members prior to World War II, Estonians had their own seminary, as well as numerous other ministries.

A notable Molokan convert, Ivan Stepanovich Prochanov,

became associated with the Saint Petersburg group and eventually became the driving force behind the Evangelical Christian wing of the movement.

A number of other major and minor elements could be amplified but will only be mentioned: the British and Foreign Bible Society, the Mennonites, and Pentecostals, as well as spontaneous local groups.

Eventually, however, two strong streams evolved, the Evangelical-Christian group under Prokhanov's strong leadership, and the Baptists under Pavlov's able leadership. Both groups were members of the Baptist World Alliance and Prokhanov was elected vice-president in 1911. In the early days, both groups experienced much persecution, including exile in Siberia for preaching. But by 1914, only fifty years after the first baptism, they numbered well over a hundred thousand. World War I created problems not only in normal suffering but also in imprisonment for some pastors who chose to do noncombatant work rather than to fight. Several Protestants were exiled.

The Communist revolution brought many changes for Baptists, especially freedom from czarist oppression. Exiles could return, church leaders reinstated, and for over a decade Baptists had their greatest freedom. The 1918 Constitution of the Russian Republic stated: "With the object of securing real freedom of conscience for the workers, the church is separated from the state, and the school from the church, but freedom of religious and antireligious propaganda is recognized for all citizens." Growth ensued, perhaps exceeding even two million.

It all changed in 1919 with an attack on all religions. The article on religion was changed to read simply, "Freedom in the exercise of religious worship and freedom of antireligious propanganda is recognized for all citizens." An additional "Law on Religious Associations" with freedom for local interpretation set the stage for close supervision of religious activities and restrictions of most. Churches had to register and supply names of members; they could not do many services, such as teaching children or conducting charitable works. This position was modified with the onset of World War II, as some concessions were made by the government to win popular support for war efforts.

Although there had been earlier unsuccessful efforts in the early 1920s to combine the Baptist groups, only in 1944 were both mainstreams united to form the "Council of Evangelical-Christians and Baptists." A year later the "Union of Christians of Evangelical Faith" (Pentecostals) joined, and the name was changed to "Council of Evangelical Christians-Baptists." It eventually included Mennonite Brethren as well, the fourth component. Each union in this All-Union Council had its own confession of faith, Prokhanov having provided a very lengthy one and the Baptist Union having used a translated, modified form of the Oncken-Købner version of the early years. When the 1944 union occurred, a formal confession was not adopted but the general wishes of the Baptists prevailed. A few used the Prokhanov Confession but it was not used by the union. A temporary compromise was found, however, in 1966 when the All-Union agreed upon the 1913 confession made by Kargel as a transitional one (that is, until a new one could be worked out). It had been used by both Unions in the 1920s and was acceptable to the Mennonites.

Kargel, a member of the Tiflis group, had been educated in the West and traveled widely, including trips to Bulgaria and Georgia. He played a major role in doctrinal questions, due to his exegetical and writing abilities. His confession, which follows, reflects a number of theological concerns of his day, as well as a definite contact with Western Protestantism. In the 1920s, the influence of English and American revivalism had been felt, especially that of the evangelist Dwight L. Moody.

After World War II, Alexander A. V. Karev emerged as the key historian, theologian, and exegete of the united group. A former pupil of, and close worker with, Prokhanov, Karev was a key leader, serving in several different roles until his death in 1971. Although a new confession is being prepared by Russian

Baptists, the Kargel confession still serves as the current or interim guide.

(Paul D. Steeves)
(Wilhelm Kahle)
(Alexei Bichkov)
(Walter Sawatsky)
(Ants Rebane)

Confession of Faith
of the
Evangelical Christians — Baptists

I. Concerning God

Ps. 90:3; Matt. 5:38; Rev. 15:4; Isa. 6:3; Gen. 17:1; Ps. 139:2-4; Acts 15:18; Ps. 11:7; Rom. 3:26; Ps. 119:68; Matt. 19:17; 1 John 4:8,16; Gen. 1:1; Col. 1:16; Ps. 3:7; John 3:16; Luke 1:28,31,35; John 3:16-17; Rom. 3:24; John 16:14,8; 3:5; 16:13

We believe in the only, true God, revealing Himself in three persons: Father, Son and Holy Spirit, which are in Oneness everlasting, perfect, holy, mighty, all-wise, righteous, good and love.

God the Father we confess as Creator of heaven and earth and of all things, visible and invisible; God the Son is the one born by the Father in eternity and by the favoured, blessed Virgin Mary; He is our Saviour and Saviour of all the world; God the Holy Spirit is the Comforter, coming from the Father, glorifying the Son, convincing the world, giving new birth to man, guiding the disciples of Christ.

II. Concerning the Word of God

2 Pet. 1:21; Ps. 148:8-9; Prov. 30:6; Mark 7:13; Heb. 1:1-2; John 5:39; 20:31; Phil. 1:27; Acts 20:32; 2 Tim. 3:15-17

We believe that all canonical books of the Old and New Testament as represented in the entire Bible, or the Holy Scripture (excluding the Apocrypha), are inspired by the Holy Spirit and given by the Lord, as indispensable, the only and completely sufficient source of knowledge about God, our redemption, and His will concerning our faith and life.

III. Concerning Man in General

We believe that God created man after His image, but that he, tempted by satan, fell into sin and came short of the glory of God. By the sin of one man all were infected, became the children of wrath, and came under punishment for sin; this means the eternal death, spiritually, physically, or the second death, that is, death after physical death.

Gen. 1:27; Rom. 3:23; 5:12,19; Eph. 6:23; Gen. 2:17; Luke 15:32; Eph. 2:1; Rom. 5:14; Matt. 25:41; Rev. 20:12-15

IV. Concerning the Redemption of Man

In the question concerning the redemption of man we believe that man cannot save himself, not by his own righteousness, not by any work and not by the help of any other man.

In the only salvation, accomplished by God Himself in Jesus Christ by means of Christ's death for all men, the Lord is offering righteousness, reconciliation, forgiveness of sins, justification and eternal life.

This work of redemption accomplished by God for man remains ineffective for him, unless the work of God works *in man*. The first has been accomplished by Christ without our help; the second has been accomplished by the Holy Spirit with the consent of man.

The Holy Spirit creates in man an inner upheaval or repentance, faith in the sacrifice of Christ and trust in the accomplished atonement, the new birth or new life as well as the adoption as sons. Also the same Holy Spirit is accomplishing the sanctification of the born again and keeping them for life eternal.

Matt. 16:26; Isa. 64:6; Rom. 10:3; Gal. 2:16; 3:10; Rom. 3:20; Ps. 49:8-9; Heb. 10:11; Acts 4:12; 2 Cor. 5:18-19; 1 Tim. 2:5-6; Matt. 20:28; 1 Pet. 1:18-19; 1 John 2:2; Heb. 2:9; Rom. 3:25; 2 Cor. 5:19-20; Col. 1:20,14; 2:13,14; Heb. 9:22; Rom. 3:24; 4:5; 2 Cor. 5:21; John 3:16; 5:24; 1 John 5:11-12; Rom. 6:23; 5:6-8; Pss. 32:3-5; 51:3-9; Isa. 53:5; Rom. 4:24-25; Eph. 2:8; Heb. 10:10-14; John 1:12-13; 3:3-8; Jas. 1:18; 1 Pet. 1:23; Rom. 8:14-16; Gal. 4:4-6; 2 Cor. 3:18; 2 Thess. 2:13; 1 Pet. 1:5; Jude 24; Rom. 6:22

V. Concerning the Church of Christ

The universal Church of Christ is built upon the foundation of the apostles and prophets, Christ Jesus Himself being the cornerstone. She consists of those who are saved, who believe, who are called to

Eph. 2:20; Acts 2:47; 4:4; 5:14; 6:7; Rom. 1:7; 1 Cor. 1:2; 2 Cor. 1:1; Eph. 1:1; Heb. 12:22-23; Rom. 12:5; 1

be saints, who are in this world as well as the saved ones who have gone to be with the Lord. Those and these are constituting one body whose head is Christ. And although the members of this church are from different nations, different situations and have different gifts, they all are one in Christ and individually members one with another.

<small>Cor. 12:27; Eph. 1:22-23; Rev. 5:9-10; Gal. 3:28; Col. 3:11; 1 Cor. 12:14-18; John 17:11,21-23; Acts 4:32; Eph. 2:15; 4:4; Rom. 12:5;</small>

The single local churches (communities) are only part of the one universal Church; they are built by the Lord in different countries, cities and local places for the uniting of the saved children of God on earth, for the unified praising of God, for the growth of the members in the knowledge of God and Christ, for upbuilding in the life of faith after the image of Christ, for the mutual participation in all this and for the spreading of the Kingdom of God on earth.

<small>John 10:16; 11:52; Rom. 15:6; 1 Cor. 14:26; Col. 3:16; Col. 2:2; Eph. 3:18-19; 4:12-15; 1 Pet. 4:10; Jude 20; Rom. 15:14; Eph. 4:16; Acts 13:1-3; Rom. 10:15; Phil. 1:5</small>

On the other hand, the Church separates from this world and, watching the purity and holiness of its members, removes the unclean out of its midst.

<small>Acts 2:40; 5:1-11,13; 1 Cor. 5:1-13</small>

VI. Concerning the Servants of Christ and of the Church

We believe that Jesus Christ, as He gave to His Church from the beginning apostles, prophets, evangelists, pastors and teachers, so He is continuing to give those in the measure of necessity until this present time. And as the Holy Spirit is granting unto them His gifts, He Himself is raising them to service, so the Church must acknowledge them and accept them, but at the same time she must break with evil-workers. In the Word of God a description of their moral qualities, their service and their reward is found.

<small>Eph. 4:11; 1 Cor. 12:4-10; Acts 13:1-3; 3 John 8-10; Phil. 3:2; Rev. 2:2; 1 Tim. 3:1-12; Titus 1:5-9; 2:7-8; Matt. 20:25-28; Acts 20:28; 1 Pet. 5:1-4; Rom. 12:7-8</small>

VII. Concerning Christ's Institutions for the Church

The Lord Jesus Christ left to His disciples two institutions: baptism and the Lord's supper, which the Church must observe as long as she exists in this

<small>Luke 22:14-15; Acts 20:7</small>

world. Both baptism and the Lord's supper are entrusted only to the disciples of Christ.

1. Baptism must be preceded by the message or teaching about salvation in Christ, repentance, faith and receiving the Holy Spirit. The significance of baptism is diverse: it is the symbol of the washing away of sins, the promise to God with a clear conscience, obedience to the Lord, the sign of burial and resurrection with Christ. From this is concluded that it cannot be given to children, just as the first disciples also were led to baptize only those who heard, who accepted the Word of God and believed in Him.

<small>Matt. 28:19; Acts 2:29-36,41; 10:47-48; Matt. 3:7-8; Acts 2:37-38; Mark 16:16; Acts 8:36-37; 10:47; 19:2-3; 22:16; 1 Pet. 3:21; Matt. 3:14-15; Luke 7:29-30; Rom. 6:2-4; Acts 8:12</small>

2. The Lord's supper has been given by the Lord Himself in remembrance of Him, especially His suffering and death paid as the price for ransom, in remembrance of His love reaching to the uttermost, and of the giving of Himself not only for us, but also to provide for our spiritual, heavenly food. Received with living faith it makes us partakers of fellowship with Him, as well as with all members of His Church.

<small>Luke 22:19; 1 Cor. 11:24-25; 1 Pet. 1:18-19; 1 Cor. 11:26; John 13:1; 15:13; Rom. 5:8; John 6:51; 1 Cor. 10:16-17</small>

VIII. Concerning Marriage

The Word of God teaches that marriage has been instituted already in paradise by the Lord and confirmed by Jesus Christ and the apostles.

<small>Gen. 1:27-28; Matt. 19:4-6; 1 Cor. 7:1-40</small>

Concerning divorce the Lord says that at the beginning there were none and that only death released one from marriage. Only one exception the Lord does admit, that is in case of adultery.

<small>Heb. 13:4; Matt. 19:6-8; Rom. 7:2; Matt. 5:32; 19:9</small>

IX. Concerning Government Authority

We believe and confess, that every true Christian must be a most faithful citizen of his government and a submissive subject to the authorities, "not only to avoid God's wrath but also for the sake of conscience." We confess with the apostle: "Let every person be subject to the governing authorities. For there is no authority except from God, and those that exist

<small>Rom. 13:5; Rom. 13:2-4; 1 Tim. 2:1-4</small>

have been instituted by God" (Rom. 13:1). So we count it a privilege to pay all of them their dues, not to resist, not to do wrong, but, on the contrary, to do what is good, to make prayers, supplications, intercessions and thanksgivings for all men, for kings and all who are in high positions.

1 Tim. 2:5; Matt. 23:8; Heb. 4:14; Matt. 22:21

In relationship to God, however, we state that one cannot suffer any human interference, having Christ Jesus as the only mediator, the only teacher, and the only High Priest; it was He who ordered us to render to Caesar those things that are Caesar's, and also ordered us to render to God what is God's.

X. Concerning the Second Coming of the Lord and His Judgment

1 Cor. 15:51-52; Matt. 24:42-44; 1 Thess. 5:2,4-10; Matt. 25:10; 24:40-41; 25:11-13; Luke 12:45-46; 1 Thess. 4:16-17

Christ is coming for His Own, invisible to the world, like a thief in the night; but those, who are watching for Him won't be caught by surprise, and those who are ready will enter with Him into Glory; those, who are not ready will be left with the unfaithful for the great tribulation. Those who have died in Him He will raise up from death; those and the others living He will gather up together to Himself so as to be always with the Lord.

Matt. 16:27; 25:31; Jude 14; Rev. 19:11-14; Matt. 24:30; John 19:37; Rev. 1:7; Matt. 25:31-46; Rev. 19:15-19; 20:4-5,7-15

But Christ will come after that with *His Own* and with His heavenly angels, and every eye will see Him. Then the judgment will begin, but only for those who live on the earth; from the unjust no one will come to life until the passing of a thousand years' reign by Christ with His Own. When the thousand years have ended, Satan will deceive the nations for a short time; then the unjust will come to life and the final judgment will take place.

[This confession was compiled by Johan Ivan Benjaminowitsch KARGEL in 1913 and confirmed by the All Union Conference in 1966.]

TR: Maria Vogel

Adult baptism in the Neckar River, Germany, in 1837.

Johann Gerhard Oncken

Julius Köbner

Gottfried Wilhelm Lehmann

I. S. Prochanov

J. Kargel

V. G. Pavlov

A. V. Karev

J. I. Zhidkov

Union of Soviet Socialist Republics
The Union of Churches of Evangelical Christians-Baptists, Dissident Baptists

A schism occurred among the Evangelical Christians-Baptists in the 1960s, one that cannot easily be explained, although it can be described. In 1960, the All-Union Council of Evangelical Christians Baptists (AUCECB, or All-Union Council) sent out two documents, a new set of statutes and a "Letter of Instructions," apparently as a result of government pressure. Both documents contained matters that many found to be contrary to Baptist principles. Restrictions were placed on children attending worship, on baptism between the ages of eighteen and thirty, evangelistic preaching was to be discouraged, and the selection of chief officers of the church had to be approved by the government. These four restrictions were coupled with a number of regulations to be met before being registered as a church. Many chose to disobey and were imprisoned as a result.

An ad hoc committee led by G. P. Vins, A. F. Prokofiev, and G. K. Krinchkov met in 1961 to call for a congress of the union in order to elect new leaders for the union and to deny the authority of the documents. The committee called itself the "Action Group for the Convening of a Congress" or "*Initsiativnaia Gruppa*" in Russian, hence the popular catch words *Initiative Baptists*. When the desired congress did not meet, the group met in 1962 to organize its own congress and declared the All-Union Council leaders to be apostate, excommunicated them from Baptist fellowship, and claimed leadership for themselves until a congress could be held.

A national congress was called by the All-Union Council leaders in 1963, and it elected the very leaders that had been excommunicated. In 1964, the Council of Prisoners' Relatives of Evangelical Christians-Baptists was created. The organization's goal was collecting information about Baptists who had been imprisoned since 1960. In 1965, the group met once more and called themselves the Union of Churches of Evangelical Christians-Baptists, hereafter called Dissident Baptists, under the leadership of the Council of Churches of Evangelical Christians-Baptists (CCECB) (that is, the former *Initsiativnaia Gruppa*). In November, 1965, they published their statutes (see Appendix 5).

The controversial 1960 statutes of the All-Union Council were rescinded both in the new constitutions of 1963 and 1966. Both Baptists and Dissident Baptists were now organized in almost the same way, except that the union (UECB) includes the office of senior presbyter or superintendent to supervise work at a regional level. The superintendent is assisted by a regional council elected at conferences of representatives of churches in a given region. The Dissident Baptists use only the regional councils and not the senior presbyter, reflecting a controversy dating back to 1911 when the office was suggested to help scattered Baptists survive under increasing czarist pressure. The idea was that such regionalization (decentralization) would help if the government arrested leaders of the union. Opposition at that time reflected fears of a bishopric; in 1930, under the severe Stalinist persecution, the plan was put into effect. It was retained in the union of 1944 but came under attack in 1961 by the Dissidents who feared it could be used by the state.

Another major difference between the constitutions exists in the fact that the Dissident Baptists have a clear statement on the separation of church and state. This reflects not only this stance but also their assertion that by cooperating with the government the All-Union Council is violating a most basic Baptist principle.

Several attempts have been made to reconcile the two groups, as well as to assist in obtaining release from prison for several Baptist pastors. A number of nonregistered churches have registered and come over to the All-Union camp. (Some, however, have registered and remained autonomous.) Unfortunately, the differences in church practices and various interpretations of unity and freedom have degenerated into a doctrinal issue. In 1970, the dissident group sent out a major declaration to all churches warning that "Your salvation is in danger if you continue to fellowship with AUCECB workers." It went on to say: "You cannot be in union with the AUCECB and in union with God at the same time." It appeared that a doctrine of a "saving church" was raised; the Baptist leadership replied that no church saves, only Christ. The dissenters were trying to indicate what they interpreted as compromising with sin. A secondary doctrine developed in the apparent necessity of a suffering church. The dissenters felt that the faithful church would be persecuted; no one would contradict their scriptural claims but questioned that they might be deliberately seeking persecution and were thusly not "being persecuted for righteousness' sake."

The Dissident Baptists list seven "Fundamental Principles of Evangelical Christians and Baptists" (CCECB), for faithfulness to which, as Pastor Vins writes "the authorities in the USSR have been persecuting us for eighteen years." The principles are:

1. The Holy Scripture (the Bible) is the only rule and guide in all matters and all questions concerning faith and life. From this it follows that preaching the Gospel of witnessing to Christ is the chief task and fundamental calling of the Church.
2. Absolute freedom of conscience.
3. Spiritual regeneration of members of the Church.
4. Baptism by Faith.
5. Independence of each separate local church.
6. The priesthood of all believers.
7. Separation of the Church from the State.

(Paul D. Steeves)
(Walter Sawatsky)
(RCDA)
(Georgi P. Vins)

Poland
The Polish Baptist Christian Union

Poland has been strongly Roman Catholic during the entire period of Baptist history in the country. This period embraces the time before World War I when the country, having been divided among Russia, Prussia, and Austria, had no political independence, the time of political independence between the two World Wars, and the time of a new political reality after World War II. The many ravages of the war did not bring remarkable changes in this respect.

The first Baptist community grew out of the pietistic movement of the nineteenth century due to the activity of a village teacher, Gottfried Alf, who, while giving leadership to small groups of people studying the Bible privately, came very near to Baptist convictions. He identified himself as a Baptist after he had come in touch with a Baptist pastor from Prussia. Twenty-six people were baptized in Adamow in 1858. This was the first Baptist church in Poland. Alf was rejected by his family, and the church was persecuted by both the official church and the state. With the passage of time, the movement spread to all language groups: Polish, Ukrainian, Bohemian, Russian, and German.

The main thrust of the work before World War I was among Germans. The interwar period was marked by a rapid growth of work among Slavic people. The Slavic Baptist Union was organized in 1921. Two Unions, Slavic and German, existed side by side with a total membership of about seventeen thousand. The two unions cooperated in many fields. Theological education was carried out, publications were issued in six languages; social work, such as hospitals, homes for aged and orphans, was started.

The outbreak of the World War II brought drastic changes to this situation. Occupation forces forbade all non-German language in worship services until the German Baptist Union intervened with the result of securing permission of worship for non-German Free Evangelical churches—all practicing believers' baptism—which were now to act as a federation. This group developed an extensive underground activity in concentration camps and areas rigidly controlled by the German army. Many people whose freedom or lives were endangered, Jews included, were helped; Bibles and Christian books were distributed, pastoral care was extended to those in need in as many cases as possible. Of course, Baptists suffered from the massive death and destruction inflicted upon the Polish people. When the war was over, only eighteen hundred members of the Federation were left alive or to be found. Many congregations were all but gone. But the remnant began relief work and evangelistic activity with great effort and enthusiasm. Scandinavian Baptists and American Baptists gave much aid, especially in the relief work.

In 1947, all other Evangelical groups drew away from the Baptists. It was also in this year that the Polish Baptist churches were legally recognized by the new government. In August of 1949, a decree dealing with the "Protection of Freedom of Conscience and Religion" guaranteed such freedom to citizens of the Polish People's Republic. This was further defined in the constitution of 1952. All religious bodies may freely exercise their functions, and no one group has—as it was the case with the Roman Catholic Church before the war—a privileged position. These two rulings affected the Catholic Church in a rather restrictive way but gave some advantages to smaller groups, such as Baptists, in comparison with their former status. Baptists carry on evangelistic work; Youth work; radio ministry; theological education; editorial work, such as printing books and issuing a monthly publication, among other activities.

Baptists in Poland had their Confession of Faith already in

1930. It was published by the Baptist Association of Mutual Help, an association, which, in the period when the Baptist church was not officially recognized by the Polish state, could undertake legal procedure on behalf of the church and act as its representative. The confession was worked out on the bases of then existing Baptist confessions in the west of Europe. It included a few articles dealing with church organization. The confession of 1930 has been adopted by the present-day Polish Baptist Church with minor changes.

(Aleksander Kircun, Jr.)

Confession of Faith of the Baptist Churches in Poland

I. God's Word

We believe that the holy books of the Old and New Testaments are truly inspired by the Holy Spirit. They contain God's authentic revelation for mankind and are the only accurate source of information about God. Also they include principles and norms of proper faith and conduct.

The Old Testament has thirty-nine books:

Genesis	Nehemiah
Exodus	Esther
Leviticus	Job
Numbers	Psalms
Deuteronomy	Proverbs
Joshua	Ecclesiastes
Judges	Song of Solomon
Ruth	Isaiah
1 Samuel	Jeremiah
2 Samuel	Lamentations
1 Kings	Ezekiel
2 Kings	Daniel
1 Chronicles	Hosea
2 Chronicles	Joel
Ezra	Amos

2 Tim. 3:16; Ex. 19:9; 2 Sam. 23:1-2; Isa. 1:2; Jer. 1:9; John 10:35; 2 Pet. 1:20-21; Heb. 1:1-2; Luke 10:16; Matt. 10:20; 1 Thess. 2:13; 1 Cor. 2:4-5,13; 2 Pet. 1:19; Ps. 119:105; Luke 16:29,31; 2 Tim. 3:15,17; John 5:39; Acts 17:11; Rom. 1:16; 1 Cor. 14:37; Gal. 1:8; Rev. 20:18

Obadiah   Zephaniah
Jonah   Haggai
Micah   Zechariah
Nahum   Malachi
Habakkuk

The New Testament has twenty-seven books:

Matthew   1 Timothy
Mark   2 Timothy
Luke   Titus
John   Philemon
Acts   Hebrews
Romans   James
1 Corinthians   1 Peter
2 Corinthians   2 Peter
Galatians   1 John
Ephesians   2 John
Philippians   3 John
Colossians   Jude
1 Thessalonians Revelation
2 Thessalonians

2. God

Deut. 6:4; 1 Cor. 8:4,6; 1 Tim. 2:5; Matt. 28:19; Gen. 1:26; 3:22; Isa. 61:1; Matt. 3:16-17; John 14:16; 2 Cor. 13:13; 1 John 5:7; 2:23; John 10:30; 4:7,10; Eph. 4:6; Matt. 6:9; Rom. 9:5; John 1:1-14; 20:28; 1 John 5:20; Heb. 1:8-10; Isa. 9:6; Jer. 23:5-6; John 5:23,58-59; 1 Cor. 2:11; Matt. 12:32; Acts 5:3-4; 2 Cor. 3:17-18; Gen. 1:2; Ps. 33:6; Acts 20:28; 1 Cor. 3:16-17; 12:11; Eph. 4:30; 1 Pet. 4:14; Ps. 90:2; Ex. 5:14; 1 Tim. 1:17; Rev. 4:8; Gen. 17:1; Rom. 16:27;

We believe that there is only one living, real, eternal God as the Father, the Son and the Holy Spirit. He is perfect, everlasting and inseparable in his nature and attributes. The Father is the true, everlasting God, the Son, the true everlasting God and the Holy Spirit, the true everlasting God—in the Holy Trinity. Yet we do not believe in three Gods, but in one who is eternal, almighty, only wise, omniscient, omnipresent God. Man can know God only through God's revelation contained in the Holy Scriptures when it is read with the help of the Holy Spirit.

EASTERN EUROPE

11:33-34; Isa. 40:28; Acts 15:18; Heb. 4:13; Ps. 139:2-4; Jer. 23:24; Ps. 139:7-10; 1 Cor. 1:21; 2:14; John 14:26; Matt. 11:25-27; Rom. 10:17

3. Sin

We believe that God created the first man in His own image i.e., a good, holy and innocent being, which was able to worship Him, to have fellowship with Him and to be happy. However, as soon as man listened to Satan and was seduced by him he sinned, drew away from God, lost the image of his Creator and fell with his body and soul in the state of death. Because all people come from Adam's seed they inherit his sinful and utterly depraved nature; they are conceived and born in sin as children of wrath. They lack the capacity and will toward that which is good and are capable of and inclined toward evil.

Gen. 1:27; Eccl. 7:29; Gen. 1:31; 2:25; 3:8,13; Rev. 20:2; John 8:44; Gen. 2:17; Matt. 8:22; Eph. 2:1; Rom. 8:6; 6:23; Col. 2:13; John 3:6; Rom. 5:12,18; Gen. 6:3; Pss. 51:7; 58:4; Eph. 2:3; Rom. 8:7; Gen. 8:21; Jer. 17:9; Mark 7:21-22; Luke 24:25; Mark 16:14

4. Redemption

We believe that God could not redeem man from the terrible consequences of his fall in any other way than by satisfying all demands of His own holy justice. Therefore God destined, from all eternity, His only Son, Jesus Christ, to be a sacrifice through which men's sins might be forgiven. When the time that had been foretold arrived, God sent His Son, Christ, to this world. Being in the form of sinful flesh, He combined within himself eternal divinity and the human nature. He had a real human soul and body which, however, was and remained completely pure and spotless. Neither in Jesus' heart nor in His body and conduct did ever any sin arise. His obedience was active when He himself had fulfilled the whole of God's law in our behalf; it was passive as He gave

Heb. 9:22; 10:5-6; 1 Pet. 1:20; Gal. 4:4; Matt. 16:16; 3:7; Rom. 8:3; Col. 2:9; 1 Tim. 3:16; Rom. 1:3-4; Matt. 26:38; Heb. 2:14; 1 Tim. 2:5; John 8:46; 1 Pet. 2:22; Heb. 4:15; Matt. 5:17; Gal. 4:4; Rom. 10:4; 5:19; Ps. 40:8-9; Matt. 20:28; Isa. 41:21; 53:4; Heb. 5:8; Phil. 2:8; Luke 22:19; Ps. 20:15-16; Isa. 53:11; Matt. 26:38; Luke 22:44; Heb. 9:28,14,26; 10:12-14; Gal. 3:13; Matt. 27:46; 2 Cor. 5:21; Isa. 53:5; Heb. 9:12; Isa. 45:17; Heb. 5:9; Isa. 53:5

His body and soul as a sacrifice for us, taking upon Himself our curse, i.e., God's wrath and the penalty for our sins.

Eph. 1:7; Col. 1:14; Matt. 26:28; Acts 20:28; Rom. 5:1; 3:24; Isa. 61:10; Jer. 23:6; 2 Cor. 5:21; 1 Cor. 15:26,54-55; John 6:40; Gen. 3:15; Col. 1:13; 2:15; 1 John 3:8; Heb. 2:14-15; Eph. 4:8; 1 Thess. 1:10; 1 John 5:11-12; John 11:25-26; 3:36; 10:28; 2 Tim. 1:10; Titus 2:14; Rom. 6:14; 1 John 3:3; Acts 15:9; Phil. 4:13,21; Rom. 7:21-22; John 19:30; Acts 2:32; Luke 24:51; Heb. 1:3; 8:1; Acts 2; John 15:26; 16:8-14; Rom. 5:5; 8:14; John 16:13-14; Heb. 4:14; 1 John 2:1; Matt. 28:20; John 14:3; 17:24

We believe that this perfect and unreserved sacrifice of Jesus Christ is the only basis of our eternal salvation. Only through this one event do we gain forgiveness for all our sins and trespasses, are justified and clothed with the garments of his righteousness, are liberated from the power of death, the devil and hell, and finally obtain eternal life. In addition we are given a gracious power to develop an aversion toward sin, in a way dying to it, and to start loving and practising virtue.

Having completed this redemptive act, Christ rose from the dead on the third day, went up to Heaven and sat at the right hand of God. From there He has sent the Holy Spirit who encourages us to accept by faith the benefits of this redemption. Jesus our great high priest, pleads with the Father on our behalf. Also He is with us always to the end of this age. Finally He will lead us into heaven where He has prepared a place for us.

5. Election to Salvation

John 3:16; 1 Tim. 2:4; Ezek. 33:11; Acts 17:30; 2 Pet. 3:9; Rom. 14:12

We believe that God desires that every man should be saved. Therefore the duty of every man is to accept the gift of salvation by sincere and obedient faith in Jesus Christ. Only a stubborn persistence in sin and a refusal to amend and to submit oneself to Christ may block a sinner's way to salvation. In this matter every man is responsible for himself before God.

6. Regeneration

Heb. 4:12; Acts 2:37; Isa. 55:10-11; 2 Cor. 7:10; John 6:37; Matt. 11:28; Rom. 3:24-25,28;

We believe and confess that man can be aroused from his spiritual death and be brought to recognize his own sin only through the Holy Spirit

EASTERN EUROPE

and God's Word. As soon as he truly repents for his sins, feels guilty and comes to Christ, man receives, through faith in Him, forgiveness and justification before God.

8:16-17; John 6:63; 3:3,5-6; Jas. 1:18; 1 Pet. 1:23; Gal. 6:15; John 1:13; 1 Cor. 2:14; Eph. 2:8

Through this work of the Holy Spirit man is born anew to a living hope and is enabled henceforth to live a new life.

7. Sanctification

We believe and confess that people who are born anew by the Holy Spirit become saints in Jesus. Due to the continuing influence of Christ's Spirit living in them, they become capable of opposing effectively temptations, from which Christians are not free, of being obedient to God and of presenting their bodies as a living sacrifice to Him.

1 Cor. 1:30; 1 Thess. 4:3,7; Heb. 12:14; 1 Pet. 1:15-16; Rom. 12:1; 1 Cor. 6:20; 1 John 1:8-9

Sanctification begins at the moment of regeneration and is subject to a growing process throughout a person's life. Its objective is to transform the person into a complete likeness of Christ. God has established certain means aiding the process of sanctification, namely, His Word, prayer and the fellowship of the saints.

Eph 4:15; 2 Cor. 7:1, 1 John 1:7; John 8:31; 2 Thess. 5:17; Acts 2:42; 4:32; Eph. 4:3

We believe that God's law is holy, just and good. The law brings the consciousness of sin and so it leads people to Christ. It remains binding in all its regulations and condemnation for all those who are not in Christ. Christians are set free from the curse and the penalties of the law because they are under the law of Christ.

Gal. 3:24; Rom. 3:19-20; Rom. 8:3-4; Gal. 4:4-5

8. Holy Baptism

The New Testament gives us ground to believe that baptism, ordered by Christ, ought to be performed in the Christian Church until His second coming. It is to be received by those who confess their faith in Jesus.

Matt. 28:19-20

Baptism is performed in the following way: A

Matt. 3:13-15; Mark

servant of God, who has been authorized to do so, immerses a believer once in water in the name of the Father, the Son and the Holy Spirit, and immediately lifts him up. Carried out in such a manner, God's order keeps its original and profound meaning.

1:9; 3:16; Acts 8:36-39; Eph. 4:5; Rom. 6:5; Col. 2:12-13

The Holy Scriptures give a clear presentation of people who may submit to this ordinance. Regardless of all external differences, such as for example nationality, they are the people who, being attracted and drawn by the Gospel and the free grace of God, turn away from their sins, come to Christ and trust Him wholeheartedly as their personal Saviour.

Mark 16:16; Acts 2:37-38,41; 5:14; 8:12; 18:8; Gal. 3:26-27

Baptism is the first proof of a man's faith in Christ and his love for Him, the first step of obedience to the Lord and an act of joining the man to His Church. It is a solemn declaration and confession of a converted sinner, who has at last realized the atrocities of sin and the state of his own condemnation, that all of his hope is now set on the death and the resurrection of Jesus Christ and that He trusts Him as the One who has set him free from the curse and the penalties for sin. Further, by this act man declares that he surrenders himself wholly, body and soul, to Christ, that he accepts His righteousness and His power, that his old sinful nature (the old man) dies forever and that he desires to live henceforth a new life with Christ.

Acts 9:6; 22:16; John 15:10,14; 1 Cor. 12:13; Acts 2:47; 1 Pet. 3:21; Heb. 10:22-23; 4:14; Acts 2:36-37; 9:5-6,9; 16:29-30; 2 Cor. 5:14; Rom. 6:23,10-11; Gal. 3:26-27; Isa. 45:23-24; Rom. 6:4-6

On the other hand baptism is also God's solemn declaration and His assurance that by the acceptance of baptism man has indeed hidden himself in Christ Jesus, i.e., he has died together with Him, has been buried and has been raised from the dead, and that his sins have been washed away and that he has become a beloved child of God with whom God is well pleased.

Rom. 6:3-4,8; Col. 2:12-13; Acts 20:12-13; 9:18-19; Matt. 3:16

Baptism should prompt within a baptized person a clear and firm awareness of being redeemed and

1 Pet. 3:21; Acts 8:39; 9:18-20; Heb. 1:9; 2

saved. This awareness is caused by God, who has sealed the believer with the Holy Spirit, for, indeed, it was through the Spirit that God first awakened that man to the genuine and saving faith in the Son of God, and in the power of His death and resurrection.   Cor. 1:21; Eph. 1:13

A peculiar notion about baptism is that it can be received only once, whereas other means of grace can be renewed and repeated in the course of the whole life of the Christian. It should therefore be made sure that this unrepeated ordinance is carried out in a proper manner.

9. The Lord's Supper

We believe that Jesus Christ has established the Lord's Supper for His Church in order that the believers, by breaking and eating bread and by drinking wine from the cup, may receive His body and blood in a spiritual way, and proclaim the Lord's death until He comes again. While celebrating this ordinance the believers remember the painful passion and death of their Saviour and realize that they themselves, as the Church, make up His holy body. We maintain that the way in which Christ's ordinance is observed must be strictly apostolic.   Matt. 26:26-28; 1 Cor. 11:23-28; Acts 2:4,46

Since a participation in the Lord's Supper should be preceded by a thorough self-examination of those who would take part in it, the Lord's Table ought to be reserved for those who have, by the grace of God, become His own and have been duly baptized.   1 Cor. 10:16-17,21; 12:13

10. The Lord's Church

In accordance with the teaching of the Holy Scriptures we believe and confess that all believing Christians make One Body of Christ. We also believe that, according to the will of the Lord Jesus and teaching given by the Apostles, all believing Christians have a duty to unite themselves in local   Eph. 1:22-23; Matt. 18:20; 1 Cor. 12:13; 1 Pet. 2:5

churches in order to maintain closer fellowship with one another.

2 Cor. 6:16-17; Eph. 2:19-22; Rev. 2:7

Churches are communities composed of voluntarily gathered disciples of Jesus, who, being baptized as believers, separate themselves from the world and submit to the will of Christ in order to encourage one another to live a life of sanctification, to spread the Kingdom of God on earth and to worship Christ.

a. Offices in the Church

Col. 1:18; Acts 14:23; 13:3; 1 Tim. 3:1-7

The supreme and the only head of the Church is Jesus Christ; the church has no visible head on earth. The New Testament acknowledges only two offices in the church: the office of an elder, i.e., a presbyter, or a bishop, and the office of a deacon. A church itself elects elders (preachers, bishops, teachers, pastors, leaders—all these are the names of one and the same office) and servants (deacons), who receive their authority through the laying on of hands by elders (ordination).

Titus 1:6-9; Acts 20:28-31; Heb. 13:17; Jas. 3:1; 2 Tim. 4:2,5; 2:15; 1 Cor. 4:1-2; Luke 10:7-8; Acts 6:1-4; 1 Tim. 3:8-11

They must possess certain qualities listed in the Holy Scriptures and perform their duties in accordance with the New Testament teaching. Like all other members of the church they must be liable to church discipline, taking however into consideration 1 Timothy 5:19.

b. Duties of the members of the Church

John 13:34-35; 1 Pet. 1:22; Heb. 10:25; Acts 2:42; 1 Cor. 16:1-2; 2 Cor. 9:6-8; Phil. 4:15

Church members have the following duties: to love one another, to endeavour to procure spiritual and physical well-being for all, to use conscientiously the gifts of God's grace and to observe the commandments which the Lord Jesus, as the Head of the body, has left for the Church. It follows that each member of the community has a duty to participate in the Lord's Supper, to attend worship services and other church meetings regularly and to contribute as much as he can to the building up of the Kingdom of God.

EASTERN EUROPE

c. Business Meeting

All church matters are settled at a business meeting, possibly by voting, in which all members exercise equal voting rights. All matters ought to be discussed in the atmosphere of the mind of Jesus, so that freedom and order are preserved in the house of God.

_{Acts 15:22-25; Matt. 23:8,11; 1 Cor. 14:33; Col. 2:5; Eph. 5:21; 1 Pet. 5:5; Matt. 18:18}

d. Reception of New Members

New members are received by voting at a business meeting and then by baptism, after the congregation has had an opportunity to learn about their spiritual standing and to hear their confession of faith. It is desirable that the voting is unanimous.

_{1 Tim. 6:12; Matt. 10:32; Rom. 10:9-10; Heb. 4:14}

e. Church Discipline

The teaching of Christ in Matthew 18:15-17 concerns each member. It is a responsibility of each member of the community both to accept brotherly admonishments and to admonish others if necessary. Admonishments should be given in the spirit of love.

_{Matt. 18:15-17}

The community has the right and the moral obligation to exclude from its number those members whose life contradicts their professed faith, providing they refuse to repent and amend, i.e., those members who consciously remain in their sins. The members who commit major sins causing others to stumble, or who continue committing sins in spite of their repeated pledges not to do so, definitely should be excluded from the church.

_{1 Cor. 5:3-13; Titus 3:10-11; 1 Tim. 1:19-20; 2 Cor. 2:6-8}

A new reception of a former (excluded) member should follow a normal procedure for receiving members, i.e., after the case has been examined, a decision should be taken by vote.

11. The Christian Day of Rest

We believe and confess that the principle of keeping one day in the week as holy comes from the will of the gracious Creator, who ordered it for the

_{Gen. 2:1-3; Ex. 20:8-11; 31:13-17; Rev. 1:10; Acts 20:7; 1 Cor. 16:1-2; Matt. 2:27}

benefit of people. God gave the seventh day of the week to the Israelites as the Sabbath and as the sign of the covenant between Himself and that nation. As the people of the New Covenant, we follow the pattern set by the first Christians and observe the first day of the week as dedicated to the Lord in a special way, because God Himself consecrated it by raising His Son from the dead, as well as by sending the Holy Spirit on that day. We feel obliged to work diligently and conscientiously fulfilling all the duties derived from our earthly citizenship on all six days of the week, but to dedicate Sunday completely to God. This means ceasing from all work which is not necessary or which does not come from the command to love one's neighbour.

Col. 2:16-17

The Lord's day should be spent in increasing the knowledge of God and true piety, in sharing Christian fellowship in a heartfelt and intelligible way, as well as contributing to the work of spreading the Kingdom of God on earth.

Ps. 118:20-24

Furthermore we emphasize that on the Lord's day every Christian should spend more time reading the Holy Scriptures for himself and teaching his children from the Book; he should also regularly attend all church services on the day. All this leads us to consider the Lord's day to be God's precious gift to the Church, absolutely necessary to its very existence.

12. Marriage

Gen. 1:27-28; 2:18,24; 1 Cor. 7:39; 1 Pet. 2:13; Phil. 4:8; Col. 3:17

We believe and confess that God established marriage in which man and woman relate to each other in a physical and moral way and educate their children. As long as both husband and wife live, the man cannot marry another woman, and the woman another man. Because marriage is also a legal status it can take place only according to the legal statutes

EASTERN EUROPE

of the given country. In spite of that the church wedding ought to be held too. According to our principle, Christians should get married only in the Lord, i.e., between believers.

We state that divorce, due to reasons not comformable to God's Word and the remarriage of divorced persons, is not allowed according to the New Testament. In the case of adultery or malicious desertion by the husband or wife, we believe that divorce is allowed according to God's Word.

Matt. 19:6-9; 1 Cor. 7:27,10-11; Rom. 7:1-4

13. Civil Authority

We believe and confess that God has established civil authorities and has authorised them to defend honest and upright people and to punish evil-doers. We feel obliged to be absolutely obedient to all their rules, providing they do not limit us in our endeavour to fulfill all our Christian duties, and to be cooperative and help by living a quiet, peaceful and godly life.

Rom. 13:1-7; 1 Pet. 2:13-14,17; Titus 3:1; Matt. 22:21; Acts 4:19-20; 5:29,42

We also feel obliged to pray for the authorities so that they may use their power in accordance with the will of God and that they might, under His leadership, keep peace and justice in the country.

1 Tim. 2:1-3

We believe that swearing is forbidden by our Lord Jesus Christ and the teaching of the Apostles. Therefore in cases of need, taking full responsibility for the truthfulness of our statements, we are ready to confirm them with simple "Yes, yes" or "No, no," just as it is recommended in the Gospel.

Matt. 5:34,37; Jas. 5:12

We also believe in accordance with the Holy Scriptures, that "the sword is not worn in vain by authorities." The authorities have the right and duty to punish evil-doers as well as to use the sword when the country needs defense. We consider it our obligation, therefore, to place ourselves at our country's disposal in the times of war if we are called to do so.

We do not see any hindrance—so far as our conscience is concerned—to hold any office with the civil authorities.

14. The Last Things

Acts 1:10-11; 1 Cor. 1:7-8; Phil. 3:20; Jas. 5:7-8; Heb. 9:28; 1 John 2:28; Titus 2:13; 2 Pet. 1:16; 1 Pet. 1:7-9; 5:4; Matt. 24:30; Luke 21:27-28; Col. 3:4; Rom. 8:23; John 5:28-29; 1 Cor. 15:16-20,23; Rev. 20:4; 5:10; 1 Cor. 15:42-43,53; Phil. 3:21; Acts 17:30-31; 1 Thess. 4:13-18; 2 Cor. 5:10; Matt. 3:12; 25:10-12; Mark 9:43-48; Luke 13:25-28; 2 Thess. 1:8-9; Rev. 14:11; 20:10-15; Luke 16:24-26; Heb. 9:27

We believe and confess that our Lord, Jesus Christ, will come again in great power and glory. We believe that the day of His appearance will be the final consummation of His redeeming work. The whole world will then know its reality and importance. Those who died in Christ will be raised again in an unblemished glory. Then the believers who are still alive shall suddenly be changed and, together with the risen ones, shall be caught up in the clouds to meet the Lord. There we shall always be with the Lord, see Him as He is, become like Him and rule with Him in His Kingdom. We also believe in the general resurrection and the judgment of the world to which all people shall have to come and stand before Christ, the Judge, and to receive wages for all they did in the days of their flesh. The Son of God will first give eternal glory to the believers and then he will pronounce a verdict of eternal condemnation on all godless. We believe, in accordance with the Holy Scriptures, that both these conditions will be eternal.

We believe that certain signs of time point to the near end of the present aeon. We remember the words of our Lord, who said: "Yes, I am coming soon," and we are waiting for Him with the prayer: "Amen. Come Lord Jesus."

TR: Marcin Piasecki
(TR: Aleksander Kircun, Jr.)

Hungary
The Baptist Union of Hungary

Baptists in Hungary trace their earliest antecedents to the Anabaptist movement from Switzerland. They note especially the work of Kristof Schröter, who started work in northern Hungary in 1523, and John Kisszebeni. Kisszebeni was sent as an emissary of Martin Luther against Schröter but became an Anabaptist himself. Another early leader was Andreas Fischer, who was martyred in 1540. In 1548, a law was issued prohibiting Anabaptist activity. But in Transylvania (East Hungary), Duke Gabor Bethlen granted many privileges. After limited freedom for over two hundred years, Anabaptists were expelled by an edict of Queen Maria Theresa in 1763.

Modern Baptist history is tied to two major impulses, the primary one being from Germany. In 1846, J. Rottmayer, K. Scharschmidt, and J. Woyka were sent by J. G. Oncken to Hungary to start missionary work. They had gone to Hamburg as carpenters in 1843, joined the Baptist church there, and returned in 1846 as missionaries. This pioneer work began very successfully, but it did not grow to a great movement due to the political and religious unrest in the country following the War of Independence (1848-1849).

The second impulse of Hungarian Baptist history is connected to Heinrich Meyer. He arrived at Budapest on March 6, 1873, as a representative of the British and Foreign Bible Society (but apparently sent also by Oncken to eastern Europe). After he had baptized several persons, he was expelled from the Bible Society. He founded the first Baptist church in Hungary in 1874. At this time he contacted Antal Novak, who was also a missionary of the Bible Society. Novak had gathered a small group of believers and asked Meyer to teach them. As a result, Meyer baptized eight persons at Gyula. Among these new members were Mihaly Kornya and Mihaly Toth, who became fellow workers. These two are called the "peasant-prophets" of the Hungarian Baptist Mission. It is reported that Kornya baptized more than eleven thousand people during his thirty years of ministry. During the first two decades, the whole Hungarian mission was under the personal leadership of Heinrich Meyer. In 1892, the first mission board was organized.

The year 1894 was a turning point in the Hungarian Baptist Mission. At this time, two young Hungarian Baptists returned from Hamburg, where they had received their theological training at the Baptist seminary. They were at once accepted as leaders of the Hungarian-speaking churches who had been striving for more independence from the German-speaking churches.

The tension between Hungarian- and German-speaking churches was connected to the question of recognition by the government and led to a division within the Baptist mission in Hungary for more than twenty years. Because of continuing troubles with the political and religious authorities, Meyer tried to gain official recognition from 1882 onward, but he did not succeed. In 1895, a law was passed dealing with religious freedom, but it contained so many restrictions and conditions that it could not be called religious freedom as Baptists understand it. Nevertheless, the Hungarian leaders saw some advantages in it and applied for recognition.

In 1900, the Hungarian churches were organized in the Union of Churches. At their convention at Ocsa in 1902, the first confession of faith was accepted. On the basis of this confession, the Hungarian Baptist Union was accepted as a "recognized" church by the government in 1905. This step led to the separation of the two Baptist groups. In 1907, a committee of the Baptist World Alliance was called to help solve this problem. This committee worked out a basis for reunion which was theoretic-

ally accepted by both sides. But in practice, it took more than ten years until the two groups were united again. On September 2, 1920, a convention was held with the representatives of all churches and the Union of Hungarian Baptist Churches was organized to conduct the "missionary affairs" of the churches. At the same time, the *Baptista Hitközseg Budapest* (Baptist Association of Budapest) regulated the judicial affairs.

In 1947, a law was passed that gave the same rights to all religious groups in the country. The convention of 1955 decided to change the name to the "Hungarian Baptist Church."

At the congress on May 25, 1967, the new confession of faith which follows, was accepted.

Johann Macher
(Emil Kiss)

Confession of Faith of the Hungarian Baptist Church

1. The Holy Scriptures

Luke 24:44; 2 Pet. 3:2,15-16; 2 Sam. 23:2; Jer. 1:9; Acts 7:36; 1 Cor. 14:37; Gal. 1:11-12; 1 Thess. 2:13; 1 Pet. 1:23,25; Ex. 24:4; Josh. 24:26; Jer. 36:1-2,4,27-28,32; Luke 1:1-4; Acts 1:1; John 21:24; Eph. 3:3; 2 Pet. 1:15-21; Pss. 12:7; 19:8-10; Prov. 30:5; John 10:35; 17:17; Rom. 3:21; Acts 18:28; Eph. 3:2,4-5; John 12:47-48; Matt. 22:29; 2 Tim. 3:15; Rom. 15:4-16,25-26; Deut. 4:2; Prov. 30:6; Jer. 23:36; 2 Tim. 3:14,16; Heb. 4:12; 2 Pet. 3:16;

We believe that the Holy Scripture (39 books of the Old Testament and 27 books of the New Testament) is God's revealed Word. This work, written by divinely inspired men, was put together by the Church under the impulse and guidance of the Holy Spirit. The providence of God has saved the Holy Scripture—both in its origin and in its transmission—from all essential errors. In its details and its totality the Holy Scripture reveals to us the most perfect divine truths. Out of it we get to know God, the way to eternal life, and those principles by which God will judge mankind. The Holy Scripture—in its context and its explanation in the light of the Holy Spirit—is an unmistakable and satisfactory regulator of the Christian life, our supreme counsellor in all things of daily life, and the most perfect touch-stone by which we may test every human tradition, teaching and exercise.

2 Thess. 3:6,10-13; 2 Tim. 3:17; Mark 7:3,5,8-9,13; Acts 17:11; 2 Thess. 2:15; 3:14

2. The One Real God

We believe that there is a living, real and eternal God who is an infinitely wise, omnipotent, omnipresent personal, spiritual reality. His perfect and holy being alone is worthy of our complete love, allegiance and obedience. The one God reveals himself in the Holy Scripture as Father, Son and Holy Spirit.

The FATHER is the origin, cause and goal of all beings. He maintains and rules the universe which He had created with His mighty Word out of the invisible.

Deut. 4:35; Isa. 44:6,8; 45:5; 1 Cor. 8:6; Jer. 10:10; Dan. 6:26; Ex. 3:14; 1 Tim. 6:15-16; Rev. 4:9; Rom. 11:33-34; 16:27; 1 Tim. 1:17; Jude 25; Gen. 17:1; Deut. 32:39; Luke 1:37; Deut. 10:14; Ps. 139:7-10; Jer. 23:23-24; John 4:24; Matt. 5:48; Titus 1:2; 1 Sam. 2:2; Rev. 15:4; Deut. 15:4; 6:5; Ps. 95:6; Rev. 4:10-11; Acts 5:29; Heb. 12:9; Matt. 5:48; 28:19; John 14:16-17; 2 Cor. 13:13; Gal. 4:4,6; Gen. 1; 2; Acts 17:24-26; 1 Cor. 15:28; John 5:17; Acts 17:28; Gen. 50:20; Pss. 96:10; 33:6,9; Heb. 11:3

The SON is the image of the invisible God through whom and for whom all things were created. He is real God who became man in order to save mankind. With regard to His divine nature He is eternal through the Father; in His human nature He was conceived of the Holy Spirit, born of the Virgin Mary on the fullness of time.

John 5:23; Col. 1:15; 2:9; Heb. 1:2-3; John 1:3; Col. 1:16; Matt. 28:18; John 1:1; Rom. 9:5; 8:3; 1 John 5:20; Phil. 2:7; 1 Tim. 2:5; Heb. 2:17-18; Ps. 2:7; Mic. 5:2; John 6:69; 8:59; 17:5; 20:31; Col. 1:15; Matt. 1:18,20-23; Luke 1:30-31, 34-35

The HOLY SPIRIT is the carrier of the personal presence of God in the created World. He sustains the order of the universe and He reveals all the rules and truths which are placed in this World. The Holy Spirit has prepared salvation, strengthened Jesus

Gen. 1:2; Ex. 35:31; Neh. 9:20,30; Job 33:4; Ps. 104:30; Hag. 2:5; 2 Cor. 3:17; 1 Pet. 4:14; Matt. 12:18,28; Luke 1:35; 4:1,14,18-19; Acts 10:38; Rom. 8:11; Heb.

Christ to be victorious over sin and death. Through Him the redemption of Christ becomes accessible for man and by Him the plan of salvation comes to its final goal.

We confess that the oneness of God and His Trinity known by revelation is not to be separated or compromised by the attempt of human arguing because this revealed truth is not to be explained but accepted by faith.

3. The Creation of Man, His Sin and Fall

We believe that God created man in His own image, good and righteous. God formed man of the dust of the earth and breathed into him the breath of life. He endowed him with wisdom and power, and put all things in this physical world under his dominion. He enabled man to have fellowship with Him as his creator and to live for His glory. He gave him freedom to refuse voluntarily the evil and to choose freely the good. But man yielded to the temptation of Satan and sinned against his creator. Through his transgression he came under the power of sin and death; both spiritually and physically he lost his divine image which he had gained in creation and now he is only partially able to use his original faculties.

4. The Salvation of Man

We believe that the salvation of sinful man is provided by the grace of Jesus Christ, the Son of God, who sacrificed himself as mediator. He fulfilled the requirements of the divine law, freely and obediently and by his death on the cross obtained perfect propitiation for our sins; he rose from death on the third day for our justification, ascended to heaven and, at the right hand of the Father, He—as the only mediator between God and man—intercedes for us. We believe that God—by His eternal, gracious decision—offers salvation through Jesus Christ to all men without respect of persons. Man is free to accept or to reject the offered grace.

9:24; 10:12; 1 Tim. 2:5; 1 John 2:1; Rom. 8:34; John 3:16; Titus 2:11; 2 Pet. 3:9; John 6:40; Mark 16:16; John 3:18; 6:54,60,66-69; 12:48

5. Faith

We believe that God in His eternal grace enables man to acknowledge Him, to understand His Holy Word with his mind, and to accept it in his heart. By the accepted Word man comes to faith and finds satisfaction with God,* gains assurance of salvation, and becomes convinced about the invisible realities.

Acts 16:14; 17:11-12; Rom. 10:17; 12:3; 1 Cor. 3:5; Heb. 4:2; 11:5-6; Rom. 8:38-39; 2 Tim. 1:12; 1 John 5:13; John 20:29; Heb. 11:1; 1 Pet. 1:8-9

Faith is, on one hand, knowledge whereby we accept the truth of God's revelations, regardless whether we are able to grasp it or not; on the other hand, it is a strong confidence in our heavenly Father. True faith is testified in good works because faith apart from works is dead.

John 6:69; Acts 24:14; Rom. 4:18-21; Heb. 11:3,7,27; Gal. 5:6; Titus 3:8; Jas. 2:19-22,25-26

(*Editorial note: the double meaning is intentional since the singular Hungarian phrase includes both God's acceptance and man's pleasure-response.)

6. Repentance and New Birth

We believe that by repentance the sinful man turns from the state of condemnation to the way of life. The repenting sinner—through the Word of God and the work of the Holy Spirit—realizes, dislikes, regrets, and confesses his sins. He flees from the righteous and just judgment of God to the only Saviour, Jesus Christ, and by faith he receives forgiveness of sins.

Ezek. 18:23,27-28; Luke 13:3; Isa. 55:7; Ezek. 20:43; Joel 2:12-13; 2 Cor. 7:10; Neh. 9:2; 1 John 1:9; Acts 5:30-31; 10:43; 26:18

We believe that the man who turns to God by faith is new-born, newly created through the Word and the Spirit of God, whereby he is enabled to love Jesus Christ and to live according to the will of God. The reality of the new birth is testified by a life lived according to the example of Jesus Christ.

Ezek. 36:26-27; John 3:5-6; Jas. 1:18; 1 Pet. 1:22-23; Rom. 8:2,6; Gal. 2:20; 5:22-25

7. Justification and Divine Sonship

<small>Titus 3:4-7; Rom. 8:1; 3:22-24,28; Gal. 2:16; Acts 13:38-39; Rom. 5:1-2,9-11</small>

We believe that justification is God's gracious act, whereby the new-born believer in the Lord Jesus Christ is acquitted from all accusations and judgments of sin and declared righteous. Justification is not gained by our own righteous deeds, but only through the sacrifice and the righteousness of Jesus Christ we receive it by faith. The fruit of justification is the relationship and peace with God.

<small>John 1:12; Eph. 1:5; 1 John 3:1; Rom. 8:14-16; 1 John 5:14; John 8:36; Eph. 2:11-13,19; Heb. 12:5-7,11; Gal. 4:7; 1 John 3:2</small>

We believe that the new-born man is not only justified by faith in Jesus Christ but he also becomes a child of God. The spirit of sonship is sent into his heart, therefore he can accede to God as his Father. God presents to him the freedom and privileges of childhood. If necessary, He will chastise him but will never forsake His child. Rather, He prepares the believer to be a co-heir of Jesus Christ in His unutterable glory in eternity.

8. Sanctification and Preservation

<small>1 Cor. 6:11; 2 Thess. 2:13; 1 Pet. 1:1-2; Phil. 3:12; 1 Thess. 4:1,3,7; 1 Pet. 2:1-2,5; 2 Cor. 7:1; Rom. 12:1; 1 Pet. 1:14-15; Matt. 26:41; John 17:17; Rom. 1:11-12</small>

We believe that sanctification is carried out by the power of the Holy Spirit, whereby the new-born man progresses gradually toward moral and spiritual perfection. The believer's sanctification is supported by self-examination, self-denial, fervent prayer, study of the Holy Scripture and exercise of Christian fellowship.

<small>John 6:39; 10:27-30; Phil. 2:12-13; Rom. 8:35,37; Eph. 3:16; Phil. 4:7; Heb. 10:39; Jas. 1:12; 1 Pet. 1:9</small>

We believe that preservation is the work of God's special providence to the believer who truthfully follows Jesus Christ. The new-born child of God is supported by the Holy Spirit, therefore he is victorious over temptations in spite of his weaknesses, and faithfully stands for Christ till the end; and finally he gains the crown of eternal life.

9. The Work of the Holy Spirit

<small>Acts 1:8; 1 Cor. 3:16; 6:19; Eph. 3:16; Luke</small>

We believe that the Holy Spirit works incessantly in the heart and life of the newly born man. He

EASTERN EUROPE

teaches, guides, counsels, reproves, encourages, and comforts the believer. He impels him to bring forth the fruits of the Spirit; He enables him to have true fellowship with God and his brethren; He entreats for him; He seals him for the day of redemption.

12:12; John 14:26; 1 Cor. 2:13; 1 John 2:20,27; John 16:13; Acts 8:29; 16:6-7; 13:2; 15:28; Heb. 3:7-8; John 16:6-7; Acts 9:31; Gal. 5:22-23; 1 John 4:13; 1 Cor. 12:13; Eph. 2:20-22; Phil. 2:1; Rom. 8:26,16-17; 2 Cor. 1:21-22; Eph. 1:13-14; 4:30

We believe that the Holy Spirit gives spiritual gifts to his redeemed and sanctified children, to be used for the glory of God, the growth of the body of Christ, and for the spiritual perfection of the church members. The Holy Spirit bestows these gifts according to his wise decision on those who strive for them. No one receives all the gifts, therefore it is necessary that the members—without disturbing the order of the church—should serve one another in humbleness with the gifts that have been granted to them for stewardship.

Eph. 4:11-13; 1 Cor. 12:11,31; 14:1; Luke 11:13; 1 Cor. 12:8-10,29-30; Rom. 12:5-6; 1 Cor. 12:7,25; 1 Pet. 4:10-11; 1 Tim. 4:14; 1 Thess. 5:19-21; 1 John 4:1; 1 Cor. 1:33,40

10. Baptism

We believe that baptism is a commandment of the Lord Jesus Christ. Baptism is a symbolic act of regeneration, it is the fruit of our faith and our obedience to our redeemer, it is a representation of oneness with Christ, and His body, the fellowship of believers. One can be baptized if the fruits of repentance can be seen in his life; one who has confessed his faith in Jesus Christ and has voluntarily asked for baptism. According to the order of Jesus Christ and the example of the apostles we baptize by immersion in the name of the Father, the Son, and the Holy Spirit.

Matt. 3:13-17; 28:19; Col. 2:11-12; John 15:10,14; Acts 2:41; 22:16; Gal. 3:27; 1 Cor. 12:13; Acts 10:47-48; 16:33-34; 8:36-38; Matt. 28:19; John 3:22-23,26; 4:1-3; Acts 2:38; 8:12

With baptism the new-born man solemnly confesses that he has broken with his sinful life, and that he surrenders his whole life to the Lord Jesus Christ. God offers assurance to the baptized believer, even

Rom. 6:11; 6:3-5; Mark 16:16; Rom. 14:23; Heb. 11:1-2

as he died and is buried to sin in baptism, so he will rise together with Christ in the newness of life. The truths represented in baptism will be realized by living faith working in the heart of the baptized believer.

11. The Lord's Supper

Luke 22:19-20; 1 Cor. 11:23-25; Acts 2:42,46; 1 Cor. 11:26; 10:16; 11:24-25

We believe that the Lord's Supper is an ordinance of Jesus Christ and is to be taken regularly, as a memorial to his infinite love, whereby we proclaim his death by deeds until he returns.

Acts 2:41-44; 1 Cor. 5:11,13; 10:14,19-21; 11:27-29

The signs of the death of the Lord Jesus can only be taken by those who are re-born and are baptized on their confession of faith, and live in good relationship with God and their fellow-men.

Acts 26:26-28

The signs of the Lord's Supper—bread and wine—symbolize the broken body and the shed blood of Christ. If we take it by faith, in remembrance of our Saviour, we enter into a spiritual union with our Lord by the Holy Spirit, because through the outward act our inward assurance is strengthened: Immanuel! God with us!

In the Lord's Supper our fellowship is demonstrated, both with Christ and with our fellow Christians.

12. The Local and the Universal Church

1 Cor. 12:13; Acts 2:41; John 10:27; Eph. 5:24; 2 Cor. 6:14,16-18

We believe that the New Testament Church is the fellowship of believers who are re-born and baptized after they have accepted Jesus Christ as their Saviour and live according to the Word of God.

Acts 2:42; 2 John 8-9; 1 John 4:1; 1 Cor. 14:3,29; Matt. 28:19-20; Acts 19:3-5; 1 Cor. 11:17-29; Acts 1:14; 2:42; Eph. 5:19-20; 1 Cor. 16:2; Heb. 13:16; Acts 11:29; Gal. 6:10; Jas. 1:27; 1 Cor. 14:40; Gal. 6:1; 1 Thess. 5:14

We confess that the true signs of the New Testament Church are: clear preaching of the Word, scriptural application of baptism and the Lord's Supper, prayer and singing, voluntary stewardship, charity and church discipline.

We believe that there is a holy, universal and invisible church, whose head is Jesus Christ, and its members are all those from different visible churches, who are cleansed in the blood of the Lamb and reborn by the Holy Spirit. We believe that our local churches are members of the universal church, living parts of the body of Christ, and in each case when they exercise biblical truths, they are visible demonstrations of the invisible church.

John 10:16; Eph. 2:19-22; Heb. 12:18,22-23; Gal. 4:26; Rev. 21:2; Eph. 1:22-23; 4:15-16; Rev. 7:9,14; 1 John 3:9-10

13. The Officers of the Church

We believe that the Lord calls pastors, elders and deacons for teaching and the care of the church, out of those who are irreprovable and conduct an exemplary life in their family, the society and the church. This call is revealed through the church when she has elections in obedience to the guidance of the Holy Spirit. The called ones are dedicated to their service with prayer and imposition of hands by the pastors and elders in the presence of the congregation, after they have testified about their faith and their call. The office holders do their service under the guidance of the Holy Spirit in line with the Holy Scripture, and according to the order of the church. The pastors and the elders are, in the first place, responsible for the spiritual needs, whereas the deacons are responsible for the material things. They should not dominate the church in their charge, however; for their good work, humble, faithful and responsible service they are worthy of double honour.

Eph. 6:11-12; 1 Tim. 3:2-13; Titus 1:5-9; Acts 6:3,5; 13:2; 1 Tim. 5:22; 6:12; Acts 6:6; 13:3; 1 Tim. 4:14; 2 Tim. 2:24-25; Acts 6:2-4; 1 Pet. 5:1-3; 1 Thess. 5:12-13; 1 Tim. 5:17-19; Heb. 13:7,17

14. Church Discipline

We believe that church discipline is ordered by God as an instrument to maintain the scriptural order of the church in morality and doctrine and to protect the healthy spiritual life of the church members. We endeavor to educate and strengthen the faithful

1 Cor. 14:40; 1 Pet. 1:14-16,22; 2:1-3,11-12; 1 John 4:1; 2 Thess. 5:14-15; 1 Tim. 4:16; Heb. 10:24; Matt. 18:15-17

members of Jesus Christ by a proper teaching of the Word. If one, in spite of this, sins, we try to admonish him with saving love, at first personally, then in the presence of witnesses and, if he does not accept this, we do it in front of the church.

Gal. 6:1; Heb. 3:12-13; 10:25; Eph. 5:11; Titus 1:13; 2 Tim. 2:26; Jas. 5:19-20; Jude 22-23; Matt. 18:17; 1 Cor. 5:11,13; 2 Thess. 3:6,14-15; 1 Tim. 1:19-20; 2 Tim. 2:25; Titus 3:10-11; 2 Cor. 2:5-8

The goal of this admonition is to bring the lost one back to the right way, to warn the light-minded and to save him from the snare of sin. Those church members who cling to their sin and despise admonition several times, we finally exclude from the church, in order that in their loneliness they might realize their spiritual misery and come back to the Saviour and the church with sincere repentance.

15. Testimony

Luke 12:8-9; John 15:26-27; Acts 1:8; 5:32; 10:42; 1 Cor. 2:13; 1 Pet. 2:9; Rom. 10:9-10; 1 John 4:15; Luke 24:47; 1 Pet. 3:15; Acts 4:13,29,33; 9:27; 18:26-28; 19:8; Eph. 6:18-19; Acts 28:30-31; 2 Cor. 5:18-20; Rom. 1:14-15; Titus 3:8; Matt. 7:21; 1 Cor. 2:4; 13:1-2; 1 Thess. 1:5; Titus 1:10-11,16; 1 John 2:3-5

We believe that the Holy Spirit empowers every new-born Christian to give testimony, and enables him to witness about the Good News, the hope he has in his heart, and the grace he experiences in his daily life, to the children of God and to those who are not yet in living fellowship with Jesus Christ. The testimony is pleasant before God and men if it does not only consist of words but is represented by deeds as well.

16. Prayer

John 4:23-24; Rom. 8:15; Jas. 4:8; Ps. 50:15; Isa. 55:6; Matt. 7:7-11; 1 Thess. 5:17; Pss. 95:6-7; 109:30; 2 Cor. 9:15; Eph. 5:19-20; Col. 1:12; Pss. 27:4; 145:18-19; Matt. 9:28; 26:41; Luke 17:5; Acts 7:34; Phil. 4:6; 2

We believe that prayer maintains and deepens the fellowship with God. God offers man the possibility of prayer. In prayer we express our adoration and our gratefulness to our Father in heaven; in prayer we draw near to God to ask forgiveness which He offered through Jesus Christ, and in prayer we bring our requests and desires to Him who is able to do all things. Prayer must come out of faith, and it must be in accordance with the will of God, revealed through Jesus Christ.

Thess. 1:11; 3:1; Heb. 4:15-16; Jas. 1:5; Matt. 21:22; Heb. 10:22; 11:6; Jas. 1:6-7; Matt. 6:5-8; Mark 11:25; John 9:31; 15:7; Jas. 4:3; 5:16; 1 Pet. 3:7,12; 4:7; 1 John 3:21-22; 5:14

17. The Lord's Day

We believe that God gave us the day of rest for our spiritual and physical recreation. On this day we should spend most of our time in devotion, worship and prayer, exercise Christian fellowship and love. On the Lord's Day we abstain from all everyday, arduous activities, except the work of charity and that of inevitable, public interest. We observe the Lord's Day—as commemoration of the resurrection of the Lord Jesus Christ and following the practice of the Apostolic Church—on the first day of the week, on Sunday.

Pss. 118:24; 84:11; 122:1; 133:1-3; Acts 2:42; 1 Cor. 16:1-2; Jas. 1:27; Mark 16:9; Acts 20:7; Col. 2:16-17; Rom. 14:5

18. Marriage

We believe that God established marriage, in order that the spouses should live in love and faithfulness together for life, to please and support each other and to bring up children. The marriage is in accordance with the will of God, when it is based on mutual and pure sympathy, when the guidance of the Spirit and the Word of God is sought, and when the partners fit together on spiritual, phychical and physical points of view.

Gen. 1:27-28; 2:18; Prov. 18:22; 19:14; 31:10,30-31; Eccl. 9:11; Song of Sol. 8:6-7; Matt. 19:4-6; 1 Cor. 7:2-5; Eph. 5:22-25,28-33; Col. 3:18-19; 1 Tim. 4:1-3; 5:14; 1 Pet. 3:1-2,7; Ps. 127:3; Prov. 22:6; Eph. 6:24; Jer. 29:6; Song of Sol. 2:7; Pss. 25:12-13; 32:8; Lev. 18:6; Deut. 7:3-4; Prov. 12:3; 2 Cor. 6:14

Divorce—except in the case of adultery—is not allowed according to the Word of God. The adulterers will not enter the Kingdom of God. The partner who is left alone after a divorce, should possibly not

Mal. 2:15-16; Matt. 5:32; Mark 10:2-12; 1 Cor. 7:10-16; 6:16-19; Gal. 5:19-20; Eph. 5:3-5; Heb. 13:4; Rev.

enter a new marriage. However we realize that "it is better to marry, than to be aflame with passion," therefore we take cognizance of such a marriage.

19. The State Power

21:8; 22:15; Rom. 7:2-3; 1 Cor. 7:9

Col. 1:16; 2:10; Rom. 13:1,3-4; Jer. 29:7; Matt. 5:13-16; 1 Tim. 2:1-2; Matt. 5:9; Heb. 12:14; Titus 3:1-2; 1 Pet. 2:13,16-17; Rom. 13:2,5-7; Mark 10:43-45; Phil. 4:8-9

We believe that state power is ordered by God to rule the country and for the benefit of the people. We confess that the Hungarian People's Republic which is called to build and protect the achievements of the socialist society enjoys the confidence and support of our church members because it serves the interests of the whole nation. Therefore, we have found our place in the socialist society of our native country and acknowledge our task in it as given by God. Our church as the representative organization and spiritual fellowship of all Baptist believers, declares that our attitude towards the state power should be based on the loyalty of citizens. We highly appreciate the separation of the State and the Church which is embodied in the Constitution as well. It is not in accord with the Holy Scripture that the followers of Jesus Christ should claim any secular power, therefore our church follows the path of service. Willingly we support the aims of the Hungarian People's Republic and in mutual respect of the ideological differences, we undertake co-operation with the state power in all those efforts which serve the progress and advance of our nation in political, economic and cultural fields.

20. The Last Things

Job. 19:25-27; John 11:25-26; Acts 24:15; Heb. 9:27; Gen. 3:19; Eccl. 12:9; Luke 23:42-43; Rom. 14:8; Phil. 1:21,23; 1 Pet. 3:18-20; Rev. 1:7; 14:13; 1 Cor. 15:35-36, 42-44, 53-54; 2 Cor.

We believe that the life of man does not cease with death. In death the soul detaches from the body. The souls of the deceased are in a conscious state; therefore the souls of the believers at once enjoy the happiness of redemption, and the souls of the unbelievers will suffer. This happiness and suffering, however will come to its final climax in the coming judgment, when the souls unite with the resurrected bodies.

We believe that Jesus Christ will return to this world visibly to everyone, in full power and glory. Then the resurrection will take place, followed by the judgment and the separation to eternal happiness or eternal pain. Satan will be cast into eternal fire, then there will be no more death, and every earthly suffering and misery will come to an end.

We believe that God will create a new heaven and a new earth where righteousness and peace will reign for ever and ever. In the re-created world, as partakers of redemption, we shall be with the Lord for ever, and then the Everlasting God will be all in all.

5:1-4; Phil. 3:20-21; Col. 3:4; Matt. 24:30; Acts 1:11; 2 Pet. 3:3-4,8-12,14-15; Rev. 1:7; Dan. 12:2-3; Matt. 25:31-34, 41-46; John 5:28-29; 1 Cor. 15:22-23; 1 Pet. 5:4; Rev. 20:11-15; Heb. 2:14; Rev. 20:10; 1 Cor. 15:26; Rev. 21:4; Rom. 8:19-21; 2 Pet. 3:13; Isa. 65:17-25; Rev. 21:1; 1 Thess. 4:17; 1 Cor. 15:28

TR: Johann Macher
TR: László Gerzsenyi

Czechoslovakia
The Baptist Union in Czechoslovakia

Modern Czechoslovakia was created in 1918 by bringing together Moravia, Bohemia, Slovakia, and Ruthenia, each of which had long and deep political and religious traditions of their own. Although some of these traditional Czech countries had been included in the Austrian-Hungarian empire and felt the heavy hand of the Counter-Reformation, a deep Protestant belief continued to exist.

Notable were the fifteenth-century Hussite movement in Bohemia, which persisted underground in spite of the death of John Hus, and the sixteenth-century Protestant Reformation, which introduced the Reformed tradition into the country. Many groups have merged into the Czech Brethren church which derived from these several traditions. The Anabaptist movement made a strong impact; Balthazar Hübmaier found refuge in Moravia from both Catholics and Protestants. Generally speaking, however, Roman Catholicism weakened most Protestant groups; many leaders were executed, and thousands fled the country. The first religious rights came in Bohemia in the Edict of Toleration of 1781, issued by Joseph II, the Holy Roman emperor.

Baptists can trace their roots to the evangelical revivals of the nineteenth century, the first contacts being through the German-speaking population, especially in the area which was then part of Austria-Hungary. A. Meeris, a colporteur of the British and Foreign Bible Society, and A. Knappe worked in Bohemia in the 1860s. The first Czechs were baptized in 1877, and a church was founded near Prague in 1885 with Henry

Novotny as leader. The Novotny family played a key role for many years among Baptists in Czechoslovakia. Later, churches were begun in Moravia amid many obstacles. A Baptist union was formed in 1919, and leaders could train abroad. Homes for children, a seminary, and social work were established in spite of great financial difficulties. Northern Baptists, British Baptists, and others gave aid, according to the London agreement of 1920.

The Constitution of 1948 guarantees freedom of conscience and stipulates in Section 16 that "everyone shall be entitled to profess privately and publicly any religious creed or be without a religious denomination." Legally all denominations have the same status and all clergy must take an oath of loyalty to the government, which also must consent to the appointment of pastors and controls their pay. In 1979, the Baptists in Czechoslovakia chose to utilize a Czech translation of the new German confession of faith (see pp. 57-76).

Yugoslavia
The Baptist Union of Yugoslavia

What we know now as Yugoslavia was created after World War I, combining the two independent kingdoms of Serbia and Montenegro with certain parts of the former Austrian-Hungarian monarchy: Croatia, Slovenia, Bosnia, Herzegovina, and the northern area of biblical Macedonia. This mosaic of peoples is typical of the current Baptist situation, as well as its history. The Reformation had some limited impact on Austria-Hungary. Islam, Roman Catholicism, and Serbian Orthodoxy were parts of this varied picture. During the period of Austria-Hungarian rule in present-day Yugoslavia, German-speaking colonists settled in many parts of northern Yugoslavia and Bosnia. Hungarians continued to move south into the Vojvodina, which was considered their southern province.

As is true in other eastern settings, there were three major streams of early Baptist influence. First, many were converted abroad, especially in Austria and Hungary, and returned to give witness. The first was apparently Franz Tabory from Novi Sad who, along with his wife, was baptized in Bucharest in 1862. Secondly, colporteurs were sent out by others, such as the British and Foreign Bible Society and Oncken. In 1863, Oncken sent August Liebig to South Russia and the Balkans by way of Serbia and Bosnia, where he baptized a few converts. In 1875, another German missionary, H. Meyer, came from his work in Hungary to baptize believers in Novi Sad. German-speaking Baptists experienced their largest growth in the ethnic villages of Vojvodina. Lay evangelists preached in other languages as well. The strong Slovak Baptist movement was a lay movement which

EASTERN EUROPE

began in farm villages by the efforts of Slovaks who returned from Hungary, America, and Slovakia. The center of Slovak work was in Backi Petrovac, a station begun by Josip Turoci and assisted by pioneer missionaries from Hungary. Slovaks make up over 30 percent of the Baptist constituency in Yugoslavia.

Much later, in the early 1920s, a third influence is seen in the arrival of Vinko Vacek, a Croatian Catholic of Czech origin, who was converted in the United States and sent out as a missionary. Southern Baptists in the United States provided his support as part of the agreement of the Baptist World Alliance London Conference in 1920. Vacek was a very effective evangelist and became instrumental in uniting all five language groups into one Baptist Union, as well as each into their own language association. He was unquestionably the most influential leader of Yugoslavian Baptists until his death in 1939. Further assistance from America was short-lived with the arrival of war. The John Allen Moores (SBC) stayed briefly in 1939 and returned over the years to help Yugoslavia to rebuild their seminary and churches after World War II.

In 1941, Yugoslavia was divided between Germany, Bulgaria, Italy, and Hungary; the Baptist Union was destroyed in the separation of its member parts. In each territory, the fate of a group was different. At the end of the war, rebuilding was slow. Not only the divisions but also Nazi pressures deterred growth, although missionary activity was maintained. The strong ties to Germany were not helpful in the aftermath of the war. Outside workers were forbidden. But freedom of religion was granted to all groups whether large or small under the new Socialist government. The seminary was rebuilt, Youth work strengthened, new churches and mission stations begun, women's work carried out, and a Baptist paper produced.

Since the Orthodox and Roman Catholics comprise three-fourths of the population, and most of the rest are Lutherans, Reformed, or nonbelievers, it is significant that such a very small group is tolerated along with others. Freedom of conscience and freedom of religion are guaranteed to citizens of the People's Republic of Yugoslavia. One is free to belong or not belong, to start religious communities, and to train ministers, as well as carry out religious tasks. Rites must be performed only in places connected to churches or temples.

The Confession of Faith of the Yugoslavian Baptist Churches reflects the setting in which it was written after the war, probably about 1948, when religious guarantees were being sought. The two lengthy prefaces are included with the confession underlining the apologetic nature and context. A further refinement in the title for Baptists in Yugoslavia was made in 1963: The Union of Baptist Churches in the Socialist Federation of Republics of Yugoslavia.

(John David Hopper)
(Stephen Orčic)

Confession of Faith of the Yugoslavian Baptist Churches

Due to the fact that different authors have accused Baptists of being heretics or a sect, maintaining that they are based on unhealthy, even unchristian principles, and also to inform those who are not familiar with our faith and those who are interested in it, we have decided to publish this work, in which the most important principles of the Baptist faith are presented, with the desire to show the ways in which the Baptist confession of faith differs from the belief of other Christian denominations. This work should at the same time emphasize that the Baptist church is not some sect whose confession of faith is ". . . a collection of erroneous teachings which endangers the eternal happiness of their followers"[1] but that it is a Christian church with sound principles of Christian faith. Likewise, we intend to give to all believers of the Baptist church a work in which are presented all fundamental truths of the Baptist faith which would serve to their spiritual edification.

The name "Baptist" derives from the Greek word "baptizein," which means "to immerse" or "to put under water"; in the modern sense it means "to baptize." Thus the name "Baptist" refers to someone who has been baptized by the biblical mode of immersion.

Baptists in the Federal Peoples' Republic of Yugoslavia are a part of a great branch of Christianity which contributed much to the advancement of freedom of spirit and conscience. They belong to a Christian family which numbers in the millions, which can be proud of its history and which has always developed in the spirit of Christ's great ideas: truth, justice, brotherhood, and equality.

I
The Fundamental Articles of the Baptist Church

Baptists take their stance solely on biblical principles, whether dealing with questions of faith or those concerning social life.

1. The Holy Scriptures are the norm for the religious and social life of Baptists. They alone, pure and unaltered, serve as the stable footing and signpost in all the different questions of life.

2. Since sin and its consequences are still the same as in the time of Christ's life on earth, the way to salvation can also be none other than that which Christ and His disciples had preached: "Repent and be converted," and "You must be born again." Therefore, Baptists preach conversion and rebirth.

3. The ecclesiastical organization is founded on democratic principles of self-management, together with the Elders. Each believer participates on a personal and voluntary basis. The relationship between Elders and believers is not one of a master to his servants but rather as a first among equals.

4. Baptists baptize only those who have become believers in Jesus Christ as their personal Saviour. The act of baptism is accomplished according to the biblical mode of immersion under water of those who have become believers, as the biblical word "baptizein" clearly indicates, and as was also practised by John the Baptist, by the Apostolic Church in Jerusalem and by Christian churches in modern times.

5. Baptists acknowledge the principle of the priesthood of all believers. Every soul can come to God directly. On the basis of Apostolic teaching, there is no other mediator between God and man than Jesus Christ alone.

6. Baptists reject any system of church taxes. Their church communities, institutions, preachers and other employees are paid through

voluntary gifts. On the basis of their conviction and experience, God's blessing only lies on those contributions that have been brought forth voluntarily and with rejoicing hearts.

7. Baptists are active Christians. They maintain the principle of the Holy Scriptures "... I will show you my faith by my works." The Christian life consists not only of an emphasis of articles of faith and repetition of religious ceremonies; it is not only a doctrine but a life. The works of Baptists as well as their whole way of life should be in harmony with the teachings of the holy gospel. Therefore, Baptists have reduced rituals to a minimum.

8. Baptists contend for freedom of conscience. Every man has the right to worship according to the dictates of his own soul. Every citizen has the right to join that denomination which stands closest to his own convictions. Only a free person can be a proper and useful member of the national community. The ideal of the freedom of conscience can—according to Baptist opinion—only be realized in a state in which church and state are separate. Jesus Christ himself acknowledges two separated spheres of human life and organization: State and Church (that is, Faith).

9. Baptists are committed to the principle of social justice. Every inhabitant of this country has the right to earn a livelihood with just payment to meet life's necessities. The work of no person should be exploited in favour of those who do not work, according to the biblical principle: "Whoever does not work, should also not eat." God's commandment, "You shall love your neighbour as yourself" is the only sure key to the solution of social problems.

II
The Articles of the Baptist Faith

1. Of the Holy Scriptures

2 Tim. 3:16; 17; 2 Pet. 1:21; 2 Sam. 23:2; Acts 1:16; 3:21; Luke 16:29-31; Deut. 4:6-8

Baptists believe that the Holy Scriptures are the will of God revealed to man, and that they are written by men inspired by the Holy Spirit, and that they are a treasure room of God's justice and teaching.

2 Tim. 3:15; Mark 16:16; John 5:38-39; Acts 11:14; Rom. 1:16; 1 Pet. 1:10-12

Thus, God is their author and they are an endless source of knowledge of God, and thus, they lead men to salvation and glory.

They are pure, true and authentic.

They contain the fundamental rules whereby God will judge men.

Therefore, they are now and forever the only God given source and norm of human knowledge and teaching.

The Holy Scriptures remain as the rule of faith and of Christian life until the end of the world.

We understand the Holy Scriptures to include all writings of the Old and New Testament with the exception of the Apocrypha which do not belong because they were never mentioned either by Jesus or by the Apostles, and because their teaching (such as rewards for works and sacrifices, prayer for the dead, etc.) contradict the teaching of Christ, and because there is no inspiration of God in them.

Pro. 3:5-6; John 17:17; Rev. 22:18-19
John 12:47-48; Luke 10:10-16; Rom. 2:2
1 John 4:1; 1 Thess. 5:20; 2 Cor. 15:5; Ps. 119:59-60; Acts 17:11; Eph. 6:17; 1 John 4:6; Jude 3
Phil. 3:16; Eph. 4:3-6; 1 Cor. 1:10; Phil. 2:1; 1 Pet. 4:11; 1 Cor. 14:11,26

2. Of God

Baptists believe on the basis of the Holy Scriptures that there is one God who is the creator, sustainer and ruler over all the seen and unseen world.

Deut. 6:4; Gen. 1:1; John 1:1-3; Pss. 147:5; 83:18; Jer. 10:10; Isa. 66:1-2; Rom. 1:20; 11:33-36; 1 Tim. 1:17; Heb. 3:4; Ex. 15:11; Isa. 6:3; Rev. 4:6,8,11; Jer. 2:12-13; Mark 12:29-30; Matt. 10:29

God presents Himself in the Holy Scriptures as Father, Son and Holy Spirit but his own being is only one and inseparable.

Eph. 4:6; 1 John 5:20; 2 Cor. 3:17; 1 John 5:7; Pss. 90:2; 139:1-10; Isa. 40:28; Matt. 11:25-27; 28:18,20; John 5:17,23; 8:58; 10:30; 17:5,10; 20:28; 2 Cor. 13:13; Eph. 2:18; Rev. 1:4-5

3. Of Jesus Christ

On the basis of the Holy Scriptures, Baptists believe that Jesus Christ is the only begotten Son of God, both true God and true man, conceived by the

John 3:16; Matt. 3:17; Luke 2:11; John 1:14; Isa. 9:6; Matt. 1:23; 1 Tim. 2:5; Phil. 2:7;

Holy Spirit and born by the virgin Mary, and that he lived a holy life without blemish, sacrificed himself and shed his blood for the redemption of the world.

<small>Acts 2:30; Isa. 7:14; Matt. 1:20,23; Luke 1:34-35; 2 Cor. 5:21; Eph. 1:7; Col. 1:14; John 1:29</small>

They believe that Jesus was resurrected on the third day, and then ascended into heaven, where he sits at the right hand of God where he intercedes for his people.

<small>1 Cor. 15:4; Matt. 16:21; 20:18-19; Luke 24:6; Mark 16:19; 1 John 2:1; Luke 24:51; Acts 1:9; Ps. 110:1</small>

Furthermore, they believe that Jesus is the only mediator between God and men.

<small>1 Tim. 2:5; Acts 4:12</small>

and that he will return to judge the living and the dead.

<small>Acts 17:31; Rev. 22:20; John 14:3; Acts 10:42</small>

4. Of the Holy Spirit

They believe, furthermore, that the Holy Spirit is the third person of the God-head, equal to God the Father and God the Son in power, in holiness and wisdom.

<small>John 5:7; Titus 3:5</small>

Sent by the Father at the request of the Son to be the Comforter and Helper of those who believe;

<small>John 15:16-17,26; Acts 5:32</small>

who teaches them God's laws and fills them with his power.

<small>Acts 1:8; Rom. 8:16; John 16:13; 14:26; Acts 2:4,38; 4:8; 1 Cor. 3:16; 2 Cor. 3:3; Gal. 5:22-23; Eph. 3:16</small>

5. Of Creation

On the basis of the Holy Scriptures and particularly the Book of Genesis they believe that God created the world

<small>Gen. 1:1; John 1:3; Acts 4:24; Rom. 1:20; Col. 1:16-17; Heb. 11:3; Rev. 10:6</small>

and that he created man according to his image.

<small>Gen. 1:27; Neh. 9:6; Acts 17:26</small>

6. Of Satan

They believe that Satan formerly was a Cherub, who rebelled against God because of arrogance and the wish to be equal to Him.

<small>Ezek. 28:14-15; Isa. 14:12-15</small>

Therefore he was expelled from heaven along with him a host of angels. Since that time he has been the tempter and seducer of men, the cause of

<small>Rev. 12:9; 1 Pet. 5:8; Matt. 4:1-3; 13:25-26; Luke 22:3; Eph. 2:2; 1 Thess. 3:5; Rev.</small>

EASTERN EUROPE

false piety and apostasy from God, as well as the cause of all evil in the world. At the end he will be overcome and thrown into the lake of fire which is prepared for him and his servants.

20:1-3,10; Ezek. 28:18; 2 Pet. 2:4; Jude 6: Rev. 12:10; 19:20

7. Of the Fall of Man

Baptists believe that man was created holy and put under the law of God, but that he has fallen out of this holy and happy state because of self-willed transgression. Therefore all men are sinners and have a tendency towards evil. As such they cannot justify themselves and are therefore condemned to eternal condemnation.

Gen. 1:27-31; 2:16-17; Eccl. 7:29; Gen. 3:17-19; 3:6-17,19-24; 6:12; Isa. 53:6; Rom. 5:19; Ps. 51:5; Rom. 5:15-19; 3:10,23-24; 2:1-16; 3:9-23; Gal. 3:10; Eph. 2:1-3; Ezek. 18:20

8. Of Salvation

On the basis of the Holy Scriptures Baptists believe that salvation is the gift of grace given by God through the saving and mediating act of His Son,

Eph. 2:8; Matt. 18:11; Rev. 15:11; Eph. 2:5-8; 1 John 4:10; John 3:16; 1:1-14; 1 Cor. 3:5-7; Heb. 4:14

who became equal with man according to the will of the Father (except in the matter of sin) and who, through his own obedience fulfilled the law and the will of God, and through his own death provided satisfaction for the sins of men.

Phil. 2:6-7; 2 Cor. 5:21; Heb. 2:9,14; Phil. 2:8; Gal. 4:4-5; Isa. 53:4-5; Matt. 20:28; Rom. 3:21-26; 4:25; 1 Cor. 15:1-3; Heb. 9:13-15; 1 John 2:2; 4:10

Resurrected from the dead, he sits at the right hand of the Father where he is the mediator of his elect people.

Heb. 1:3; Col. 3:1-4; Heb. 8:1; 7:25-26; 1 John 2:1

Furthermore, Baptists believe that this salvation is free, offered by means of the holy gospel to all men; all can take part in this salvation through repentance and conversion, through the faith in the Lord Jesus Christ.

9. Of New Birth

Baptists believe that only through the Word of God and the Holy Spirit can man come to the realization of sin. When he sincerely repents for his sins and turns to Christ, he receives through faith the

Heb. 4:12; Isa. 55:10-11; Acts 2:37; John 6:63; Acts 10:44,46; 1 Cor. 2:4-5,14; Eph. 2:1-5,8;

forgiveness of sins and justification before God. By this means man is reborn through the Holy Spirit and thus he despises sin and lives a new life.

<small>Rom. 3:24-25; Acts 26:17-18; Rom. 3:28; John 3:5-6; Jas. 1:18; Gal. 6:15; John 1:13; Eph. 5:8; 1 Pet. 1:23; Acts 16:14-15</small>

10. Of Sanctification

On the basis of the Holy Scriptures Baptists believe that reborn souls are sanctified through the gift of the Holy Spirit. Through this they are enabled to fight against sin and to preach the kingdom of God in this world. Sanctification begins with rebirth and continues throughout all of life; its' goal is the transformation into the image of Christ.

<small>1 Cor. 1:30; John 17:19; Rom. 6:22; Gal. 5:22; Rom. 12:1; Eph. 4:22-24; 1 Thess. 4:7; Col. 3:5-10; 1 Pet. 1:15-16; 2 Cor. 7:1</small>

11. Of Baptism

On the basis of the Holy Scriptures Baptists believe that baptism is a commandment given by Christ, and that it is to be done in the biblical manner of a singular immersion in water in the name of the Father, the Son and the Holy Spirit. Only those can be baptized who have accepted Jesus Christ as their personal Saviour and who have confessed their faith before the church with a testimony. The believer testifies by his baptism that he believes in the death and resurrection of Jesus Christ, that he has surrendered himself body and soul to Christ—and that he has buried the old man and is resurrected to new life with Christ. Baptism should also confirm the believer in his assurance that he is saved and accepted into the community of believers and that, as such, he has become a member of the Church of Christ. Thus baptism is a seal of faith and a symbol of rebirth; it is carried out by the church with new born souls until the return of Jesus Christ.

<small>Matt. 28:19; Mark 16:16; Acts 2:38; 8:12; 16:32,34; 18:8; Eph. 4:5; Acts 8:36-37; Mark 16:16; Acts 22:16; 1 Pet. 3:21; Col. 2:12-14; Rom. 6:3,6,8; 2 Cor. 1:21-22; Eph. 1:13; Gal. 3:27; 5:24</small>

12. Of the Lord's Supper

On the basis of the Holy Scriptures they believe that the Lord's Supper is an institution of the Lord

<small>Matt. 26:26,28; Mark 14:22-24; Luke</small>

Jesus Christ, at which occasion believers remember his death. When they take part in the Lord's Supper they bear witness that salvation has been accomplished by Jesus Christ and that they have accepted it. At the same time they express their deep thankfulness for the salvation received. The Lord's Supper is at the same time a symbol of communion with Christ and his church. It is a ceremony which should be continued until the return of Christ and which serves for the cultivation of unity and love among the believers. It prepares the believers for the return of Jesus Christ. All baptized members may take part in the Lord's Supper, after a thorough examination of themselves. The Lord's Supper is served with bread and wine.

22:17-20; Acts 2:46; 20:7; 1 Cor. 11:26; 10:17; Acts 2:42; 1 Cor. 10:16,21; 11:27-30

13. Of the Community of Believers (The Church Community)

A. Baptists believe on the basis of the Holy Scriptures that all believers form together the body of Christ. They believe that, according to the will of God and the instructions of the Apostle, and in order to care for the spiritual education of each individual believer, it is necessary to join together in a local community which signifies the visible and public Church of Christ. Such a community consists of those followers of Christ who have voluntarily joined themselves together, who are born again and baptized, and who are, according to the intention of Christ, members of His body and ambassadors of His thoughts as they are sent into the world to spread His kingdom. Baptists believe in the independence of the local community: each congregation independently resolves questions in its own area of work under the leadership of the Holy Spirit. They believe, furthermore, that in addition to the moral development and spiritual edification of its members, as well as missionary activity, the local community is responsible

Eph. 1:22-23; Matt. 18:20; 16:18; 1 Cor. 12:18-27; Eph. 4:1; 1 Pet. 2:5; John 10:16; Acts 2:1,41,46-47; see the whole Book of Acts; 1 Cor. 12:12-17; 16:1,19; 2 Cor. 6:16-17; 1 Thess. 5:11-23; Mark 16:15; Acts 2:42-47; Acts 16:5; 15:41; 1 Cor. 1:27; 2 Cor. 8:1; Eph. 2:19-22; Col. 2:19; Eph. 4:3-16; Acts 2:44-47; 1 Cor. 16:1-19; Phil. 2

Col. 1:18; Acts 14:23; Matt. 20:25-27; 23:8; Eph. 4:15; Phil. 1:1; Titus 1:5; Acts 13:3; 6:6; 1 Tim. 4:14; 5:22; Titus 1:5-9; Matt. 7:15; Acts 20:28,31; Rom. 16:17-18; 1 Cor. 4:1-2; 3:9,11-13; Gal. 1:8-9; 1 Tim. 4:14; 5:17-18; 3:8-10; Gal. 6:6; 2 Tim. 4:2,5; 2:15; 1 Tim. 6:3-5; Jas. 3:1

John 13:34-35; Acts 2:42; Pss. 26:8; 27:4; 84:1; 122:1; John 15:12,17; Rom. 12:15; 2 Cor. 9:6-8; Gal. 5:6; 1 Thess. 5:14; 1 Pet. 1:22; 1 John 2:4; 3:11,16-18; 2 John 6

Acts 15:22-25; Matt. 18:17-18; 1 Cor. 14:33,40; Eph. 5:21; Col. 2:5; 1 Pet. 5:5

1 Tim. 6:12; Matt. 10:32; Rom. 10:9-10;

for social justice, striving to improve social conditions first of all among its own members.

B. They believe on the basis of the Holy Scriptures that the Lord Jesus Christ is the supreme head of the church. The New Testament knows only two kinds of servants in New Testament churches (i.e. the local communities): Elders and Deacons. The church itself elects its Elders (preachers, pastoral counsellors, teachers, etc.—all different names for one and the same ministry), and Deacons, who are set aside for their service through laying on of hands. The laying on of hands (ordination) can be carried out only for those who possess all the virtues which the New Testament requires of them. They must do their service conscientiously and fervently according to the instructions given in the Epistles to Timothy and Titus.

C. On the basis of the Holy Scriptures they believe that it is the task of the members of the church to share hearty love among one another, to actively participate in acquiring and spreading spiritual goods as well as social justice inside and outside the church community. Furthermore they do this in utilizing responsibly all divine gifts of His grace and doing so in obedience to the rules which God gave to his church. Therefore it is the duty of every member to take part in the Lord's Supper, to attend all meetings (worship service, prayer meeting, Bible study, business meeting) regularly. It is furthermore his duty to give his share continuously, voluntarily and according to his own material possibilities to the building up of the kingdom of God here on earth.

D. They believe on the basis of the Holy Scriptures that the church should solve all current questions in meetings of the members where all members have equal right to vote.

E. The acceptance of new members into the congregation can only be accomplished after a testimony of their conversion and faith in Jesus Christ as Lord and when the members vote in favour of acceptance.   Heb. 4:14

F. Every member has the duty to submit oneself to the rule of Matthew 18:15-17 according to which each member should admonish the others in brotherly love, but where one is also obliged to accept the admonitions of others. It is the right and the duty of the church to expel those members from its ranks whose lives are not in accordance with the teaching of the Holy Scriptures and the Articles of Faith which it confesses. Expulsion can be accomplished only after repeated and fruitless admonitions and if the admonished member is unwilling to reject his sinful life and if he does not sincerely repent for the trangression he committed. By expulsion he loses all rights which he had in the church, although the church allows him to continue to attend its worship services. He is also dismissed from all offices in the church. Reacceptance follows the same procedure as with the acceptance of new members on the grounds of the testimony of the excluded member.   Matt. 18:15-17; 1 Cor. 5:3-13; 2 Cor. 2:6-8; 1 Tim. 1:19-20; 6:3-5; 2 Thess. 3:6; Titus 3:10-11

14. Of Sunday as the Day of Rest

Baptists believe that Sunday, the first day of the week, corresponds to the day of rest which the first Christian church celebrated. Sunday should be consecrated for rest and should serve as spiritual recuperation. On this day not only should physical work be avoided but also everything which could disturb the peace of this day. Instead, works of mercy and the Lord's work should be done eagerly in order to prepare for the rest that is promised to the people of God.   Rev. 1:10; Acts 20:7; Ps. 118:24; Matt. 28:1; John 20:19,26; Acts 2:1; 1 Cor. 16:1-2; Col. 2:16-17; Mark 2:27; Heb. 10:25; Gen. 2:3; Ex. 20:8; Matt. 12:10-12; 10:24-25

15. Of Marriage

Baptists believe on the basis of the Holy Scriptures that marriage has been instituted by God. The   Gen. 1:27-28; 2:18,24; 1 Cor. 7:2-39; Eph.

husband can have only one wife, and the wife only one husband. Wherever marriage is regulated by the state, it shall be carried out according to the existing laws, but it is recommended not to omit the ceremony in a church. Baptists believe that only such a marriage can be fully blessed and be happy which has begun in the name of God and with both partners as believers. Divorce for reasons which are not in accordance with the teaching of the Holy Scriptures and marriage with persons so divorced is not considered permissible.

Refs: 5:22-23; Heb. 13:4; Matt. 19:6,9; 1 Kings 11:1-8; Neh. 13:23-28; 2 Cor. 6:14-15

16. Of the Relation to the Public Authorities

Baptists believe that the public authorities were instituted by God for justice, in order to secure peace and good order and in order to punish those elements that are harmful and dangerous for society. They believe also that one should pray for the government according to the commandment of the Holy Scriptures, that one should honour it and submit oneself to it according to one's own conscience and as a testimony before the world, except in those cases which contradict the teaching of Christ, because Christ is the one and only Lord of the conscience and of human souls.

Refs: Rom. 13:3; Gen. 9:6; Ex. 18:21-23; Deut. 16:18-19; 2 Sam. 23:3; Rom. 13:1-7; 1 Pet. 2:13-14; Matt. 22:21; 1 Tim. 2:1-3; Titus 3:1; 1 Pet. 2:13-17; Rev. 19:16; Ps. 72:11; Dan. 3:15-18; 6:7-10; Matt. 10:28; Acts 4:18-20; 5:29; Phil. 2:10-11

17. Of the Return of the Lord Jesus Christ

On the basis of the Holy Scriptures Baptists believe that the Lord Jesus Christ will come again to judge the living and the dead. The return will be in power and glory when he comes as the Lord over all lords; when the whole world will recognize his glory and majesty and be a witness to his final victory over Satan.

Refs: Acts 1:11; Matt. 16:27; Phil. 3:20; Heb. 9:28; 10:37; Col. 3:4; Matt. 25:31; 1 Cor. 1:7-8; 11:26; 1 John 2:28; Rev. 1:8; 3:11

18. Of the Resurrection

On the basis of the Holy Scriptures Baptists believe in a physical resurrection. This body will be-

Refs: Job 19:25,27; John 5:29; 1 Cor. 15:52-53;

come spiritually transfigured because only such a body can inherit the new earth which God has prepared for the believers in eternity.

Dan. 12:2-3; Jude 14—15; Ps. 16:10; 1 Pet. 5:4; 1 Thess. 4:16-17

19. Of Judgment and the Eternal Life

On the basis of the Holy Scriptures Baptists believe that the Day of the Lord will occur with the return of the Lord Jesus Christ. Then all men, the living and the dead, must appear before God's judgment and they will receive proper reward for their lives and their works. The believers will be accepted for eternal blessedness, while the unbelievers will be condemned to eternal punishment. The Holy Scriptures reveal clearly that both the conditions of "eternal blessedness" and "eternal punishment" are unending in their length. Baptists believe that the "signs of time" point towards an early end of this world. They hold fast the word of the Lord Jesus: ". . . Surely, I am coming soon." And therefore believers cry: "Yes, come, Lord Jesus!"

Rom. 14:10-12; Acts 17:31; 2 Cor. 5:10; Rev. 22:12; Matt. 25: 31-34,41; Rev. 22:20,7; 1:3; 3:11

TR: Rut Lehotsky
TR: James Williams
(TR: Ulrike Ross)

Note

1. Stj. Bakšić, *The Baptists and Their Heresies,* p. 5.

Romania
The Baptist Union of the Republic of Socialist Romania

Baptists in Romania value the early Anabaptist heritage in their area and particularly the many congregations in Transylvania. In spite of severe persecution at different times, they survived until 1762 when most emigrated to Russia as a result of oppression under Maria Theresa's reign.

One sees modern Baptist beginnings in several sources in the mid-1800s. Karl Scharschmidt, an immigrant who had been baptized by Oncken in 1845, was, along with his wife Augusta, very active in Bucharest. In 1864, four converts were baptized in the Dimbovita River and a German-speaking Baptist congregation was formed, meeting in a house on Popa Rusa Street. Oncken himself visited the newly built chapel in 1869.

A second way of spreading the Baptist faith was through Russian Baptist immigrants, primarily from the South Ukraine. They reached the Dobrogea area in 1862 and established a Baptist church in Cataloi. A. Liebig, a member of the Bucharest church, worked with the immigrants. In 1870, the first Russian converts were baptized and formed a church in Tulcea.

The conversion and subsequent ministry of Constantin Adorian was another help for Baptist development in Romania. Baptized in the German church in Bucharest, Adorian studied at the seminary in Hamburg and returned to become pastor of the Romanian Baptist church in Bucharest in 1912. His contemporary, Radu Tasca from Arad, worked among Romanians in Dobrogea, organizing several churches.

In Transylvania, the main pioneer was Antal Noval, a tailor

and colporteur of the British and Foreign Bible Society. In 1871, he came to J. Lajo's home Bible-study group in Salonta Mare to discuss believers' baptism. Consequently six persons were baptized by the Baptist Missionary from Budapest, H. Meyer. They formed a Hungarian-speaking Baptist church in Salonta Mare. A little later (1885), a Romanian-speaking church was formed in Chess (Crisana) under the noble leadership of Mihai Kornyea. Growth in Transylvania was rapid. By 1910, there were 147 churches.

The new Baptist denomination developed its statutes and received state recognition in 1905. The Baptist union was formed in 1919, the year after Transylvania united with Romania. In 1920, the first Baptist assembly was held. There were by this time four major language groups: Romanian, Russian, Hungarian, and German. The Baptist Theological Seminary was founded for pastoral training in 1921, with assistance from Southern Baptists in the United States.

Baptists in Romania suffered much persecution in several phases. The Law of Cults in 1928 brought some toleration but was interpreted to prevent the Baptist movement. This time of difficulty reached its climax with law number 927/28 of December 1942, which called for the abolition of the Baptist cult. All properties were confiscated. With the breakup of the fascist dictatorship in August 1944, a new law was issued (Nr. 553, in November 1944) which recognized the Baptists as a free-functioning denomination.

The new constitution for socialist Romania was accepted in 1948 and grants "freedom of religious worship; the religious denominations shall be free to organize themselves and may freely function." It also permitted schools and organizations. Later laws interpreted this in more detail, noting financial limits and permitting participation in international meetings of a purely religious nature. The constitution was revised in 1952, giving the Orthodox church equal status with others (that is, it was no longer privileged). The confession of faith of Romanian Baptists reflects something of its historical context and was last reissued in 1974.

(Ioan Bunaciu)
(TR:Rodica Cocar)

Confession of Faith of the Romanian Baptist Churches

1. The Doctrine of the Bible — God's Word

Gal. 1:11; 1 Pet. 1:12; 2 Tim. 3:16; John 10:35; Joel 2:28; Matt. 10:20; 1 Cor. 2:10; 11:23; Eph. 1:13; 2 Tim. 1:13; Rom. 10:17; Ps. 119:105

We believe and affirm that the Holy Scripture of the Old and New Testament are inspired by the Holy Spirit. They are the written word of God, a godly revelation to mankind, the unmistakable source of the awareness of God.

The Bible — the word of God written by the inspiration of the Holy Spirit — is the only rule and norm of faith and behaviour in this life.

Matt. 15:6; John 17:17; 5:39; Isa. 34:16; Acts 17:11; John 20:31

In religious matters, the Bible is the only authority; it is sufficient for our teaching and there is no need for support from tradition.

2. The Doctrine of God

Gen. 1:1; Eph. 4:6; Mal. 2:10; John 13:15; Rom. 1:14-20; 11:36; Ps. 94:9; Acts 17:24; 1 Cor. 13:14; Matt. 28:19; 1 John 5:7; John 6:27; 1 Pet. 1:2; Matt. 11:25; Mark 14:36; Luke 22:42; 23:34,45; Acts 2:33; Rom. 15:6; 1 Cor. 8:6
Matt. 16:16; John 1:1; Luke 3:32; Acts 8:37; 9:20; 2 Cor. 1:19; 1 John 2:24; 3:23; 4:15; John 20:31
John 4:24; 2 Cor.

We believe and affirm that there is one God the Creator, the Sustainer and the Ruler of all things.

In the Bible we discover God as the Father, Son and Holy Spirit, completely one in their being and not separated in their being and not separated in their oneness.

(1.) God the Father

(2.) God the Son, Jesus Christ

(3.) God the Holy Spirit

3:3,17; Job 33:4; Isa. 48:16; 1 Cor. 2:12; John 15:26; 14:26; Luke 11:13; Acts 5:32

3. The Doctrine of Man

We believe and affirm that God created man after his own image. The human body's material part is from the dust of the earth; the spiritual part is from God. God made man perfect and without sin, but with a free will to choose between good or evil.

Gen. 1:27; 2:7

Through the fall into sin man is under the curse and he became unable to do the will of God. Through natural birth everyone inherits the seed of sin, an inclination toward sin, and a sinful nature. Man is now free and is thus responsible to God for all his actions, words and thoughts. All men must die, but after death follows judgment and eternal reward.

Gen. 1:31; Eccl. 7:29; Gen. 2:13; Ps. 107:17; Deut. 30:15; Rom. 5:12,19; 7:17-18; 5:6; 7:20-23; Rom. 14:12; Matt. 12:36; 2 Cor. 5:10; Heb. 9:27

4. The Doctrine of Sin

We believe and affirm that man was created by God in His own image to give Him glory and a happy life in Him, and that man was lured by the devil, becoming disobedient to the command of God and, consequently, sin and the curse entered the world. Sin is nonconformity to the moral law of God in action, disposition or attitude.

Gen. 3:13; 1 John 5:16; Rom. 14:23; Jas. 4:17; John 8:34; Rom. 6:13; Eccl. 7:29; Ps. 51:4; Eph. 2:1-3; Deut. 9:7; 1 John 3:7

(1.) The Universality of Sin: All Men Are Sinners

Rom. 3:23; Eccl. 7:20; John 15:16; Rom. 5:12; 1 John 1:8; 1 Kings 8:46

(2.) The Consequence of Sin: Spiritual Death

Rom. 6:23; 5:12; Gen. 2:17; Jas. 1:15

5. The Doctrine of Salvation

We believe and affirm that salvation is the deliverance of persons from the consequences of their breaking divine law. It involves human nature and acts done by Him. Man cannot save himself. He can-

Jer. 2:22; Rom. 1:20; Amos 9:2-3; Rom. 3:20; Isa. 64:6; Jer. 13:23

not wash himself clean of sin; he cannot hide himself from the consequences of sin.

He cannot earn merits through good deeds to cover his guilty past and to earn salvation.

Titus 1:11; Eph. 2:8-9; Acts 15:11; Titus 2:5

Salvation is by God's grace. It is a free grace without merit; good deeds are salvation's fruits.

Acts 4:12; 1 John 2:2; Isa. 52:5; Eph. 1:7; 2 Cor. 5:18; Rom. 3:24-25; 1 John 2:2; Titus 1:11; 1 Tim. 2:4

The means of salvation is our Lord Jesus who was crucified in our place. There is no other means (crucifixes, mysteries, saints).

This salvation which was accomplished on the cross can be freely obtained and is for all people, all nations and all social classes.

Mark 1:15; Luke 13:3; Acts 2:38; 17:30; 16:31

For a sinner to experience this salvation he must fulfill two conditions: repentance and faith. These are eternally inseparable.

—Repentance means to recognize the sin, to be sorry about it, although having it, as well as to confess it to God and to turn back to Him.

—Faith means the sinner's receiving the grace of God through Jesus Christ to salvation and everlasting life.

6. The Doctrine of the New Birth

John 3:7

' We believe and affirm that the new birth is the regeneration of life which gives us a holy, spiritual attitude and mood. It involves the entire character: intellect, feeling and will. Thus, every sinner must be born again to become a true believer. Man cannot be born again or changed by his own power.

Jer. 13:23; John 15:5; Matt. 6:16-18; Rom. 8:7; Matt. 12:36

Without being born again all the efforts to do good deeds for which God will reward on the Judgment Day cannot have any meaningful result. By way of natural birth we inherit a carnal inner state which produces sin's fruits. We are like a wild tree which cannot bring forth good fruits. It does not matter how much care it has; its fruits are wild. Only by being in Christ will the natural mind change.

1 Pet. 1:23; Isa. 1:18;

The new birth is a divine work done by God in a

sinner's life enabling him to do His will. For a sinner to be born again he has to repent, to believe and to receive salvation through grace. Then God accomplishes the work of the new birth through his word and through the Holy Spirit. *John 3:5; Eph. 2:10*

The new birth is not a superior life but a radical change of life. It is not the change of effect but of determinant cause. It is not the cleansing of the exterior but of the interior life. *1 Cor. 5:17; Rom. 6:4; Col. 3:9-10*

The new birth offers us the traits of God's children; we have the same Godly mind and are able to live according to God's will. As it is in our normal life so it is with the new birth, the second mind, the old mind continues to exist: the old flesh is crucified—stopped to act—and the new mind is developing and produces good fruits. The new state is quite different from the old one. This is the situation with those who are born again and who will show the quality of a child of God. *John 3:6; Gal. 5:22-23; Matt. 7:17*

Through the new birth we become heirs of God. The right to an everlasting inheritance is founded on the new relationship with God. Whoever is not born again is not a child of God and does not have right to an everlasting inheritance. *Rom. 8:17; John 3:3*

7. The Doctrine of the Church

We believe and affirm that according to the New Testament, the Church of Christ is made up of the totality of all believers, from all races, nationalities, social states and from all history. This is the universal Church. The universal Church is not an earthly organization which can be seen, but is a living spiritual body made up of those who are saved, of those who have believed in Jesus Christ and have been born again. *Heb. 12:23; Acts 20:28; Matt. 16:18; Eph. 1:22-23*

In the Greek language the word "church" (ἐκκλησία) meant a gathering of those called to be interested in public matters. This word was adopted not only for the universal Church but also for the local church, independently organized by the followers of Christ in a town who gathered together for worship.

<small>Matt. 18:20; Rom. 16:5; 1 Cor. 16:19; Col. 4:15; Acts 8:1; Gal. 1:22; 1 Cor. 1:2</small>

According to the New Testament teaching the local church is a voluntary union of a group of believers from a locality, born again, and baptized on the basis of their personal witness of their faith in Jesus Christ as their Saviour. They come together to worship God, to build themselves up spiritually and to keep the Christian faith by Christian teaching (according to the New Testament teaching) and to cooperate in spreading the word of God.

In the beginning the church gathered in private homes.

<small>Col. 1:18; Eph. 1:22-23; 5:23; 1 Pet. 5:3</small>

The direct leadership of the church belongs to Jesus Christ through the Holy Spirit. Hierarchy is not recognized. Those who have specific tasks are only servants of the church and not rulers for ordaining.

<small>Matt. 23:8; Eph. 5:3; Acts 2:41</small>

The right to be a member is not inherited but is received individually through a new birth. Acceptance in a local church is on a voluntary and personal basis after baptism which in turn is based on a testimony about one's faith in Jesus Christ. Members call each other "brothers" and are equal with each other in terms of rights and obligations with no consideration whatsoever to which race, nationality or social level they belong.

<small>Mark 16:15; Eph. 4:12; 1 Cor. 14:4-5,12; Eph. 3:19</small>

The local church organization is based on the principle of autonomous democracy. The program has as its aim the establishment of the kingdom of God in human hearts; the churches are means chosen by God by which this aim is fulfilled. The churches are responsible for glorifying God, for spreading the gospel and for helping in the spiritual growth of each member through brotherly fellowship.

8. The Servants of the Church

We believe and affirm that in the New Testament churches there were several kinds of special servants, but that they had only two classes of servants who led in the spiritual and material matters of the churches: elders (presbyter, pastors, bishops) and deacons. — Phil. 1:1

1. The titles of "bishop," "presbyter," and "pastor" were given to the highest servants of the New Testament churches. All of their callings are for one and the same duty: spiritual supervision and ruling the church. To be able to have such responsibility one must have the qualities described by Paul in 1 Timothy 3:1-7 and Titus 1:5-9. — Acts 20:17,28; 1 Tim. 3:1-7; Titus 1:5-9

   The method of election is shown by the Greek word "$\chi\epsilon\iota\rho\text{o}\tau\text{o}\nu\acute{\epsilon}\omega$" which means to vote by raising the hand. This election is made by the church when it is together for this purpose. — Acts 14:23

   The pastor can be disciplined also when his guilt is very well founded. — 1 Tim. 5:19

2. The deacons have the duty of helping the pastor in managing the material affairs of the church. They are responsible for cultivating financial giving and for calling for philanthropic actions. They are to have the qualities mentioned in 1 Timothy 3:8-13. — 1 Tim. 3:8-13

   They receive their task by the laying on of hands. — Acts 6:6; 13:3; 1 Tim. 4:14; 1 Pet. 2:5,9; Rev. 1:6

   We believe and affirm, according to the New Testament, that the priesthood is not a special class but a quality for every believer; it is universal. Every believer is a priest. Everyone has the right to come directly to God through Jesus Christ without any other intercessor. Everyone has the right to offer spiritual sacrifices.

9. The New Testament's Symbols

We believe and affirm that the New Testament church has two symbols: Baptism and the Lord's Supper. They are not sacraments.

Matt. 28:19

1. Baptism. The Greek word for baptism is βαπτίξω, which means immersion and indicates the means of baptism as being immersion and in no way sprinkling with water. Immersion is done only once and in the name of the Trinity.

Rom. 6:4

Baptism is the symbol of the burial of the old man and the resurrection of the new man so that he may walk in newness of life.

Acts 8:13-21; 1 Pet. 3:21

Baptism does not cleanse sins; this is done only by the blood of Jesus Christ. Baptism is a public witness of one person that he is already cleansed.

Mark 16:16; Acts 2:38; 8:36-37

A person must receive salvation before baptism to have a good conscience; he has to fulfill salvation's conditions: repentance and faith. Children cannot affirm that they have fulfilled these conditions and therefore cannot be admitted to baptism.

Matt. 26:26-28; Luke 22:19; 1 Cor. 11:24-25; Acts 2:41-42; 1 Cor. 11:28

2. Lord's Supper. The Lord's Supper is the symbol of the Lord's death in our place. It is composed of bread and wine but not mixed. The broken bread reminds us of the body of Christ which was broken for us; the wine reminds us of his blood shed for the cleansing of our sin. The Lord's Supper does not have the effect of forgiving sins. It only reminds us that for the forgiveness of our sins the Lord's body had to be broken and his blood shed. For this reason he commanded us to have Holy Communion. The Lord's Supper can be taken by all those who have confessed their faith in the Lord Jesus and have been baptized. At

each Lord's Supper the believer is to examine himself.

10. The Lord's Day—Sunday

We believe and affirm that Sunday is a Christian practice which must be kept continually and which must be spent in worship, in spiritual meditation both publicly and at home. Distinguishable from the Old Testament Hebrews who kept the seventh day, the Christians belong to the New Covenant and have to keep the first day of the week (Sunday) which was sanctified by God by the resurrection of his Son from the dead, and by the sending of the Holy Spirit.

Mark 16:9; Luke 24:1-6; John 20:1; Acts 2:1-4; Rev. 1:10; Acts 20:7; 1 Cor. 16:2; Ps. 118:24; Lev. 23:15-16

The early Christians kept it as a day of worship. On this day we are to rest from work and bodily pleasure; we are permitted to do only the necessary things and to have pity on others. We do not have festivals for saints.

11. Discipline in the Church

We believe and affirm that the church has the right to exhort brotherly discipline to members who have gone astray from Christian teaching of the word of God—in attitude, teaching and life. Discipline includes admonishing, removal of church rights and exclusion from the church. One is invited back into fellowship only after a personal testimony.

Matt. 18:15-17; Titus 3:10; 2 Thess. 3:6; 1 Cor. 5:11-13

12. Prayer

We believe and affirm that prayer is a close fellowship of man with God. It is a matter of personal honesty, opening our innermost being to the Lord. For this reason we do not have prayer books and do not encourage others to commit prayers to memory.

Pss. 62:8; 142:2; Phil. 4:6

Prayers can be for thanksgiving, supplication and intercession. Prayers are addressed to the Father in the name of the Lord Jesus Christ. He is the only

1 Tim. 2:1; Eph. 5:20; John 16:23; 1 Tim. 2:5; Matt. 6:6; 14:23; 26:26,39; Acts 2:42;

mediator between man and God. We do not believe in prayers to the saints. Such are not according to the Holy Scriptures. Prayer is absolutely necessary to the spiritual life, to upbuilding and strengthening, for facing temptation and for overcoming the enemy (Satan).

Prayers for the dead were not practiced in Christian churches. We believe that they have no value because the dead have gone to their appropriate place immediately after death and that there is no possibility of changing from one place to another.

13. Holiness

We believe and affirm that sanctification is a progressive work done by God through the Holy Spirit in the life of the saved. It begins at the new birth and by means of it we remain in his will. It means the cleansing of sin and a life for God through a separation from the world. The cleansing of sin is accomplished by the blood of the Lord Jesus Christ.

Being separated from the world and being kept for God is done by the word of God and through the Holy Spirit who gave us power to resist temptation and to live according to his will. Sanctification has two parts: God's and man's. God, through his Holy Spirit, influences our will and gives us power; man accepts for himself the will and power of God.

14. Marriage

We believe and affirm that, according to the Scriptures, marriage was constituted by God. Marriage is an act of free will through which a man and a woman agree to live together their whole life. The man is allowed to have only one woman as wife; likewise the woman is allowed to have only one man as husband. After the death of one the other can marry again.

Bearing in mind that marriage is also a civil act it is done according to state law and after that follows the blessing of the church. We believe that Christians should be married only with other Christians. Marriage is not to be broken by divorce; divorce is forbidden for believers. We believe that the Holy Scripture allows for divorce in the case of proven adultery or when one tries to leave the home. In this case Scripture allows the other one to marry again.

2 Cor. 6:14; 1 Cor. 7:39; Matt. 2:16; 19:6; Matt. 19:9; 1 Cor. 7:15

15. Christian Giving

We believe and affirm that, according to the teaching of the Word of God and the practice of the early church, church members have the obligation morally to give freely to the work of the kingdom:

2 Cor. 9:6-7; Ex. 25:2; 35:5; 1 Cor. 2:5; Rom. 12:8

1. To sustain the workers of the kingdom so that they lack nothing,
2. To help poor orphans and widows, and
3. To build the churches.

Phil. 4:16-18; Titus 3:13; 2 John 6; 1 Cor. 9:14; Matt. 10:10; 1 Tim. 5:18; Acts 11:29; Rom. 15:27; 1 Cor. 16:1; John 12:7-8; Matt. 25:40; Deut. 4:29; Jas. 1:27; Ex. 35:21; 1 Chron. 29:19; Ezra 2:68-69

16. Our Mediator Before God

We believe and affirm that Jesus Christ is the only divinely appointed mediator between God and man. He took on human nature but was without sin. He suffered and died on the cross for the salvation of sinners. He was buried and rose on the third day. He ascended to the Father and sits at His right hand where he is living forever, mediating for His people. He is the only mediator, prophet and king of His church.

1 Tim. 2:5; Heb. 8:7; 9:15-24; 12:24; Heb. 7:25; Acts 7:25,56; Ps. 110:1; 1 Pet. 3:22; Rom. 8:34; 1 John 2:1

17. Keeping the Saints in Grace

We believe and testify that a believer saved by the sacrifice of the Lord Jesus Christ, after repen-

Isa. 41:10-13; Jude 24; 1 Pet. 1:5; 2 Pet. 2:9; 1

tance and belief, is kept in this state of grace by the power of God until the moment of disbelief (when he freely chooses to leave this keeping). For this purpose He gave the Holy Spirit to believers to comfort them, to enlighten them, and to bring them to maturity. This collaboration of the Holy Spirit and man can be seen in all parts of his life as long as he remains in grace. The will of such men is filled by the divine will; their battle with temptation and sin is supported by the power of God.

Cor. 10:13; Phil. 1:6; John 10:28; Rom. 8:26

18. Church and State

We believe and affirm that the authority of the state is clothed by God with power for maintaining order and for punishment for wrongdoing. According to the teaching of the word of God we are to obey civil laws, to fulfil our duties as citizens and to pray for all authorities of the state.

Titus 3:1; Rom. 13:1-7; 2 Pet. 2:13-17; 1 Tim. 2:1-3

19. The Hereafter

1. The Intermediary State (the situation of the soul after death).

We believe and affirm that at physical death the body, which is but dust, is buried in a tomb but the soul, which is from God (spirit), goes to heaven. In that "world" there are two states completely different and completely apart: one of joy, rest and happiness called heaven, Abraham's bosom, "heavenly house," etc., and another of anguish and suffering called hell, the place of anguish. After death the souls of those who were saved and have peace with God go to heaven; the souls of sinners go to hell. Both states are conscious and awaiting the judgement. They do not have bodies.

1. The state of the saved.

Luke 16:22; 23:43; 1 Cor. 5:1,7-8; Rev. 6:9-10; 7:9,14

2. The state of sinners. Luke 16:23; 2 Pet. 2:9,4; Matt. 8:12; 13:49-50; 2 Pet. 2:17

2. The Second Coming.

We believe and affirm that, according to the teaching of the New Testament, our Lord Jesus Christ ascended to heaven and he will come again in glory and radiance for the judgement of both the living and the dead. His coming will be seen by all but the exact time is known only by God the Father. At his coming the dead will be raised, the living believers will be changed in the twinkling of an eye and will be raptured to meet the Bridegroom. Acts 1:11; Matt. 24:30; Mark 13:26; Luke 21:27; John 14:3; 1 Thess. 1:10; 4:16; Rev. 1:7; Matt. 24:36

3. The Resurrection of the Dead.

We believe and affirm that at the second coming of the Lord the dead will rise to go to the judgement seat. The resurrected body will be a new one like the resurrected body of Jesus. With this body they will inherit everlasting life—for those who were saved, everlasting happiness, for sinners everlasting punishment. John 5:28-29; Acts 24:15; 1 Cor. 15:42,52-53; Phil. 3:21; Rev. 20:13

4. The Last Judgement.

We believe and affirm that every person will be judged by God through our Lord Jesus Christ and will receive a reward or punishment according to the kind of life he led on earth. Acts 17:30-31; Rom. 2:16; 2 Cor. 5:10; Rev. 20:12; Acts 24:25

5. The State after Judgement.

We believe and affirm that according to the New Testament teaching the saved will inherit everlasting life but the sinners will be sent to everlasting anguish, to eternal punishment in their entire being, body and soul.

Matt. 25:46; Rev. 21:3,7; 22:3-5; Matt. 25:34

1. The state of the saved.

Matt. 25:46; 26:41; Rev. 14:10-11; 21:8; 20:15

2. The state of sinners.

TR: Nicolae Gheorghita

Bulgaria
The Union of Baptist Churches in Bulgaria

Baptist beginnings in Bulgaria date back to the later half of the nineteenth century and can be attributed to at least five basic influences: (1) German refugees and immigrants from South Russia from 1867 onward, many of whom were fleeing the religious persecution there (Vasili Pavolvo was a notable effective refugee preacher in this time.); (2) colporteur work of the British and Foreign Bible Society (Jakob Klundt, for example); (3) Bulgarians who traveled abroad returning with Baptist convictions (Peter Doycheff was a key person.); (4) missionary endeavors, such as that of P. E. Petrick, a man of Slavic origin who had served in India for many years and who came under the sponsorship of the North American Baptist General Conference, a group which gave much help and assistance when possible; (5) the spontaneous Bible study groups that sprang up without evangelistic efforts.

The first Baptist church was founded in 1880 in Ruse; the church in the capital city of Sofia was founded in 1897. Bulgarians had the first gypsy Baptist church, as well as other outreach in a predominantly Eastern Orthodox land. Numbers have never been large and conditions have limited the work at various periods in Bulgarian history. They have a courageous witness in the major cities and in many mission points in villages throughout the country.

The constitution of 1947 assures religious freedom of conscience and religion; the Law on Religious Denominations of 1949 and the Statute of the Church of 1951 supplement the constitution and encourage strict governmental supervision of the freedom permitted. Baptists in Bulgaria had a confession of faith prior to World War II but have had no current one since that time.

VI
English-Speaking

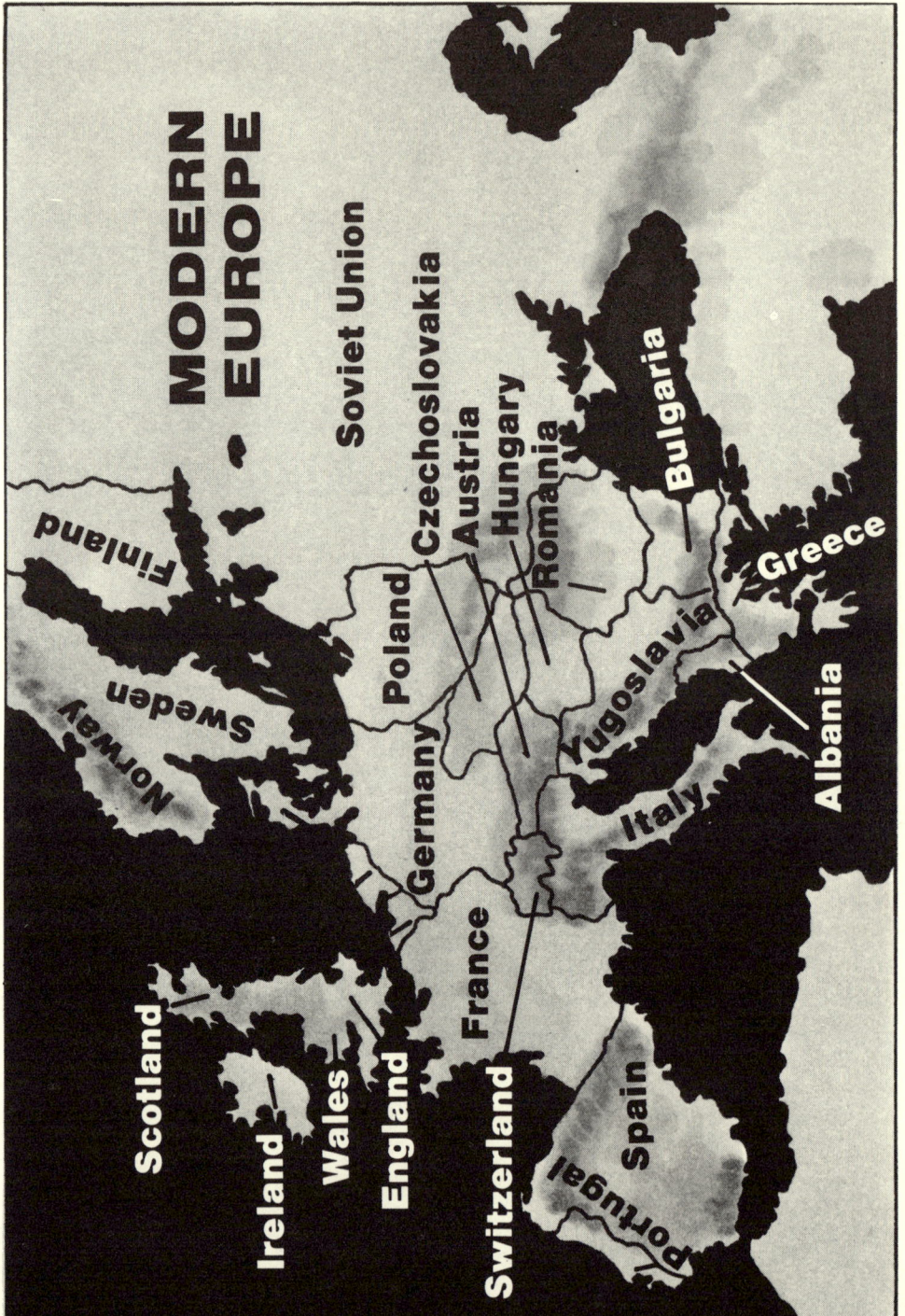

Europe
The European Baptist Convention—EBC, English Language

Europe has also experienced the birth and growth of a non-indigenous group of Baptists who have united to form the European Baptist Convention (EBC), English language. These EBC churches were founded by many post-World War II groups of English-speaking people who lived in Europe for different periods of time. Drawn together for fellowship, Bible study, prayer, worship, and Sunday School work, two churches in Germany in 1958 formed the "Association of Baptists in Continental Europe" (ABCE). The membership grew to forty-three churches in several countries. Primarily led by laymen, they met in homes on their own initiative, but eventually saw the need for organized coordination and leadership. In 1961, the ABCE and German Baptist Union asked the Foreign Mission Board of the Southern Baptist Convention for an appointee to serve as district missionary and fraternal representative to the German Union (since most of the churches were located in Germany). Over several years, four men served as "associated missionaries," helping find pastors, preaching, and being pastor to the pastors.

In 1964, the growing association became a convention (EBC) and underlined its indebtedness to Southern Baptist principles since the majority of its members came from that heritage. A restructuring of the organization eventually resulted in the office of an executive secretary whose duty it is to work for the EBC and relate to the European Baptist Federation and Baptist World Alliance. Although the EBC supports and identifies itself with the Southern Baptist Convention, it is also actively engaged in direct support of mission work in Europe.

The confession of faith utilized by the Southern Baptists (and thus, the EBC churches) is "The Baptist Faith and Message" of 1963, seen in Appendix 3.

VII
Appendixes

Appendix 1

The Apostles' Creed

The Apostles' Creed is one of the oldest and most commonly used confessions of all Christian groups. No one knows its exact original date, although some claimed that it was agreed upon by Jesus' apostles after Pentecost. It is most probably an expansion of (or collection of) early baptismal confessions. It is close to the baptismal creed recorded by Hippolytus in the early third century. Its universal appeal is probably due not only to its antiquity but also to its concise summary of early Christian teaching. The translation below follows the recent German translation. Some European Baptist unions have specifically mentioned their agreement with, or presupposing use of, the Apostles' Creed.

I believe in God, the Father, the Almighty, the creator of Heaven and Earth, and in Jesus Christ, His only begotten Son, our Lord, conceived through the Holy Spirit, born of the Virgin Mary, suffered under Pontius Pilate, was crucified, died and was buried, descended into the realm of death, on the third day resurrected from the dead ascended into heaven; He sits at the right hand of God, the almighty Father: from there he will come to judge the living and the dead. I believe in the Holy Spirit, the Holy Christian Church, the communion of the Saints, forgiveness for sins, resurrection of the dead and eternal life. Amen.

The German text of this version of the Apostle's Creed is the result of an extensive, scholarly translation from early texts by an ecumenical commission of officially appointed representatives of most major church groups (both Catholic and Protestant) in the

German-speaking areas of Europe. Baptists and other Free Church groups took part in the work. Some differences will be seen by one who is familiar with the more traditional English translation: "realm of death" is chosen rather than "hell"; "resurrected from the dead" replaces "rose again from the dead," and the Protestants utilized "the Holy Christian Church" whereas the Roman Catholics maintained the traditional wording "Holy Catholic Church."

Appendix 2

The Nicene Creed

The Nicene Creed, like the Apostles' Creed, is one of the fairly universal Christian creeds. Named for the Council of Nicea (AD 325) it actually developed over several years in response to the Arian heresy which threatened to split the early Christian church over the nature of Christ. Sometimes popularly called the "Niceno-Constantinopolitan Creed" to reflect further modification at the Council of Constantinople in 381, it continued to be changed to match current theological crises concerning the nature of Christ and the Trinity. The famous Filioque clause was added at the Third Council of Toledo in 589, effectively ending the Arian arguments. The translation below is that of the English *Book of Common Prayer*. The Baptist union of Norway "affirms the content" of the Nicene and Apostolic Creeds.

I believe in one God the Father Almighty, Maker of heaven and earth, And of all things visible and invisible:

And in one Lord Jesus Christ, the only begotten Son of God, Begotten of His Father before all worlds, God of God, Light of Light, Very God of very God, Begotten, not made, Being of one substance with the Father, by whom all things were made: Who for us men, and for our salvation came down from heaven, and was made incarnate by the Holy Ghost of the Virgin Mary, And was made man. And was crucified also for us under Pontius Pilate. He suffered and was buried, And the third day he rose again according to the Scriptures, And ascended into heaven, And sitteth on the right hand of the Father. And he shall come again with glory to judge both the quick and the dead: Whose kingdom shall have no end.

And I believe in the Holy Ghost, the Lord and the giver of life, Who proceedeth from the Father and the Son, Who with the Father and the Son together is worshipped and glorified, Who spake by the prophets. And I believe one Catholic and Apostolic Church. I acknowledge one Baptism for the remission of sins. And I look for the Resurrection of the dead, And the life of the world to come. Amen.

Appendix 3

The Baptist Faith and Message

(Adopted by Baptists in Spain, Portugal, Greece, and the EBC)

Four groups of Baptists in Europe utilize "The Baptist Faith and Message" statement of the Southern Baptist Convention: Spain, Portugal, Greece, and the European Baptist Convention (EBC). Except for the EBC churches, which are scattered in several different countries and use English anyway, these groups have translated this confession into their languages and have used it for necessary local recognition. Portugal modified it slightly. The availability of the confession due to the presence of Southern Baptist missionaries obviously played a role in their choice.

First published and approved by the Southern Baptist Convention in 1963, the confession was a modification of the 1925 version, and sought to meet "certain needs" of the new generation, even as the former version had updated the New Hampshire Confession of Faith.

The preamble to "The Baptist Faith and Message" is an integral part of the original in that it gives five statements that qualify the nature and function of the confession. These are carried over from the former confession and present a modest, noncreedal attitude toward confessions and underline not only their subordination to the Scriptures but also their lack of "finality or infallibility." The original preamble is presented below along with the confession, in order to present the reader with a more accurate context of the original.

Report of Committee On Baptist Faith and Message

Throughout its work your committee has been conscious of the contribution made by the statement of "The Baptist Faith and Message" adopted by the Southern Baptist Convention in 1925. It quotes with approval its affirmation that "Christianity is supernatural in its origin and history. We repudiate every theory of religion which denies the supernatural elements in our faith."

Furthermore, it concurs in the introductory "statement of the historic Baptist conception of the nature and function of confessions of faith in our religious and denominational life." It is, therefore, quoted in full as part of this report to the Convention.

"(1) That they constitute a consensus of opinion of some Baptist body, large or small, for the general instruction and guidance of our own people and others concerning those articles of the Christian faith which are most surely held among us. They are not intended to add anything to the simple conditions of salvation revealed in the New Testament, viz., repentance towards God and faith in Jesus Christ as Saviour and Lord.

"(2) That we do not regard them as complete statements of our faith, having any quality of finality or infallibility. As in the past so in the future Baptists should hold themselves free to revise their statements of faith as may seem to them wise and expedient at any time.

"(3) That any group of Baptists, large or small have the inherent right to draw up for themselves and publish to the world a confession of their faith whenever they may think it advisable to do so.

"(4) That the sole authority for faith and practice among Baptists is the Scriptures of the Old and New Testaments. Confessions are only guides in interpretation, having no authority over the conscience.

"(5) That they are statements of religious convictions, drawn from the Scriptures, and are not to be used to hamper freedom of thought or investigation in other realms of life."

The 1925 Statement recommended "the New Hampshire Confession of Faith, revised at certain points, and with some additional articles growing out of certain needs . . . ." Your present committee has adopted the same pattern. It has sought to build upon the structure of the 1925 Statement, keeping in mind the "certain needs" of our generation. At times it has reproduced sections of the Statement without change. In other instances it has substituted words for clarity or added sentences for emphasis. At certain points it has combined articles, with minor changes in wording, to endeavor to relate certain doctrines to each other. In still others—e.g., "God" and "Salvation"—it has sought to bring together certain truths contained throughout the 1925 Statement in order to relate them more clearly and concisely. In no case has it sought to delete from or to add to the basic contents of the 1925 Statement.

Baptists are a people who profess a living faith. This faith is rooted and grounded in Jesus Christ who is "the same yesterday, and to-day, and for ever." Therefore, the sole authority for faith and practice among Baptists is Jesus Christ whose will is revealed in the Holy Scriptures.

A living faith must experience a growing understanding of truth and must be continually interpreted and related to the needs of each new generation. Throughout their history Baptist bodies, both large and small, have issued statements of faith which comprise a consensus of their beliefs. Such statements have never been regarded as complete, infallible statements of faith, nor as official creeds carrying mandatory authority. Thus this generation of Southern Baptists is in historic succession of intent and purpose as it endeavors to state for its time and theological climate those articles of the Christian faith which are most surely held among us.

Baptists emphasize the soul's competency before God, freedom in religion, and the priesthood of the believer. However, this emphasis should not be interpreted to mean that there is an absence of certain definite doctrines that Baptists believe, cherish, and with which they have been and are now closely identified.

It is the purpose of this statement of faith and message to set forth certain teachings which we believe.

The Baptist Faith and Message

Southern Baptist Convention

I. The Scriptures

The Holy Bible was written by men divinely inspired and is the record of God's revelation of Him- Ex. 24:4; Deut. 4:1-2; 17:19; Josh. 8:34; Pss.

19:7-10; 119:11,89,105, 140; Isa. 34:16; 40:8; Jer. 15:16,36; Matt. 5:17-18; 22:29; Luke 21:33; 24:44-46; John 5:36; 16:13-15; 17:17; Acts 2:16 ff.; 17:11; Rom. 15:4; 16:25-26; 2 Tim. 3:15-17; Heb. 1:1-2; 4:12; 1 Pet. 1:25; 2 Pet. 1:19-21

self to man. It is a perfect treasure of divine instruction. It has God for its author, salvation for its end, and truth, without any mixture of error, for its matter. It reveals the principles by which God judges us; and therefore is, and will remain to the end of the world, the true center of Christian union, and the supreme standard by which all human conduct, creeds, and religious opinions should be tried. The criterion by which the Bible is to be interpreted is Jesus Christ.

II. God

There is one and only one living and true God. He is an intelligent, spiritual, and personal Being, the Creator, Redeemer, Preserver, and Ruler of the universe. God is infinite in holiness and all other perfections. To Him we owe the highest love, reverence, and obedience. The eternal God reveals Himself to us as Father, Son, and Holy Spirit, with distinct personal attributes, but without division of nature, essence, or being.

A. God the Father

Gen. 1:1; 2:7; Ex. 3:14; 6:2-3; 15:11 ff.; 20:1 ff.; Lev. 22:2; Deut. 6:4; 32:6; 1 Chron. 29:10; Ps. 19:1-3; Isa. 43:3,15; 64:8; Jer. 10:10; 17:13; Matt. 6:9 ff.; 7:11; 23:9; 28:19; Mark 1:9-11; John 4:24; 5:26; 14:6-13; 17:1-8; Acts 1:7; Rom. 8:14-15; 1 Cor. 8:6; Gal. 4:6; Eph. 4:6; Col. 1:15; 1 Tim. 1:17; Heb. 11:6; 12:9; 1 Pet. 1:17; 1 John 5:7

God as Father reigns with providential care over His universe, His creatures and the flow of the stream of human history according to the purposes of His grace. He is all powerful, all loving, and all wise. God is Father in truth to those who become children of God through faith in Jesus Christ. He is fatherly in His attitude toward all men.

B. God the Son

Gen. 18:1 ff.; Pss. 2:7 ff.; 110:1 ff.; Isa. 7:14;

Christ is the eternal Son of God. In His incarnation as Jesus Christ he was conceived of the Holy

Spirit and born of the virgin Mary. Jesus perfectly revealed and did the will of God, taking upon Himself the demands and necessities of human nature and identifying Himself completely with mankind yet without sin. He honored the divine law by His personal obedience, and in His death on the cross He made provision for the redemption of men from sin. He was raised from the dead with a glorified body and appeared to His disciples as the person who was with them before His crucifixion. He ascended into heaven and is now exalted at the right hand of God where He is the One Mediator, partaking of the nature of God and of man, and in whose Person is effected the reconciliation between God and man. He will return in power and glory to judge the world and to consummate His redemptive mission. He now dwells in all believers as the living and ever present Lord.

53; Matt. 1:18-23; 3:17; 8:29; 11:27; 14:33; 16:16,27; 17:5; 27; 28:1-6,19; Mark 1:1; 3:11; Luke 1:35; 4:41; 22:70; 24:46; John 1:1-18,29; 10:30,38; 11:25-27; 12:44-50; 14:7-11; 16:15-16,28; 17:1-5,21-22; 20:1-20,28; Acts 1:9; 2:22-24; 7:55-56; 9:4-5,20; Rom. 1:3-4; 3:23-26; 5:6-21; 8:1-3,34; 10:4; 1 Cor. 1:30; 2:2; 8:6; 15:1-8,24-28; 2 Cor. 5:19-21; Gal. 4:4-5; Eph. 1:20; 3:11; 4:7-10; Phil. 2:5-11; Col. 1:13-22; 2:9; 1 Thess. 4:14-18; 1 Tim. 2:5-6; 3:16; Titus 2:13-14; Heb. 1:1-3; 4:14-15; 7:14-28; 9:12-15,24-28; 12:2; 13:8; 1 Pet. 2:21-25; 3:22; 1 John 1:7-9; 3:2; 4:14-15; 5:9; 2 John 7-9; Rev. 1:13-16; 5:9-14; 12:10-11; 13:8; 19:16

C. God the Holy Spirit

The Holy Spirit is the Spirit of God. He inspired holy men of old to write the Scriptures. Through illumination He enables men to understand truth. He exalts Christ. He convicts of sin, of righteousness and of judgment. He calls men to the Saviour, and effects regeneration. He cultivates Christian character, comforts believers, and bestows the spiritual gifts by which they serve God through His church. He seals the believer unto the day of final redemption. His presence in the Christian is the assurance of God to bring the believer into the fulness of the stature of Christ. He enlightens and empowers the believer and the church in worship, evangelism, and service.

Gen. 1:2; Judg. 14:6; Job 26:13; Pss. 51:11; 139:7 ff.; Isa. 61:1-3; Joel 2:28-32; Matt. 1:18; 3:16; 4:1; 12:28-32; 28:19; Mark 1:10,12; Luke 1:35; 4:1,18-19; 11:13; 12:12; 24:49; John 4:24; 14:16-17,26; 15:26; 16:7-14; Acts 1:8; 2:1-4, 38; 4:31; 5:3; 6:3; 7:55; 8:17,39; 10:44; 13:2; 15:28; 16:6; 19:1-6; Rom. 8:9-11,14-16, 26-27; 1 Cor. 2:10-14; 3:16; 12:3-11; Gal. 4:6;

III. Man

Eph. 1:13-14; 4:30; 5:18; 1 Thess. 5:19; 1 Tim. 3:16; 4:1; 2 Tim. 1:14; 3:16; Heb. 9:8,14; 2 Pet. 1-21; 1 John 4:13; 5:6-7; Rev. 1:10; 22:17

Gen. 1:26-30; 2:5,7,18-22; 3; 9:6; Ps. 1; 8:3-6; 32:1-5; 51:5; Isa. 6:5; Jer. 17:5; Matt. 16:26; Acts 17:26-31; Rom. 1:19-32; 3:10-18,23; 5:6,12,19; 6:6; 7:14-25; 8:14-18,29; 1 Cor. 1:21-31; 15:19,21-22; Eph. 2:1-22; Col. 1:21-22; 3:9-11

Man was created by the special act of God, in His own image, and is the crowning work of His creation. In the beginning man was innocent of sin and was endowed by His Creator with freedom of choice. By his free choice man sinned against God and brought sin into the human race. Through the temptation of Satan man transgressed the command of God, and fell from his original innocence; whereby his posterity inherit a nature and an environment inclined toward sin, and as soon as they are capable of moral action become transgressors and are under condemnation. Only the grace of God can bring man into His holy fellowship and enable man to fulfill the creative purpose of God. The sacredness of human personality is evident in that God created man in His own image, and in that Christ died for man; therefore every man possesses dignity and is worthy of respect and Christian love.

IV. Salvation

Gen. 3:15, Ex. 3:14-17; 6:2-8; Matt. 1:21; 4:17; 16:21-26; 27:22 to 28:6; Luke 1:68-69; 2:28-32; John 1:11-14,29; 3:3-21,36; 5:24; 10:9,28-29; 15:1-16; 17:17; Acts 2:21; 4:12; 5:11; 16:30-31; 17:30-31; 20:32; Rom. 1:16-18; 2:4; 3:23-25; 4:3 ff.; 5:8-10; 6:1-23; 8:1-18,29-39;

Salvation involves the redemption of the whole man, and is offered freely to all who accept Jesus Christ as Lord and Saviour, who by His own blood obtained eternal redemption for the believer. In its broadest sense salvation includes regeneration, sanctification, and glorification.

A. Regeneration, or the new birth, is a work of God's grace whereby believers become new creatures in Christ Jesus. It is a change of heart wrought by the Holy Spirit through conviction of sin, to which

APPENDIXES

the sinner responds in repentance toward God and faith in the Lord Jesus Christ.

Repentance and faith are inseparable experiences of grace. Repentance is a genuine turning from sin toward God. Faith is the acceptance of Jesus Christ and commitment of the entire personality to Him as Lord and Saviour. Justification is God's gracious and full acquittal upon principles of His righteousness of all sinners who repent and believe in Christ. Justification brings the believer into a relationship of peace and favor with God.

B. Sanctification is the experience, beginning in regeneration, by which the believer is set apart to God's purposes, and is enabled to progress toward moral and spiritual perfection through the presence and power of the Holy Spirit dwelling in him. Growth in grace should continue throughout the regenerate person's life.

C. Glorification is the culmination of salvation and is the final blessed and abiding state of the redeemed.

10:9-10,13; 13:11-14; 1 Cor. 1:18,30; 6:19-20; 15:10; 2 Cor. 5:17-20; Gal. 2:20; 3:13; 5:22-25; 6:15; Eph. 1:7; 2:8-22; 4:11-16; Phil. 2:12-13; Col. 1:9-22; 3:1 ff.; 1 Thess. 5:23-24; 2 Tim. 1:12; Titus 2:11-14; Heb. 2:1-3; 5:8-9; 9:24-28; 11:1 to 12:8,14; James 2:14-26; 1 Pet. 1:2-23; 1 John 1:6 to 2:11; Rev. 3:20; 21:1 to 22:5

V. God's Purpose of Grace

Election is the gracious purpose of God, according to which He regenerates, sanctifies, and glorifies sinners. It is consistent with the free agency of man, and comprehends all the means in connection with the end. It is a glorious display of God's sovereign goodness, and is infinitely wise, holy, and unchangeable. It excludes boasting and promotes humility.

All true believers endure to the end. Those whom God has accepted in Christ, and sanctified by His Spirit, will never fall away from the state of grace, but shall persevere to the end. Believers may fall into sin through neglect and temptation, whereby they grieve the Spirit, impair their graces and comforts, bring reproach on the cause of Christ, and temporal

Gen. 12:1-3; Ex. 19:5-8; 1 Sam. 8:4-7,19-22; Isa. 5:1-7; Jer. 31:31 ff.; Matt. 16:18-19; 21:28-45; 24:22,31; Luke 1:68-79; 2:29-32; 19:41-44; 24:44-48; John 1:12-14; 3:16; 5:24; 6:44-45,65; 10:27-29; 15:16; 17:6,12,17-18; Acts 20:32; Rom. 5:9-10; 8:28-39; 10:12-15; 11:5-7,26-36; 1 Cor. 1:1-2; 15:24-28; Eph. 1:4-23; 2:1-10; 3:1-11; Col. 1:12-14; 2 Thess. 2:13-14; 2 Tim. 1:12;

judgments on themselves, yet they shall be kept by the power of God through faith unto salvation.

12:2; 1 Pet. 1:2-5,13; 2:4-10; 1 John 1:7-9; 2:19; 3:2

VI. The Church

A New Testament church of the Lord Jesus Christ is a local body of baptized believers who are associated by covenant in the faith and fellowship of the gospel, observing the two ordinances of Christ, committed to His teachings, exercising the gifts, rights, and privileges invested in them by His Word, and seeking to extend the gospel to the ends of the earth.

This church is an autonomous body, operating through democratic processes under the Lordship of Jesus Christ. In such a congregation members are equally responsible. Its Scriptural officers are pastors and deacons.

The New Testament speaks also of the church as the body of Christ which includes all of the redeemed of all the ages.

Matt. 16:15-19; 18:15-20; Acts 2:41-42,47; 5:11-14; 6:3-6; 13:1-3; 14:23,27; 15:1-30; 16:5; 20:28; Rom. 1:7; 1 Cor. 1:2; 3:16; 5:4-5; 7:17; 9:13-14; 12; Eph. 1:22-23; 2:19-22; 3:8-11-21; 5:22-32; Phil. 1:1; Col. 1:18; 1 Tim. 3:1-15; 4:14; 1 Pet. 5:1-4; Rev. 2—3; 21:2-3

VII. Baptism and the Lord's Supper

Christian baptism is the immersion of a believer in water in the name of the Father, the Son, and the Holy Spirit. It is an act of obedience symbolizing the believer's faith in a crucified, buried, and risen Saviour, the believer's death to sin, the burial of the old life, and the resurrection to walk in newness of life in Christ Jesus. It is a testimony to his faith in the final resurrection of the dead. Being a church ordinance, it is prerequisite to the privileges of church membership and to the Lord's Supper.

The Lord's Supper is a symbolic act of obedience whereby members of the church, through partaking of the bread and the fruit of the vine, memorialize the death of the Redeemer and anticipate His second coming.

Matt. 3:13-17; 26:26-30; 18:19-20; Mark 1:9-11; 14:22-26; Luke 3:21-22; 22:19-20; John 3:23; Acts 2:41-42; 8:35-39; 20:7; Rom. 6:3-5; 1 Cor. 10:16,21; 11:23-29; Col. 2:12

VIII. The Lord's Day

The first day of the week is the Lord's Day. It is a Christian institution for regular observance. It commemorates the resurrection of Christ from the dead and should be employed in exercises of worship and spiritual devotion, both public and private, and by refraining from worldly amusements, and resting from secular employments, work of necessity and mercy only being excepted.

Ex. 20:8-11; Matt. 12:1-12; 28:1 ff.; Mark 2:27-28; 16:1-7; Luke 24:1-3,33-36; John 4:21-24; 20:1,19-28; Acts 20:7; 1 Cor. 16:1-2; Col. 2:16; 3:16; Rev. 1:10

IX. The Kingdom

The Kingdom of God includes both His general sovereignty over the universe and His particular kingship over men who willfully acknowledge Him as King. Particularly the Kingdom is the realm of salvation into which men enter by trustful, childlike commitment to Jesus Christ. Christians ought to pray and to labor that the Kingdom may come and God's will be done on earth. The full consummation of the Kingdom awaits the return of Jesus Christ and the end of this age.

Gen. 1:1; Isa. 9:6-7; Jer. 23:5-6; Matt. 3:2; 4:8-10,23; 12:25-28; 13:1-52; 25:31-46; 26:29; Mark 1:14-15; 9:1; Luke 4:43; 8:1; 9:2; 12:31-32; 17:20-21; 23:42; John 3:3; 18:36; Acts 1:6-7; 17:22-31; Rom. 5:17; 8:19; 1 Cor. 15:24-28; Col. 1:13; Heb. 11:10,16; 12:28; 1 Pet. 2:4-10; 4:13; Rev. 1:6,9; 5:10; 11:15; 21—22

X. Last Things

God, in His own time and in His own way, will bring the world to its appropriate end. According to His promise, Jesus Christ will return personally and visibly in glory to the earth; the dead will be raised; and Christ will judge all men in righteousness. The unrighteous will be consigned to Hell, the place of everlasting punishment. The righteous in their resurrected and glorified bodies will receive their reward and will dwell forever in Heaven with the Lord.

Isa. 2:4; 11:9; Matt. 16:27; 18:8-9; 19:28; 24:27,30,36,44; 5:31-46; 26:64; Mark 8:38; 9:43-48; Luke 12:40,48; 16:19-26; 17:22-37; 21:27-28; John 14:1-3; Acts 1:11; 17:31; Rom. 14:10; 1 Cor. 4:5; 15:24-28,35-58; 2 Cor. 5:10; Phil. 3:20-21; Col. 1:5; 3:4; 1 Thess. 4:14-18; 5:1 ff.; 2 Thess. 1:7 ff.; 2; 1 Tim. 6:14; 2 Tim. 4:1,8; Titus 2:13; Heb. 9:27-28; Jas. 5:8; 2 Pet. 3:7 ff.; 1 John 2:28;

3:2; Jude 14; Rev. 1:18; 3:11; 20:1 to 22:13

Gen. 12:1-3; Ex. 19:5-6; Isa. 6:1-8; Matt. 9:37-38; 10:5-15; 13:18-30,37-43; 16:19; 22:9-10; 24:14; 28:18-20; Luke 10:1-18; 24:46-53; John 14:11-12; 15:7-8; 16; 17:15; 20:21; Acts 1:8; 2; 8:26-40; 10:42-48; 13:2-3; Rom. 10:13-15; Eph. 3:1-11; 1 Thess. 1:8; 2 Tim. 4:5; Heb. 2:1-3; 11:39 to 12:2; 1 Pet. 2:4-10; Rev. 22:17

Deut. 4:1,5,9,14; 6:1-10; 31:12-13; Neh. 8:1-8; Job 28:28; Pss. 19:7 ff.; 118:11; Prov. 3:13 ff.; 4:1-10; 8:1-7,11; 15:14; Eccl. 7:19; Matt. 5:2; 7:24 ff.; 28:19-20; Luke 2:40; 1 Cor. 1:18-31; Eph. 4:11-16; Phil. 4:8; Col. 2:3,8-9; 1 Tim. 1:3-7; 2 Tim. 2:15; 3:14-17; Heb. 5:12 to 6:3; Jas. 1:5; 3:17

Gen. 14:20; Lev. 27:30-32; Deut. 8:18; Mal. 3:8-12; Matt. 6:1-4,19-21; 19:21;

XI. Evangelism and Missions

It is the duty and privilege of every follower of Christ and of every church of the Lord Jesus Christ to endeavor to make disciples of all nations. The new birth of man's spirit by God's Holy Spirit means the birth of love for others. Missionary effort on the part of all rests thus upon a spiritual necessity of the regenerate life, and is expressly and repeatedly commanded in the teachings of Christ. It is the duty of every child of God to seek constantly to win the lost to Christ by personal effort and by all other methods in harmony with the gospel of Christ.

XII. Education

The cause of education in the Kingdom of Christ is co-ordinate with the causes of missions and general benevolence, and should receive along with these the liberal support of the churches. An adequate system of Christian schools is necessary to a complete spiritual program for Christ's people.

In Christian education there should be a proper balance between academic freedom and academic responsibility. Freedom in any orderly relationship of human life is always limited and never absolute. The freedom of a teacher in a Christian school, college, or seminary is limited by the pre-eminence of Jesus Christ, by the authoritative nature of the Scriptures, and by the distinct purpose for which the school exists.

XIII. Stewardship

God is the source of all blessings, temporal and spiritual; all that we have and are we owe to Him. Christians have a spiritual debtorship to the whole

APPENDIXES

world, a holy trusteeship in the gospel, and a binding stewardship in their possessions. They are therefore under obligation to serve Him with their time, talents, and material possessions; and should recognize all these as entrusted to them to use for the glory of God and for helping others. According to the Scriptures, Christians should contribute of their means cheerfully, regularly, systematically, proportionately, and liberally for the advancement of the Redeemer's cause on earth.

23:23; 25:14-29; Luke 12:16-21,42; 16:1-13; Acts 2:44-47; 5:1-11; 17:24-25; 20:35; Rom. 6:6-22; 12:1-12; 1 Cor. 4:1-4; 6:19-20; 12; 16:1-4; 2 Cor. 8—9; 12:15; Phil. 4:10-19; 1 Pet. 1:18-19

XIV. Cooperation

Christ's people should, as occasion requires, organize such associations and conventions as may best secure cooperation for the great objects of the Kingdom of God. Such organizations have no authority over one another or over the churches. They are voluntary and advisory bodies designed to elicit, combine, and direct the energies of our people in the most effective manner. Members of New Testament churches should cooperate with one another in carrying forward the missionary, educational, and benevolent ministries for the extension of Christ's Kingdom. Christian unity in the New Testament sense is spiritual harmony and voluntary cooperation for common ends by various groups of Christ's people. Cooperation is desirable between the various Christian denominations, when the end to be attained is itself justified, and when such cooperation involves no violation of conscience or compromise of loyalty to Christ and His Word as revealed in the New Testament.

Ex. 17:12; 18:17 ff.; Judg. 7:21; Ezra 1:3-4; 2:68-69; 5:14-15; Neh. 4; 8:1-5; Matt. 10:5-15; 20:1-16; 22:1-10; 28:19-20; Mark 2:3; Luke 10:1 ff.; Acts 1:13-14; 2:1 ff.; 4:31-37; 13:2-3; 15:1-35; 1 Cor. 1:10-17; 3:5-15; 12; 2 Cor. 8—9; Gal. 1:6-10; Eph. 4:1-16; Phil. 1:15-18

XV. The Christian and the Social Order

Every Christian is under obligation to seek to make the will of Christ supreme in his own life and in human society. Means and methods used for the im-

Ex. 20:3-17; Lev. 6:2-5; Deut. 10:12; 27:17; Ps. 101:5; Mic. 6:8; Zech. 8:16; Matt. 5:13-16,

43-48; 22:36-40; 25:35; Mark 1:29-34; 2:3 ff.; 10:21; Luke 4:18-21; 10:27-37; 20:25; John 15:12; 17:15; Rom. 12—14; 1 Cor. 5:9-10; 6:1-7; 7:20-24; 10:23 to 11:1; Gal. 3:26-28; Eph. 6:5-9; Col. 3:12-17; 1 Thess. 3:12; Phil.; Jas. 1:27; 2:8

provement of society and the establishment of righteousness among men can be truly and permanently helpful only when they are rooted in the regeneration of the individual by the saving grace of God in Christ Jesus. The Christian should oppose in the spirit of Christ every form of greed, selfishness, and vice. He should work to provide for the orphaned, the needy, the aged, the helpless, and the sick. Every Christian should seek to bring industry, government, and society as a whole under the sway of the principles of righteousness, truth, and brotherly love. In order to promote these ends Christians should be ready to work with all men of good will in any good cause, always being careful to act in the spirit of love without compromising their loyalty to Christ and His truth.

XVI. Peace and War

Isa. 2:4; Matt. 5:9,38-48; 6:33; 26:52; Luke 22:36,38; Rom. 12:18-19; 13:1-7; 14:19; Heb. 12:14; Jas. 4:1-2

It is the duty of Christians to seek peace with all men on principles of righteousness. In accordance with the spirit and teachings of Christ they should do all in their power to put an end to war.

The true remedy for the war spirit is the gospel of our Lord. The supreme need of the world is the acceptance of His teachings in all the affairs of men and nations, and the practical applications of His law of love.

XVII. Religious Liberty

Gen. 1:27; 2:7; Matt. 6:6-7,24; 16:26; 22:21; John 8:36; Acts 4:19-20; Rom. 6:1-2; 13:1-7; Gal. 5:1,13; Phil. 3:20; 1 Tim. 2:1-2; Jas. 4:12; 1 Pet. 2:12-17; 3:11-17; 4:12-19

God alone is the Lord of the conscience, and He has left it free from the doctrines and commandment of men which are contrary to His Word or not contained in it. Church and state should be separate. The state owes to every church protection and full freedom in the pursuit of its spiritual ends. In providing for such freedom no ecclesiastical group of denomination should be favored by the state more than others. Civil government being ordained of God, it is the duty of Christians to render loyal obedience thereto in all things not contrary to the revealed will of God. The church should not resort to the civil power to carry on its work. The gospel of Christ contemplates spiritual means alone for the pursuit of its ends. The state has no right to impose penalties for religious opinions of any kind. The state has no right to impose taxes for the support of any form of religion. A free church in a free state is the Christian ideal, and this implies the right of free and unhindered access to God on the part of all men, and the right to form and propagate opinions in the sphere of religion without interference by the civil power.

Appendix 4

A Norwegian Postscript

A lively public debate about the authority of the Bible occurred in the 1960s in Norway with charges by some non-Baptists that some Baptist theologians were not "orthodox" in their teaching about the Bible. A special committee drafted the statement below and presented it to the pastor's conference in September 1966. Since that time it has been widely cited and referred to in debates and publications. Although not formally acted upon by the national assembly of Baptists, it is generally regarded as an authoritative Baptist document.

(Peter Eidberg)

Statement Concerning the Bible

In the last years even the Baptists have had a debate concerning their view of the Bible. The following statements represent certain views generally held by Norwegian Baptists.

1. We believe that the Bible is God's inspired word, given to us as a historical document. It is the final content of God's revelation; it speaks of a divine creation, gives us the law and the prophetic word and leads us to Jesus Christ and the apostolic time.
2. We believe that the center of God's revelation is Jesus Christ. In him the Scripture has its highest authority and on him it must be tested.
3. We believe however that only a formal confession of the Bible is not enough. A true understanding of the Bible also includes a true understanding of the great truths of salvation. As an example we

mention the Scripture's view of Jesus Christ who is God who became flesh, who died and arose for our salvation.
4. We believe that the Holy Spirit is the Word's life principle. The Word and the Spirit cannot be separated. The Spirit's testimony is Jesus Christ and as the Scripture says, "He [the Spirit] shall take from me and proclaim for you."
5. We believe that the gospel is God's offer of salvation which every individual must accept or reject. The gospel is always relevant and reaches its purpose when people come into fellowship with God.

Appendix 5
Statutes of the UCECB (Dissident) Baptists

The controversy among Soviet Baptists over registration and other matters led eventually to the formation of the UCECB (Union of Churches of Evangelical Christians—Baptists) or Dissident Baptists. They first compiled the statutes published below in 1965 when they formally separated from the All-Union Council of Evangelical Christians—Baptists. They were reprinted on a secret press in 1974 and seem to serve as a guideline for dealing with local authorities, as well as an internal guideline.

Keston College in England which specializes in the study of religious communities in the Soviet Union and Eastern Europe gives a brief commentary as a preface to their translation of the statutes. It says in part:

These statutes are interesting from several points of view. They are called the statutes of the "Union" of Evangelical Christians—Baptist Churches. A study of the text of the statutes reveals that this "Union" includes registered and unregistered churches which recognize the leadership of the Council of Churches (here defined as a body of 15-17 ministers, with its headquarters in Moscow). Such a Union does not exist in reality—it simply reflects the attitude of the reform Baptist leadership, which sees itself as the true representative of the whole ECB movement in the Soviet Union.

Although the wording of the statutes bears an occasional resemblance to Soviet legislation on religion, there are a number of clear deviations which constitute a greater or lesser challenge to the state. For example, paragraph 33 states that official registration may not be a pretext for the violation of the separation of church and state: in other words, even if a church is granted registration, it will not comply with

APPENDIXES

any regulations which infringe its independence. Also paragraph 43 states that the finances of a local church are administered by the church at its own discretion. This is an open challenge to Soviet regulations which forbid certain uses of church finances, for example for charitable purposes.

At the same time, it must be noted again that these statutes underline the basically loyal civil attitude of the reform Baptists (see for example paragraph 35, last section).

(Keston College, Translation service No. 6, 1976)

The statute translation following is that of RCDA.

Statutes of the Union of Churches of Evangelical Christians-Baptists (Dissidents)

I. The UCECB

1. General Information
   1) The Union of Churches of Evangelical Christians-Baptists is a voluntary association of independent and equal churches, confessing the Evangelical Baptist creed, which is based upon the Holy Scriptures—the Books of the Old and New Testaments (canonical).
   2) The only statutes for the spiritual activity of the UCECB is the Word of God (the Bible). The present statutes are a collection of rules necessary for the conduct of those aspects of the activity which relate to the civil and legal norms of life.
   3) On the basis of the principle of the separation of church and state, the Union of Churches of ECB, its administrative organs and departments, and its member churches are completely free in their spiritual and internal activity and are associations of like-minded believing citizens which are independent of the state.

2. Goals and Tasks of the Union

"I press toward the mark for the high calling" (Phil. 3:13-14). "After ye have done the will of God, ye might receive the promise" (Heb. 10:36).
   4) The Union of Churches of ECB sets before itself the goals and

tasks established by the Lord for His disciples:
a) to preach the Gospel of Jesus Christ to all people (Mark 16:15-16);
b) to achieve a higher spiritual level of holiness and Christian piety for all the people of God (Rev. 22:11; 2 Tim. 3:17);
c) to achieve the association and unity of all churches and of all ECB believers, on the basis of purity and holiness, in a single brotherhood in Christ (John 17:21; Eph. 4:13).

3. The Composition and Structure of the Union

"From whom the whole body fitly joined together and compacted by that which every joint supplieth, according to the effectual working in the measure of every part, maketh increased of the body unto the edifying itself in love" (Eph. 4:16).

5) The Union of Churches of ECB unites all legally registered and unregistered local ECB churches active on all the territory of the USSR. Religious associations of other denominations, which are similar in faith, may be received into the body of the Union of Churches of ECB on the condition that they recognize the doctrines of the Evangelical Christians-Baptists and are governed by the Word of God in life, ministry and activity.
6) A local church informs the governing organ of the Union (The Council of Churches of ECB) of its decision to join the Union of Churches of ECB, by declaration.
7) Each local church enjoys the right to withdraw from the Union of Churches of ECB freely.
8) The Union of Churches may have fraternal fellowship with ECB churches and associations of other denominations of similar faith that are not members of the Union of Churches of ECB, provided that they are governed by the doctrines of the Evangelical Christians-Baptists.

4. Leadership of the Union

"Without counsel, purposes are disappointed: but in the multitude of counsellors they are established" (Prov. 15:22). "And the apostles and elders came together for to consider this matter" (Acts 15:6).

9) The highest governing organ, determining all the activity of the

APPENDIXES

union, is the All-Union Congress of Evangelical Christians-Baptists.

10) For the execution of the decisions of the congress and the conduct of the activity of the Union in the period between congresses, the All-Union Congress elects a Council of Churches of Evangelical Christians-Baptists (CCECB), composed of 15-17 ministers of ECB churches.

11) The Council of Churches of ECB organizes departments: evangelists, publication, etc.

12) The regular All-Union Congress is called once every three years. The standards of representation at the All-Union Congress, and also the place and time of its convocation, are determined by the Council of Churches of ECB.

5. Ministry and Activity of the Council of Churches of Evangelical Christians-Baptists

"The care of all the churches" (2 Cor. 11:28). "And whatsoever ye do in word or deed, do all in the name of the Lord Jesus" (Col. 3:17).

13) The ministry and activity of the Council of Churches of ECB are determined by the goals and tasks, established by the congress and expressed in the present statutes, and they should be carried out in full accordance with the teachings of Jesus Christ.

14) The Council of Churches is responsible for:
   a) giving spiritual and organizational help to local churches, and the district and inter-district fraternal councils. The CCECB maintains ties with them both through correspondence and through visitation by its representatives;
   b) publication and supply for the ECB churches of the necessary religious literature;
   c) organization of Bible and choir directing courses and seminars;
   d) conduct, within the limits of the law, of external representation of the ECB churches both in the USSR and abroad.

15) The Council of Churches of ECB has a seal and stamp.

16) The location of the offices of the Council of Churches of ECB is the City of Moscow.

17) The Council of Churches gives account for all its activity to the All-Union Congress of representatives of Evangelical Christians-Baptist churches.

6. Finances of the Union

"Praying us with much intreaty that we would receive the gift, and take upon us the fellowship of the ministering to the saints" (2 Cor. 8:4).
18) The finances of the Union consist of:
   a) voluntary assignments and contributions of local ECB churches;
   b) voluntary contributions of individual persons;
   c) other income received.
19) Auditing of the finances of the Union is carried out by an Auditing Commission, elected by the Congress and composed of three persons. The commission reports the results of its audit to the regular All-Union Congress of representatives of Evangelical Christians-Baptist Churches.

7. Termination of the Activity of the Union

20) A resolution concerning the termination of the activity of the Union is accepted exclusively by the All-Union Congress of representatives of ECB churches, as the highest governing organ of the Union of Churches of ECB.

II. District (Territorial) and Inter-District Associations of ECB Churches

"Every purpose is established by counsel" (Prov. 20:18).
"For the perfecting of the saints, for the work of the ministry, for the edifying of the body of Christ" (Eph. 4:12).
21) All spiritual and organizational activity in the provinces is carried out by district (territorial) and inter-district associations of ECB churches in the person of their governing organs.
22) The governing organs of the associations are the conferences of representatives of ECB churches that are members of the given association and the fraternal council of the associations elected by the conferences.
23) The period of the conferences and the number of members of the district (territorial) and inter-district fraternal councils are determined by the conferences of the representatives of ECB churches comprising the associations.
24) In their spiritual and organizational activity, district (territorial) and inter-district fraternal councils are governed by the Word of God,

by the decision of the conferences of their associations, and by the objectives and tasks of the Union of Churches of ECB (Par. 4), and they give account to:
a) district (territorial) and inter-district conferences of representatives of the ECB churches;
b) the Council of Churches of ECB.
25) Expenses connected with the activity of district (territorial) and inter-district associations are covered out of the finances received from local churches for the Union of Churches of ECB.

III. The Local ECB Church

"That thou mayest know how thou oughtest to behave thyself in the house of God, which is the church of the living God, the pillar and ground of the truth" (1 Tim. 3:15).

8. Objectives and Tasks of the Local Church

26) The ECB Church is an association of believing citizens of the Evangelical Baptist creed, united for joint satisfaction of their spiritual needs and having the goal of the preaching of the Gospel of Jesus Christ for the salvation of sinners and the achievement of holiness and Christian piety by believers, expressed in love for God and neighbor (Mark 16:15-16; 1 Thess. 4:3; Mark 12:30-31).
27) For the accomplishment of these stated objectives the ECB church conducts meetings for the preaching of the Gospel, prayer, study of the Holy Scriptures and other spiritual requirements. Congregational and choral singing, with musical accompaniment, is an integral part of divine worship.
28) All citizens, including children, are guaranteed free attendance at worship services.
29) Worship services of local ECB churches are conducted on Sundays, Christian holidays, and on other days of the week according to the authorization of the church.
30) The premises for worship services of the ECB church may be granted both by the state and by private individuals.
31) The ECB church participates in district (territorial), inter-district, and all-union conferences and congresses of ministers of ECB churches and is linked with other local ECB churches both in its

own district and beyond its boundaries; by its particpation it comprehensively supports the activity of the Council of Churches of ECB.

9. Relationship to the Government

"My kingdom is not of this world" (John 18:36).
"Render therefore unto Caesar the things which are Caesar's; and unto God the things that are God's" (Matt. 22:21).

32) The local ECB church is an association of likeminded believing citizens, completely free and independent of the state.
33) The election and dismissal of ministers, the reception of members and their excommunication, the conduct of religious rites, general and members' meetings are conducted by the church in observation of the principle of the separation of church and state. Registration of the ECB churches with the organs of government should not serve as an occasion for violation of the principle of the independence of the church from the state.

10. Composition of the Local Church and the Obligations of the Members of the Church

"For we are his workmanship, created in Christ Jesus unto good works, which God hath before ordained that we should walk in them" (Eph. 2:10).

34) Each person who has believed in Christ as his personal Saviour, has turned to God in repentance, has received water baptism upon profession of faith, and is guided by the Word of God in his life may be a member of the ECB church.
35) Guided by the Word of God, the member of the church is called:
—to grow in knowledge of the Lord Jesus Christ (2 Pet. 3:18).
—to witness regarding Christ by word and life (Rom. 1:16).
—to act in his relationship with people according to the teaching of Christ: (Matt. 7:12), and do not do toward others what you do not wish for yourself (Acts 15:20).
—to labor conscientiously, "doing with his hands the thing that is useful, so that he will have something to give to him who is in need" (Eph. 4:28), for it is said in the Scripture: "if anyone does not wish to work, he shall not eat" (2 Thess. 3:10).
—to take active part in the life of the church, and to perform

service according to his calling (Rom. 12:6-11); not to miss meetings (Heb. 10:25) and to bear responsibility for the spiritual condition of the church and its members (Gal. 6:1-2).

—to manifest concern for relatives and to be a model in the family, to preserve peace and holiness (Heb. 12:14), to educate his children in the teachings and admonition of the Lord (Eph. 6:4), and to strive to serve the Lord with all his house (Josh. 24:15).

—to manifest submission to the civil laws according to the teaching of Jesus Christ: 'render to Caesar what is Caesar's, and to God what is God's (Mark 12:17), and to pray for the government, that it will exercise the authority entrusted to it in accordance with the will of God in order to preserve peace and justice (Rom. 13:5,7; Titus 3:1; Acts 5:20; 1 Tim. 2:1-4).

11. Administration of the Local Church

"Take heed therefore unto yourselves, and to all the flock, over the which the Holy Ghost hath made you overseers, to feed the church of God which he hath purchased with his own blood" (Acts 20:28).

36) The highest organ of administration of the local ECB church is the members' meeting of the given church.
37) All important questions, such as reception of members, excommunication, election of ministers, and others, are decided by the members' meeting of the church.
38) For conduct of the daily ministry and spiritual education of the members, the church elects a presbyter, deacons, and a church council comprised of as many members as the church itself stipulates. In their activity, the presbyter, deacons and church council are responsible to the members' meeting.
39) All church institutions, such as baptism, marriage, burial, prayers for the sick and prayers for children are conducted by the presbyter and ministers elected for this by the church.
40) Both members of the given church and ministers of other churches, on authorization of the church council, may participate in preaching and worship services.
41) The presbyter of the given church bears the chief responsibility for the conduct of worship services.
42) External representation of the local church in matters relating to registration, conclusion of agreements for the use of property, etc.,

are carried out by three members of the church, elected by the church. The final decision of questions related to registration and relations with governmental organs resides in the members' meeting of the church.

12. Finances of the Local Church

"Every man according as he purposeth in his heart, so let him give; not grudgingly, or of necessity; for God loveth a cheerful giver" (2 Cor. 9:7).

43) Finances of the local church consist of the voluntary contributions of believers and are disbursed for the needs of the work of God under supervision of the church itself.
44) The local church keeps an inventory book, in which is entered the property received from the state as well as that which has been purchased and donated.
45) An audit of the finances and material valuables is conducted by an auditing commission, elected by the church, comprised of three members. The commission notifies the church of the results of its audit.

13. Closing of a Local Church

46) The activity of a local ECB church may be terminated only upon decision of the members' meeting of the given church.

Council of Churches of
Evangelical Christians-Baptists

November 30, 1965   Translated from the Russian

Published with permission of Religion in Communist-Dominated Areas (RCDA)

Appendix 6
The Lausanne Covenant

Introduction

We, members of the Church of Jesus Christ, from more than 150 nations, participants in the International Congress on World Evangelization at Lausanne, praise God for his great salvation and rejoice in the fellowship he has given us with himself and with each other. We are deeply stirred by what God is doing in our day, moved to penitence by our failures and challenged by the unfinished task of evangelization. We believe the Gospel is God's good news for the whole world, and we are determined by his grace to obey Christ's commission to proclaim it to all mankind and to make disciples of every nation. We desire, therefore, to affirm our faith and our resolve, and to make public our covenant.

1. The Purpose of God

We affirm our belief in the one-eternal God, Creator and Lord of all the world, Father, Son and Holy Spirit, who governs all things according to the purpose of his will. He has been calling out from the world a people for himself, and sending his people back into the world to be his servants and his witnesses, for the extension of his kingdom, the building up of Christ's body, and the glory of his name. We confess with shame that we have often denied our calling and failed in our mission, by becoming conformed to the world or by withdrawing from it. Yet we rejoice that even when borne by earthen vessels the gospel is still a precious treasure. To the task of making that treasure known in the power of the Holy Spirit we desire to dedicate ourselves anew.

Isa. 40:28; Matt. 28:19; Eph. 1:11; Acts 15:14; John 17:6,18; Eph. 4:12; 1 Cor. 5:10; Rom. 12:2; 2 Cor. 4:7

2. The Authority and Power of the Bible

2 Tim. 3:16; 2 Pet. 1:21; John 10:35; Isa. 55:11; 1 Cor. 1:21; Rom. 1:16; Matt. 5:17-18; Jude 3; Eph. 1:17-18; 3:10,18

We affirm the divine inspiration, truthfulness and authority of both Old and New Testament Scriptures in their entirety as the only written word of God, without error in all that it affirms, and the only infallible rule of faith and practice. We also affirm the power of God's word to accomplish his purpose of salvation. The message of the Bible is addressed to all mankind. For God's revelation in Christ and in Scripture is unchangeable. Through it the Holy Spirit still speaks today. He illumines the minds of God's people in every culture to perceive its truth freshly through their own eyes and thus discloses to the whole church ever more of the many coloured wisdom of God.

3. The Uniqueness and Univerality of Christ

Gal. 1:6-9; Rom. 1:18-32; 1 Tim. 2:5-6; Acts 4:12; John 3:16-19; 2 Pet. 3:9; 2 Thess. 1:7-9; John 4:42; Matt. 11:28; Eph. 1:20,21; Phil. 2:9-11

We affirm that there is only one Saviour and only one gospel, although there is a wide diversity of evangelistic approaches. We recognize that all men have some knowledge of God through his general revelation in nature. But we deny that this can save for men suppress the truth by their unrighteousness. We also reject as derogatory to Christ and the gospel every kind of syncretism and dialogue which implies that Christ speaks equally through all religions and ideologies. Jesus Christ, being himself the only God-man, who gave himself as the only ransom for sinners, is the only mediator between God and man. There is no other name by which we must be saved. All men are perishing because of sin, but God loves all men, not wishing that any should perish but that all should repent. Yet those who reject Christ repudiate the joy of salvation and condemn themselves to eternal separation from God. To proclaim Jesus as "the Saviour of the world" is not to affirm that all men are either automatically or ultimately saved, still less to affirm that all religions offer salvation in Christ. Rather it is to proclaim God's love for a world of sinners and to invite all men to respond to him as Saviour and Lord in the wholehearted personal commitment of repentance and faith. Jesus Christ has been exalted above every other name; we long for the day when every knee shall bow to him and every tongue shall confess him Lord.

4. The Nature of Evangelism

To evangelize is to spread the good news that Jesus Christ died for our sins and was raised from the dead according to the Scriptures, and that as the reigning Lord he now offers forgiveness of sins and the liberating gift of the Spirit to all who repent and believe. Our Christian presence in the world is indispensable to evangelism, and so is that kind of dialogue whose purpose is to listen sensitively in order to understand. But evangelism itself is the proclamation of the historical, biblical Christ as Saviour and Lord, with a view to pursuading people to come to him personally and so be reconciled to God. In issuing the gospel invitation we have no liberty to conceal the cost of discipleship. Jesus still calls all who would follow him to deny themselves, take up their cross, and identify themselves with his new community. The results of evangelism include obedience to Christ, incorporation into his church and responsible service in the world.

1 Cor. 15:3-4; Acts 2:32-39; John 20:21; 1 Cor. 1:23; 2 Cor. 4:5; 5:11,20; Luke 14:25-33; Mark 8:34; Acts 2:40,47; Mark 10:43-45

5. Christian Social Responsibility

We affirm that God is both the Creator and Judge of all men. We therefore should share his concern for justice and reconciliation throughout human society and for the liberation of men from every kind

Acts 17:26,31; Gen. 18:25; Isa. 1:17; Ps. 45:7; Gen. 1:26-27; Jas. 3:9; Lev. 19:18; Luke 6:27,35; Jas. 2:14-16; John 3:3,5;

of oppression. Because mankind is made in the image of God, every person, regardless of race, religion, colour, culture, class, sex or age, has an intrinsic dignity because of which he should be respected and served, not exploited. Here too we express penitence both for our neglect and having sometimes regarded evangelism and social concern as mutually exclusive. Although reconciliation with man is not reconciliation with God, nor is social action evangelism, nor is political liberation salvation, nevertheless we affirm that evangelism and socio-political involvement are both part of our Christian duty. For both are necessary expressions of our doctrines of God and man, our love for our neighbour and our obedience to Jesus Christ. The message of salvation implies also a message of judgment upon every form of alienation, oppression and discrimination, and we should not be afraid to denounce evil and injustice wherever they exist. When people receive Christ they are born again into his kingdom and must seek not only to exhibit but also to spread its righteousness in the midst of an unrighteous world. The salvation we claim should be transforming us in the totality of our personal and social responsibilities. Faith without works is dead.

Matt. 5:20; 6:33; 2 Cor. 3:18; Jas. 2:20

6. Church and Evangelism

We affirm that Christ sends his redeemed people into the world as the Father sent him, and that this calls for a similar deep and costly penetration of the world. We need to break out of our ecclesiastical ghettos and permeate non-Christian society. In the church's mission of sacrificial service evangelism is primary. World evangelization requires the whole church to take the whole gospel to the whole world. The church is at the very centre of God's cosmic pur-

John 17:18; 20:21; Matt. 28:19-20; Acts 1:8; 20:27; Eph. 1:9-10; 3:9-11; Gal. 6:14,17; 2 Cor. 6:3-4; 2 Tim. 2:19-21; Phil. 1:27

APPENDIXES

pose and is his appointed means of spreading the gospel. But a church which preaches the cross must itself be marked by the cross. It becomes a stumbling block to evangelism when it betrays the gospel or lacks a living faith in God, a genuine love for people, or scrupulous honesty in all things including promotion and finance. The church is the community of God's people rather than an institution, and must not be identified with any particular culture, social or political system, or human ideology.

7. Cooperation in Evangelism

We affirm that the church's visible unity in truth is God's purpose. Evangelism also summons us to unity, because our oneness strengthens our witness, just as our disunity undermines our gospel of reconciliation. We recognize, however, that organizational unity may take many forms and does not necessarily forward evangelism. Yet we who share the same biblical faith should be closely united in fellowship, work and witness. We confess that our testimony has sometimes been marred by sinful individualism and needless duplication. We pledge ourselves to seek a deeper unity in truth, worship, holiness and mission. We urge the development of regional and functional cooperation for the furtherance of the church's mission, for strategic planning, for mutual encouragement, and for the sharing of resources and experience.

<small>John 17:21,23; Eph. 4:3-4; John 13:35; Phil. 1:27; John 17:11-23</small>

8. Churches in Evangelistic Partnership

We rejoice that a new missionary era has dawned. The dominant role of western missions is fast disappearing. God is raising up from the younger churches a great new resource for world evangelization, and is thus demonstrating that the responsibility

<small>Rom. 1:8; Phil. 1:5; 4:15; Acts 13:1-3; 1 Thess. 1:6-8</small>

to evangelize belongs to the whole body of Christ. All churches should therefore be asking God and themselves what they should be doing both to reach their own area and to send missionaries to other parts of the world. A re-evaluation of our missionary responsibility and role should be continuous. Thus a growing partnership of churches will develop and the universal character of Christ's church will be more clearly exhibited. We also thank God for agencies which labour in Bible translation, theological education, the mass media, Christian literature, evangelism, missions, church renewal and other specialist fields. They too should engage in constant self-examination to evaluate their effectiveness as part of the Church's mission.

9. The Urgency of the Evangelistic Task

John 9:4; Matt. 9:35-38; Rom. 9:1-3; 1 Cor. 9:19-23; Mark 16:15; Isa. 58:6-7; Jas. 1:27; 2:1-9; Matt. 25:31-46; Acts 2:44-45; 4:34-35

More than 2,700 million people, which is more than two-thirds of mankind, have yet to be evangelized. We are ashamed that so many have been neglected; it is a standing rebuke to us and to the whole church. There is now, however, in many parts of the world an unprecedented receptivity to the Lord Jesus Christ. We are convinced that this is the time for churches and para-church agencies to pray earnestly for the salvation of the unreached and to launch new efforts to achieve world evangelization. A reduction of foreign missionaries and money in an evangelized country may sometimes be necessary to faciliate the national church's growth in self-reliance and to release resources for unevangelized areas. Missionaries should flow ever more freely from and to all six continents in a spirit of humble service. The goal should be, by all available means and at the earliest possible time, that every person will have the opportunity to hear, understand, and receive the

APPENDIXES

good news. We cannot hope to attain this goal without sacrifice. All of us are shocked by the poverty of millions and disturbed by the injustices which cause it. Those of us who live in affluent circumstances accept our duty to develop a simple life-style in order to contribute more generously to both relief and evangelism.

10. Evangelism and Culture

The development of strategies for world evangelization calls for imaginative pioneering methods. Under God, the result will be the rise of churches deeply rooted in Christ and closely related to their culture. Culture must always be tested and judged by Scripture. Because man is God's creature, some of his culture is rich in beauty and goodness. Because he is fallen, all of it is tainted with sin and some of it is demonic. The gospel does not presuppose the superiority of any culture to another, but evaluates all cultures according to its own criteria of truth and righteousness, and insists on moral absolutes in every culture. Missions have all too frequently exported with the gospel an alien culture, and churches have sometimes been in bondage to culture rather than to the Scripture. Christ's evangelists must humbly seek to empty themselves of all but their personal authenticity in order to become the servants of others, and churches must seek to transform and enrich culture, all for the glory of God.

Mark 7:8-9,13; Gen. 4:21-22; 1 Cor. 9:19-23; Phil. 2:5-7; 2 Cor. 4:5

11. Education and Leadership

We confess that we have sometimes pursued church growth at the expense of church depth, and divorced evangelism from Christian nurture. We also acknowledge that some of our missions have been too slow to equip and encourage national leaders to

Col. 1:27-28; Acts 14:23; Titus 1:5,9; Mark 10:42-45; Eph. 4:11-12 assume their rightful responsibilities. Yet we are committed to indigenous principles, and long that every church will have national leaders who manifest a Christian style of leadership in terms not of denomination but of service. We recognize that there is a great need to improve theological education, especially for church leaders. In every nation and culture there should be an effective training programme for pastors and laymen in doctrine, discipleship, evangelism, nurture and service. Such training programmes should not rely on any stereotyped methodology but should be developed by creative local initiatives according to biblical standards.

12. Spiritual Conflict

Eph. 6:12; 2 Cor. 4:3-4; Eph. 6:11,13-18; 2 Cor. 10:3-5; 1 John 2:18-26; 4:1-3; Gal. 1:6-9; 2 Cor. 2:17; 4:2; John 17:15

We believe that we are engaged in constant spiritual warfare with the principalities and powers of evil, who are seeking to overthrow the church and frustrate its task of world evangelization. We know our need to equip ourselves with God's armour and to fight this battle with the spiritual weapons of truth and prayer. For we detect the activity of our enemy, not only in false ideologies outside the church, but also inside it in false gospels which twist Scripture and put man in the place of God. We need both watchfulness and discernment to safeguard the biblical gospel. We acknowledge that we ourselves are not immune to worldliness of thought and action, that is, to a surrender to secularism. For example, although careful studies of church growth, both numerical and spiritual, are right and valuable, we have sometimes neglected them. At other times, desirous to ensure a response to the gospel, we have compromised our message, manipulated our hearers through pressure techniques, and become unduly preoccupied with statistics or even dishonest in our use of them. All this is worldly. The church must be in the world; the world must not be in the church.

13. Freedom and Persecution

It is the God-appointed duty of every government to secure conditions of peace, justice and liberty in which the church may obey God, serve the Lord Christ, and preach the gospel without interference. We therefore pray for the leaders of the nations and call upon them to guarantee freedom of thought and conscience, and freedom to practise and propagate religion in accordance with the will of God and as set forth in the Universal Declaration of Human Rights. We also express our deep concern for all who have been unjustly imprisoned, and especially for our brethren who are suffering for their testimony to the Lord Jesus. We promise to pray and work for their freedom. At the same time we refuse to be intimidated by their fate. God helping us, we too will seek to stand against injustice and to remain faithful to the gospel, whatever the cost. We do not forget the warnings of Jesus that persecution is inevitable.

1 Tim. 1:1-4; Acts 4:19; 5:29; Col. 3:24; Heb. 13:1-3; Luke 4:18; Gal. 5:11; 6:12; Matt. 5:10-12; John 15:18-21

14. The Power of the Holy Spirit

We believe in the power of the Holy Spirit. The Father sent his Spirit to bear witness to his Son; without his witness ours is futile. Conviction of sin, faith in Christ, new birth and Christian growth are all his work. Further, the Holy Spirit is a missionary spirit; thus evangelism should arise spontaneously from a Spirit-filled church. A church that is not a missionary church is contradicting itself and quenching the Spirit. Worldwide evangelization will become a realistic possibility only when the Spirit renews the church in truth and wisdom, faith, holiness, love and

1 Cor. 2:4; John 15:26-27; 16:8-11; 1 Cor. 12:3; John 3:6-8; 2 Cor. 3:18; John 7:37-39; 1 Thess. 5:19; Acts 1:8; Pss. 85:4-7; 67:1-3; Gal. 5:22-23; 1 Cor. 12:4-31; Rom. 12:3-8

power. We therefore call upon all Christians to pray for such a visitation of the sovereign Spirit of God that all his fruit may appear in all his people and that all his gifts may enrich the body of Christ. Only then will the whole church become a fit instrument in his hands, that the whole earth may hear his voice.

15. The Return of Christ

Mark 14:62; Heb. 9:28; Mark 13:10; Acts 1:8-11; Matt. 28:20; Mark 13:21-23; John 2:18; 4:1-3; Luke 12:32; Rev. 21:1-5; 2 Pet. 3:13; Matt. 28:18

We believe that Jesus Christ will return personally and visibly, in power and glory, to consummate his salvation and his judgment. This promise of his coming is a further spur to our evangelism, for we remember his words that the gospel must first be preached to all nations. We believe that the interim period between Christ's ascension and return is to be filled with the mission of the people of God, who have no liberty to stop before the End. We also remember his warning that false Christs and false prophets will arise as precursors of the final Antichrist. We therefore reject as a proud, self-confident dream the notion that man can ever build a utopia on earth. Our Christian confidence is that God will perfect his kingdom, and we look forward with eager anticipation to that day, and to the new heaven and earth in which righteousness will dwell and God will reign forever. Meanwhile, we rededicate ourselves to the service of Christ and of men in joyful submission to his authority over the whole of our lives.

Conclusion

Therefore, in the light of this our faith and our resolve, we enter into a solemn covenant with God and with each other, to pray, to plan and to work together for the evangelization of the whole world. We call upon others to join us. May God help us by his

APPENDIXES

grace and for his glory to be faithful to this our covenant! Amen, Alleluia!

(Published with the permission of World Wide Publications)

Appendix 7

STATISTICS 1980

Taken in part from 1980 Baptist World Alliance Statistics with permission

Country/Union	Churches	Church Members	Publications	Youth Work	Women's Work	European Baptists Mission Society (EBM)	Foreign Missions	Home m./Evangelism	Social Ministry	Sunday Sch./Education	Baptist World Alliance	Bible School/Seminary
1. England (Baptist Union of Great Britain and Ireland)	2,091	174,578	X		X		X	X	X	X	X	X
2. Scotland (Baptist Union of Scotland)	157	14,429	X	X	X			X	X	X	X	X
3. Wales (Baptist Union of Wales)	638	37,770	X	X	X		X	X	X	X		X
4. Ireland (Baptist Union of Ireland)	90	7,676	X	X			X	X	X	X		X
5. Germany, Democratic Republic (Union of Evangelical Free Churches in the GDR)	215	21,193	X									X
6. Germany, Federal Republic (Union of Evangelical Free Churches in the FRG)	356	68,012	X	X	X	X	X	X	X	X	X	X
7. Switzerland (Union of Baptist Churches in Switzerland)	15	1,425	X		X	X	X	X	X	X	X	X (Int.)
8. Austria (Baptist Union of Austria)	9	691						X			X	
9. The Netherlands (Union of Baptist Churches in the Netherlands)	81	11,951	X	X	X	X		X			X	X
10. Denmark (Baptist Union of Denmark)	41	6,362	X	X	X	X	X	X	X	X	X	X
11. Norway (Norwegian Baptist Union)	64	6,299	X	X	X	X	X	X	X	X	X	X
12. Sweden (Baptist Union of Sweden)	422	21,651	X	X	X	X	X	X	X	X	X	X
13. Sweden (Orebro Mission)	234	19,000	X		X	X			X			X
14. Finland (Finnish Baptist Union, Finnish-Speaking)	10	771	X			X					X	

APPENDIXES

15. Finland (Swedish-Speaking Baptist Union of Finland)	24	1,712	X						
16. Italy (Baptist Christian Union of Italy)	80	4,200	X		X	X		X	
17. Spain (Baptist Evangelical Union of Spain)	61	4,800	X	X	X	X	X	X	X
18. Portugal (Portuguese Baptist Convention)	52	2,800	X	X	X	X	X	X	X
19. France (Federation of Baptist Evangelical Churches)	28	2,997	X	X	X	X	X	X	X
20. Belgium (Union of Evangelical Baptist Churches)	8	512	X	X		X		X	
21. Evangelical Association of French-Speaking Baptist Churches	26	2,000	X			X			
22. Greece	1	28							
23. Soviet Union (All Union Council of Evangelical Christians-Baptists)	5,000	545,000	X			X		X	X (Corr.)
24. Poland (Polish Baptist Christian Union)	55	2,539	X						
25. Hungary (Baptist Union of Hungary)	200	12,000	X	X		X	X	X	X
26. Czechoslovakia (Baptist Union in Czechoslovakia)	28	3,978							
27. Yugoslavia (Baptist Union of Yugoslavia)	61	3,484	X	X		X	X	X	X
28. Romania (Baptist Union of the Republic of Socialist Rumania)	662	160,000	X	X		X	X	X	X
29. Bulgaria (Union of Baptist churches in Bulgaria)	10	650							
30. Europe (European Baptist Convention-EBC, English Language)	43	3,847	X	X	X	X	X	X	

Editorial Note: The figures for the Baptist Union of Wales do not include South Wales and North Wales area figures which are already included in those for the Baptist Union of Great Britain and Ireland.

Appendix 8
Declaratory Statement,
Adopted By the Baptist Union Assembly
April 23, 1888

The Baptist Union of Great Britain and Ireland struggled with both growth and controversy during the nineteenth century; some of the latter centered around the expressed need in a few quarters for a clearer statement of faith. The Statement of 1888 below represents a compromise to avoid a split within the union during the "Downgrade" controversy. It is reproduced from E. A. Payne, *The Baptist Union, A Short History* (1958) with permission of the Carey Kingsgate Press, Ltd.

Whilst expressly disavowing and disallowing any power to control belief or restrict inquiry, yet in view of the uneasiness produced in the churches by recent discussions, and to show our agreement with one another, and with our fellow Christians on the great truths of the Gospel, the Council deem it right to say that:

(a) Baptised in the name of the Father, and of the Son, and of the Holy Ghost, we have avowed repentance towards God and faith in the Lord Jesus Christ—the very elements of a new life; as in the Lord's Supper we avow our union with one another, while partaking of the symbol of the Body of our Lord, broken for us, and of the Blood shed for the remission of sins. The Union, therefore, is an association of churches and ministers, professing not only to believe the facts and doctrines of the Gospel, but to have undergone the spiritual change expressed or implied in them. This change is the fundamental principle of our church life.

(b) The following facts and doctrines are commonly believed by the Churches of the Union:

1. The Divine Inspiration and Authority of the Holy Scriptures as the supreme and sufficient rule of our faith and practice: and the right and duty of individual judgment in the interpretation of it.

APPENDIXES

2. The fallen and sinful state of man.

3. The Deity, the Incarnation, the Resurrection of the Lord Jesus Christ, and His Sacrificial and Mediatorial Work.

4. Justification by Faith—a faith that works by love and produces holiness.

5. The Work of the Holy Spirit in the conversion of sinners, and in the sanctification of all who believe.

6. The Resurrection; the Judgment at the Last Day, according to the words of our Lord in Matthew 25:46.[1]

[1] It should be stated, as an historical fact, that there have been brethren in the Union, working cordially with it, who, whilst reverently bowing to the authority of Holy Scripture and rejecting dogmas of Purgatory and Universalism, have not held the common interpretation of these words of our Lord.

Bibliography

Association Evangélique d'Eglises Baptistes de Langue Francaise 1921-1971: Notice Historique publié à l'occasion du Cinquantenaire. Crémines (CH): Roos SA, 1971.

The Baptist World Congress. London, July 11-19, 1905: Authorised Record of Proceedings. London: Baptist Union Publication Department, 1905.

Bächtold, T. "Johann Gerhard Oncken and Baptist Beginnings in Switzerland." B. D. Treatise, Baptist Theological Seminary, Rüschlikon 1970.

Balders, G. *Theurer Bruder Oncken: Das Leben Johann Gerhard Onckens in Bildern und Dokumenten*. Wuppertal and Kassel: Oncken Verlag, 1978.

Donat, R. *Wie das Werk begann: Entstehung der deutschen Baptisten-Gemeinden*. Kassel: Oncken Verlag, 1978.

Franks, J. D. (ed.) *European Baptists Today*. Rüschlikon: Blaublatt AG, 1950, 1952.

Gutsche, W. *Westliche Quellen des russischen Stundismus: Anfänge der evangelischen Bewegung in Russland*. Kassel: Oncken Verlag, 1956.

Hopper, J. D. "A History of Baptists in Yugoslavia 1862-1962." Ph.D. Treatise, Southwestern Baptist Theological Seminary, Forth Worth, 1977.

Hughey, J. D. *Europe-A Mission Field?* Nashville: Convention Press, 1972.

_____. *Die Baptisten: Einführung in Lehre, Praxis und Geschichte*. Kassel: Oncken Verlag, 1959.

_____. and R. Thaut. "Die Baptisten." *Theologische Realenzyklopädie*, Band V, 190-197. Berlin: Walter de Gruyer, 1980.

Kahle, W. *Evangelische Christen in Russland und der Sovetunion: Ivan Stephanovic Prochanov (1869-1935) und der Weg der Evangeliumschristen und Baptisten*. Wuppertal and Kassel: Oncken Verlag, 1978.

Lehmann, J. *Geschichte der deutschen Baptisten*. Hamburg and Kassel: Verlagshaus der deutschen Baptisten, 1900.

Lumpkin, W. L. *Baptist Confessions of Faith*. Valley Forge, 1959, Rev. Ed. 1969.

McGlothlin, W. J. *Baptist Confessions of Faith*. Philadelphia: American Baptist Publication Society, 1911.

BIBLIOGRAPHY

Murray, D. B. *The First Hundred Years: The Baptist Union of Scotland.* Glasgow: The Baptist Union of Scotland, 1969.

Payne, E. A. *The Baptist Union: A Short History.* London: Carey Kingsgate Press LTD., 1958.

Reiling, J. "Baptist Beginnings in the Netherlands." *The Baptist Quarterly*, XXVII, 2, Apr. 1979:62-68.

Rudén, E. and G. Lahrson. "An Outline of Baptist Life on the European Continent." American Baptist Foreign Mission Society and Woman's American Baptist Foreign Mission Society, 1963. (Mimeographed)

Rushbrooke, J. H. *The Baptist Movement in the Continent of Europe.* London: The Kingsgate Press, 1923.

Steeves, P. D. "The Russian Baptist Union, 1917-1935: Evangelical Awakening in Russia." Ph.D. Dissertation, University of Kansas, 1976.

Torbet, R. G. *A History of the Baptists.* Valley Forge: The Judson Press, 1950, Revised Ed. 1963.

Wagner, W. I. *New Move Forward in Europe: Growth Patterson of German Speaking Baptists in Europe.* South Pasedena: William Carey Library, 1978.

Westin, G. *The Free Church Through the Ages.* Nashville: Broadman Press, 1958.

Index 1: Scripture

Genesis
1: 61, 106, 189
   1 106, 125, 137, 154, 207, 208, 218, 246, 251
   2 125, 174, 189, 247
   26-30 248
   26 106, 174, 190, 269
   27-31 209
   27 61, 71, 126, 138, 155, 157, 175, 182 190, 197, 208, 213, 219, 226, 254, 269
   28 61, 157, 182, 190, 197, 213, 226
   31 126, 138, 175, 219
2: 61
   1-3 181
   3 213
   5 248
   7 190, 219, 246, 248, 254
   13 219
   15 61
   16 209
   17 155, 175, 209, 219
   18-22 248
   18-25 71
   18 182, 197, 213
   24 182, 213
   25 175
3: 190, 248
   1-17 59
   6-17 209
   8 175
   13 175, 219
   15 176, 248
   17-19 190, 209
   19-24 209
   19 198
   22 174
   27,28 70
4: 7 190
   21,22 273
5: 1 190
6: 3 175
   12 209
8: 21 175
9: 6 214, 248
12: 1-3 62, 249, 252
14: 1 137
   20 252
17: 1 106, 154, 174, 189
18: 1 246
   25 269
50: 20 189

Exodus
3: 14-17 248
   14 189, 246
5: 14 174
6: 2-3 246

2-8 248
7: 14 138
9: 5 138
15: 11 106, 207, 246
17: 12 253
18: 17 ff. 253
   21-23 214
19: 5,6 62, 252
   5-8 249
   9 173
20: 1-17 61, 63
   1 246
   3-17 253
   8 213
   8-11 181, 251
   11 137
24: 4 126, 188, 245
25: 2 227
31: 13-17 181
35: 5 227
   21 227
   31 189
53: 4,5 138
   6 138
   10 138
55: 4,5 138

Leviticus
6: 2-5 253
18: 6 197
19: 2 137
   18 269
22: 2 246
23: 15,16 225
27: 30-32 252

Deuteronomy
4: 1 245, 252
   2 188, 245
   5 127, 252
   6-8 206
   9 252
4: 14 252
   29 227
   35 189
6: 1-10 252
   4 125, 137, 174, 207, 246
   5 137, 189
   7-19 64
   20-25 64
7: 3-4 197
   7,8 62
8: 18 252
9: 7 219
10: 12 253
   14 189
15: 4 189
16: 18,19 214
17: 19 245
18: 15 138

   18 126
24: 16 126, 138
27: 17 253
29: 29 190
30: 15 219
   19 138, 190
31: 12,13 252
   24 ff. 137
32: 6 246
   39 189

Joshua
8: 34 245
24: 14 190
   15 190, 265
   26 188

Judges
7: 21 253
14: 6 247

1 Samuel
2: 2 189
   3 137
8: 4-7 249
   19-22: 249
10: 6 127

2 Samuel
13: 2 125
23: 1 173
   2 126, 137, 173, 188, 206
   3 214

1 Kings
8: 46 219
   47,48 126
   60 137
11: 1-8 214

1 Chronicles
29: 10 246
   19 227

Ezra
1: 3-4 253
2: 68,69 227, 253
5: 14,15 253
6: 3 137

Nehemiah
4: 253
8: 1-8 252
   1-5 253
   10 60
9: 2 191
   6 208
   20 189
   30 189
13: 23-28 214

INDEXES

Job
19: 25 214
25,26 141, 198
27 198, 214
26: 13 247
27: 3 190
28: 28 252
33: 4 125, 189, 219

Psalms
1: 248
2: 7 189, 246
3: 7 154
8: 3-6 248
4-7 190
4 106
6 61
11: 7 154
12: 7 188
16: 10 215
19: 1-3 246
7-10 246, 252
8-10 188
20: 15,16 175
24: 8-10 125
25: 12,13 197
26: 8 212
27: 4 196, 212
32: 1-5 248
1,2 139
3-5 155
5 139
8 197
51 139
33: 6 106, 174, 189
9 106, 189
37: 3 137
40: 7 137
8,9 175
45: 7 125, 269
8 125
49: 8,9 155
50: 15 196
51: 3-9 155
3 126
4 126, 219
5 209, 248
7 126, 138, 175
11 247
53: 4 126, 138
58: 4 175
62: 8 225
9 137
67: 1-3 275
78: 5 126
83: 18 207
84: 1 212
11 197
85: 4-7 275
90: 2 137, 174, 207
3 154
94: 9 218
95: 6 189, 196
7 196

96: 10 189
101: 5 253
102: 25-28 137
104: 24 106
30 189
107: 17 219
109: 30 196
110: 1 208, 227, 246
115: 16 190
118: 11 252
20-24 182
24-197 213, 225
119: 11 246
68 154
89 246
105 173, 218, 246
140 246
122: 1 197, 212
126: 5,6 108
127: 3 197
133: 1-3 197
139: 1-12 137
1-10 207
2-4 154, 175
7-10 175, 189, 247
16 137
145: 1-13 137
17 137
147: 5 106, 137, 207
148: 8,9 154

Proverbs
3: 5 137, 207
6 207
13,14 252
4: 1-10 252
8: 1-7 252
11 252
12: 3 197
15: 14 252
22 260
18: 22 197
19: 14 197
20: 18 262
22: 6 197
28: 13 139
30: 5 188
6 154, 188
31: 10 197
30,31 197

Ecclesiastes
7: 19 252
20 219
29 175, 190, 209, 219
9: 11 197
12: 9 198

Song of Solomon
2: 7 197
8: 6,7 197

Isaiah
1: 2 173

17 269
18 220
2: 4 251, 254
5: 1-7 249
6: 1-8 252
3 106, 154, 207
5 248
7: 14 208, 246
8: 20 126
9: 6 106, 174, 207, 251
7 251
11: 2 125
12: 2 125
14: 12-15 208
34: 16 218, 246
40: 8 246
28 106, 175, 207, 267
41: 10-13 227
21 175
42: 5 190
43: 3 246
15 246
21 190
44: 6 189
8 189
45: 5 106, 189
12 190
17 175
23,24 178
46: 9 106
48: 16 219
50: 6 190
52: 5 220
53: 247
4 126, 209
5 126, 155, 175, 209
6 126, 209
11 175
55: 6 196
7 191
10 176, 209
11 176, 209, 268
58: 1 127
6,7 272
61: 1-3 247
1 174
10 176
64: 6 155, 219
8 246
65: 17-25 199
66: 1,2 207

Jeremiah
1: 9 173, 188
2: 12,13 207
22 219
10: 10 106, 189, 207, 246
13: 23 219, 220
15: 16 246
36 246
17: 5 248
13 246
23: 5 174, 251
6 174, 176, 251

23	189	
24	175, 189	
36	188	
29:	6	196
	7	72, 198
31:	31-34	62, 249
36:	1	188
	2	188
	4	188
	27,28	188
	32	188

Ezekiel

11:	19	139
18:	20	107, 209
	23	74, 191
	27,28	191
20:	43	191
28:	14,15	208
	18	209
33:	7	127
	11	176
36:	26,27	191
37:	14	127

Daniel

3:	15-18	214
6:	26	189
7:	13,14	128
9:	24	125
12:	1-3	128
	2	126, 141, 199, 215
	3	108, 141, 199, 215

Joel

2:	12,13	139, 191
	26	140
	28-32	247
	28	218
	29	140

Amos

7:	15	127
9:	2,3	219

Micah

5:	2	189
6:	8	190, 253

Haggai

2:	5	189

Zechariah

7:	12	127
8:	16	253

Malachi

2:	10	218
	15,16	197
3:	6	137
	8-12	252

Matthew

1:	18-23	247

18	189, 247	
20	208	
20-23	189	
21	248	
23	138, 207, 208	
2:	16	227
	27	181
3:	2	251
	7	157, 175
	8	157
	12	184
	13-17	193, 250
	13-15	177
	14	157
	15	157
	16	174, 178, 247
	17	174, 207, 247
4:	1-3	208
	1	247
	4	126
	8-10	251
	17	248
	23	251
5:	2	252
	8	73
	9	198, 254
5:	10-12	275
	13-16	69, 198, 253
	15,16	108
	17	138, 175, 190, 246, 268
	18	137, 246, 268
	20	270
	31-46	251
	32	157, 197
	34	183
	37	183
	38-48	254
	38	154
	43-48	70, 254
	45	61
	48	189
6:	1-4	252
	5-8	197
	6	225, 254
	7	254
	9	174, 246
	10	108
	12	64, 73
	16-18	220
	19-21	252
	24	254
	33	65, 254, 270
7:	7-11	196
	11	246
	12	264
	15	212
	17-21	127
	17	221
	21	196
	21-23	141
	24 ff.	252
8:	12	229
	22	175
	29	247

9:	10-13	57
	28	196
	35-38	272
	37,38	252
10:	5-15	252, 253
	10	227
	20	173, 218
	24,25	213
	28	214
	29	207
	32	74, 181, 212
11:	25-27	175, 207
	25	218
	27	247
	28	176, 268
12:	1-12	251
	10-12	213
	18	189
	25-28	251
	28-32	247
	32	174
	28	125, 189
	36	141, 219, 220
	37	141
13:	1-52	251
	4-23	138
	18	30, 252
	25,26	208
	37-43	252
	49	128, 229
	50	229
14:	23	225
	33	247
15:	6	218
	19	138
16:	15-19	250
	16	175, 218, 247
	16-20	141
	18	211, 221, 249
	19	249, 252
	21	208
	21-26	248
	24-27	138
	26	155, 248, 254
	27	109, 158, 214, 247, 251
17:	5	138, 247
	24	129
	27	129, 247
18:	5-20	132
	8,9	251
	11	209
	15-20	250
	15-18	143
	15-17	181, 195, 213, 225
	15	68
	17	127, 131, 196, 212
	17-20	141
	18	74, 181, 212
	19	250, 270
	20	65, 127, 179, 211, 222, 250, 270
19:	4-6	157, 197
	4	190
	6-9	183

INDEXES

    6-8 157
    6 214, 227
    9 157, 214, 227
    14 107
    17 154
    21 252
    28 251
20: 1-16 253
    18 208
    19 190, 208
    25 212
    25-28 156
    26 212
    27 212
    28 155, 175, 190, 209
21: 22 197
    28-45 249
22: 1-10 253
    9 246, 252
    10 252
    21 129, 158, 183, 214, 254, 264
    29 188
    36-40 254
23: 8 158, 181, 212, 222
    9 246
    11 181
    23 253
24: 14 252
    15-42 126
    22 249
    27 251
    30 138, 158, 184, 199, 229, 251
    31 138, 249
    36 229, 251
    40,41 158
    42-44 158
    44 251
25: 10 13, 158
    10-12 184
    11-13 158
    14-29 108, 253
    31-46 109, 141, 158, 251, 272
    31-44 199
    31-34 215
    31 158, 214
    34 230
    35 254
    40 227
    41-46 199
    41 138, 155, 215
    45 74
    46 26, 230, 281
26: 26-30 250
    26-29 128
    26-28 66, 140, 179, 224
    26 210, 225
    28 176, 210
    29 251
    36-39 139
    38 175
    39 225
    41, 192, 196, 230
    52 254
    64 251
27: 22 to 28:6 248
    46 175
28: 1-6 247
    1 129, 213, 251
    5,6 108
    16-20 64
    18 61, 189, 207, 276
    19 62, 65, 76, 107, 108, 125, 128, 129, 137, 140, 141, 157, 174, 177, 189, 193, 194, 210, 218, 224, 246, 247, 252, 253, 267,
    18 20, 127, 252
    20 107, 140, 141, 176, 177, 194, 207, 252, 253, 276

Mark
1: 1 247
    5 128
    9-11 246, 250
    9 128, 178
    10 128, 247
    12 247
    14 251
    15 57, 139, 220, 251
    29-34 254
2: 3 253
    3 ff. 254
    27 213, 251
    28 251
3: 11 247
    13-15 127
    31-35 64
7: 3 189
    5 189
    8 189, 273
    9 189, 273
    13 154, 189
    20-23 59
    21 175
    22 175
8: 34 269
    38 128, 139, 251
9: 1 251
    43-48 184, 251
10: 2-12 197
    7-9 71
    13-16 71
    21 254
    42-45 273
    43-45 198, 269
    45 58
11: 25 197
12: 17 265
    29-33 125
    29-31 60
    29 207
    30 137, 207, 263
    31 263
13: 10 276
    21-23 276
    26 229
14: 22-26 250
    22-25 128
    22-24 140, 210
    36 218
    62 276
16: 1-7 251
    1 129
    9 197, 225
    14 175
    15,16 108, 140, 260
    15 64, 211, 222, 263, 272
    16 107, 128, 157, 178, 191, 193, 206, 210, 224, 263
    19 139, 190, 208

Luke
1: 1-40 188
    2-4 63
    26-35 126
    28 154
    30 189
    31 154, 189
    34 189, 208
    35 139, 154, 189, 208, 247
    37 189
    68-79 249
    68,69 248
2: 10 125
    11 125, 207
    28-32 187, 249
    40 252
3: 10 65
    21-22 250
    32 218
4: 1 189, 247
    14 189
    18-21 254
    18 189, 247, 275
    19 189, 247
    41 247
    43 251
5: 8 58
6: 27 269
    35 269
7: 29 157
    30 157
8: 1 251
9: 2 251
    35 139
10: 1-20 127
    1-18 252
    1 ff. 253
    7,8 180
    10-16 207
    16 173
    27-37 254
11: 13 193, 219, 249
    17-20 138
12: 8,9 196
    12 193, 249
    16-21 253

```
        31   251                    1-3   137, 207              44   139, 249
        32   251, 276               1-14  107, 126, 139, 174,   45   249
        40   251                          209                   51   157
        42   253                    1-18  247                   54   191
        45,46  158                  3    189, 208               60   191
        48   251                    4    61                     63   177, 209
    13: 3-5  126, 139               11-14  248                  65   139, 249
        3    191, 220                12   107, 127, 155, 192, 249  66-69  191
        25-28  141, 184              13   107, 127, 155, 177,   69   189, 191
    14: 16-24  74                         210, 249           7: 37-39  275
        25-33  269                   14   126, 207, 249      8: 34   59, 219
    15: 32   155                     29   208, 247, 248         36   57, 192, 254
    16: 1-13  253                3:  3    127, 177, 221, 251, 269  44   175
        19-26  251                  3-21  248                   46   175
        22   228                    3-8   155                   58   207
        23   229                    5    127, 154, 177, 190, 191,  59   189
        24-26  184                        210, 221, 269      9: 4    272
        26   226                    6    127, 175, 177, 191, 210,  31   197
        29-31  206                        221, 275              39-41  60
        29   173                    7    220, 275          10: 9    248
        31   173                    8    275                    15   139
    17: 5    196                    16-19  268                  16   139, 156, 195, 211
        20,21  251                   16   58, 107, 127, 139, 154,  27-30  192
        22-37  251                        155, 176, 191, 207, 209,  27-29  249
    19: 41-44  249                        249                   27   194
    20: 25   129, 254                17   154                   28   176, 228, 248
    21: 27   128, 184, 229, 251      18   138, 191, 276         29   248
        28   184, 251                22   193                   30   126, 174, 207, 247
        33   246                     23   193, 250              35   173, 188, 218, 268
    22: 3    208                     26   193                   38   247
        14-20  128                   34   139              11: 23-25  141
        14,15  156                   36   74, 127, 138, 139, 176,  25-27  247
        16-20  66                         248                   25,26  176, 198,
        16   75                  4:  1-3  193, 276              52   156
        17-20  211                   1,2  128, 129, 174     12: 7,8  227
        19   140, 157, 175, 194,     21-24  251                 44-50  247
             224, 250                22   62                    47   188, 207
        20   140, 194, 250           23   196                   48   188, 191, 207
        24   139                     24   106, 189, 196, 218,  13: 1-17  69
        36   254                          246, 247              1    157
        38   254                     42   268                   15   218
        42   190                 5:  7    208                   34,35  180, 212
        44   175                     13   191                   35   271
        70   247                     17   106, 189, 207     14: 1-3  251
    23: 42   198, 251                21   106                   2    75, 139
        43   198                     22-29  141                 3    128, 139, 176, 208, 229
    24: 1-3  251                     22   139                   6-13  246
        1-6  225                     23   106, 174, 189, 207    6    139
        1    129                     24   65, 75, 138, 155, 248,  7-11  247
        6    208                          249                   9,10  106, 126
        25   175                     26   246                   11,12  252
        27   137                     27-29  139                 16   140, 174, 189, 247
        30-35  66                    28   109, 184, 199, 229    17   140, 189, 247
        33-36  251                   29   109, 184, 199, 214, 229  19   73
        44-48  249                   36   246                   23   106
        44-46  246                   38   206                   26   140, 175, 193, 208,
        44   137, 188                39   60, 63, 126, 137, 154,      219, 247
        46   247                          173, 206, 218     15: 1-16  248
        46-53  252                   46   126                   1-8  64
        47   196                     58,59  174                 5    220
        49   140, 247            6:  27   218                   7    197, 252
        51   176, 208                37   139, 176              8    252
                                     38   190                   10   178, 193
    John                             39   139, 141, 192         12   212, 254
    1:  1   189, 218                 40   139, 176, 191         13   157
```

INDEXES

    14 178, 193
    16 208, 219, 249
    17 208, 212
    18-21 275
    26 106, 140, 176, 190,
        196, 208, 219, 247, 275
    27 196, 275
16:    252
    6 193
    7-14 247
    7 140, 193
    8-14 176
    8-11 275
    8 127, 140, 154
    13 140, 154, 176, 190,
        193, 208, 246
    14 140, 154, 176, 190, 246
    15 246, 247
    16 247
    23 225
    28 247
17: 1-8 246
    1-5 247
    2 139
    3 137
    4 58
    5 139, 189, 207
    6 139, 249, 267
    10 207
    11-23 271
    11 156
    12 249
    15 252, 254, 274
    17 139, 188, 192, 207,
        218, 226, 246, 248, 249
    18 249, 267, 270
    19 210
    21-23 156
    21 247, 260, 271
    22 69, 247
    23 271
    24 74, 176
18: 36 251, 264
19: 30 176
    37 158
20: 1-20 247
    1 129, 225, 251
    19-28 251
    19 108, 213
    21 252, 269, 270
    22 65
    25 139
    26 129, 213
    27 139
    28 174, 207, 247
    29 191
    31 63, 154, 189, 218
21: 15-17 108
    24 188

Acts
1: 1 126, 188
    2 63
    6 251
    7 73, 246, 251

    8-11 276
    8 63, 140, 192, 196, 208,
        247, 252, 270, 275
    9-11 139
    9 208, 247
    10-12 109
    10 184
    11 72, 128, 184, 190, 199,
        214, 229, 251
    13 253
    14 194, 253
    15-26 130, 131
    16 126, 137, 206
2:    63, 176, 252
    1-4 225, 247
    1 211, 213, 253
    4 179, 208
    16 246
    21 248
    22-24 247
    23,24 139
    29-36 157
    30 208
    32-39 269
    32 139, 176
    33 218
    36 58, 178
    37 157, 176, 178, 209
    38-41 127, 128, 140
    38 65, 76, 129, 157, 178,
        193, 208, 210, 220, 224,
        247
    40-42 108
    40 156, 226, 269
    41-47 141, 211
    41-46 107
    41-44 194
    41 75, 129, 140, 157, 178,
        193, 194, 211, 222, 224,
        250
    42-47 69
    42 66, 128, 140, 177, 180,
        194, 197, 211, 212, 224,
        225, 250
    44-47 76, 211, 253
    44 272
    45 272
    46 140, 179, 194, 211
    47 66, 129, 155, 178, 211,
        250, 269
3: 3,4 126
    18-21 126
    19 139
    21 126, 137, 206
4: 2 141
    4 155
    8 208
    12 62, 155, 208, 220, 248,
        268
    13 196
    18-20 214
    19 83, 254, 275
    20 183, 254
    24 208
    29 196

    31-37 253
    31 65, 247
    32 156, 177
    33 196
    34,35 272
5: 1-11 156, 253
    11 248
    3 174, 247
    4 174
    11-14 250
    13 129, 141, 156
    14 129, 141, 155, 178
    20 265
    29 183, 189, 214, 275
    30 191
    31 191
    32 196, 208, 219
    42 183
6: 1-4 180
    1-6 131, 142
    2-5 127
    2-7 141
    2 195
    3-6 130, 250
    3 195, 247
    4 127, 195
    5 131, 195
    6 195, 212, 223
    7 155
7: 1 141
    4,5 141
    25 227
    34 196
    36 188
    55 247
    56 227, 247
8: 1 222
    12 129, 140, 156, 178,
        193, 210
    13-21 224
    15 127
    17 247
    26-40 252
    29 193
    35-39 250
    35-40 107
    36-38 65, 193
    36-39 128, 140, 178
    36 75, 157, 210, 224
    37 157, 210, 218, 224
    39 178, 247
9: 4 247
    5 178, 247
    6 178
    9 178
    18-20 178
    18 178
    19 141, 178
    20 218, 247
    26-31 141
    26 129, 131
    27 131, 196
    31 193
10: 38 189
    42-48 252

BAPTISTS IN EUROPE

```
42   74, 126, 139, 196, 208          34   193, 210                     11,12  192
43   191                             40   129                          14-20  218
44   209, 247                    17: 11   126, 137, 173, 189,          14,15  196
46   209                                  191, 207, 218, 246           16-18  248
47   128, 140, 157, 193              12   191                          16     62, 75, 173, 206, 264,
48   140, 157, 193                   22-31 251                                268
11: 2-4  131                         24-26 106, 189                    18-32  268
    14   206                         24   218, 253                     18     59
    18   131                         25   253                          19-32  248
    19-26 108, 129                   26-28 248                         19     190
    22   131                         26   61, 190, 208, 269            20     190, 207, 208, 219
    24   127                         27   190                          21     190
    25   127                         28   189, 190                 2:  1      209
    26   127                         30   139, 176, 184, 220,          2-16   141, 209
    29   131, 194, 227                    229, 248                     2      207
    30   130                         31   139, 141, 184, 208,          4      248
12: 5    236                              215, 229, 248, 251, 269      5-11   138
13: 1-3  129, 156, 250, 271      18: 8    129, 178, 210                5      128
    1    127                         10   129                          16     74, 229
    2    193, 195, 247, 252, 253     26   196                      3:  2      126, 137
    3    180, 195, 212, 223, 252,    27   131, 196                     9-12   190
         253                         28   188, 196                     9-23   209
    29   107                     19: 1-6  247                          10-18  248
    38,39 192                        1-5  129                          10     209
14: 17   61                          2,3  157                          18     190
    22   65                          3-5  140, 194                     19     126, 177
    23   127, 130; 180, 212,         8    196                          20     155, 177, 219
         223, 250, 273               9    127, 141                     21-31  69
    27   127, 250                20: 127                               21-29  59
15:      69                          7    108, 128, 129, 140, 156,     21-28  107
    1-35 253                              181, 197, 211, 213, 224,     21-26  209
    1-30 250                              250, 251                     21     188
    2-4  130                         12,13 178                         22-30  139
    3    127, 129, 131                17-36 142                        22-24  58, 192
    4    129, 131                    17-28 127, 130                    22     126
    6    127, 260                    17   141, 223                     23-26  247
    9    176                         20   139                          23     155, 209, 219, 248
    11   220                         21   107, 139                     24     154, 155, 176, 209, 210,
    12   131                         27   270                                 220, 248
    14   267                         28   174, 176, 250, 265           25     126, 139, 155, 176, 210,
    18   154, 175                    28-31 141, 156, 180, 212,                220, 248
    20   264                              221, 223                     26     139, 154
    22-25 181, 212                   31   212                          28     176, 192, 210
    22   127, 129, 130, 131          32   154, 248, 249            4:  3      248
    23   127, 130, 131               35   253                          4-8    107
    28   193, 247                21: 127                               4      139
    30   129, 131                    17   142                          5      139, 155
    33   127, 131                    18   127, 130, 142                15     126
    41   211                     22: 16   140, 156, 178, 193, 210      16     107
16: 4    130, 141                24: 14   191                          17     61
    5    141, 211, 250               15   109, 128, 141, 198, 229      18-21  191
    6    247                         25   229                          24     155
    6,7  193                     26: 17   210                          25     58, 155, 190, 209
    14   129, 191, 210               18   139, 191, 210            5:  1-9    127
    15   129, 210                    26-28 194                         1      107, 139, 176, 192
    18   141                     28: 20   76                           2      192
    25-34 107                        30,31 196                         5      127, 140, 176, 190
    26-27 141                                                          6-21   247
    29   179                    Romans                                 6-8    155
    30-33 129                    1:  2    126, 137                     6      219, 248
    30   179, 248                    3    139, 175, 247                8-10   248
    31   220, 248                    4    126, 139, 175, 247           8      157
    32   210                         7    155, 250                     9-11   192
    33   128, 140, 193                8    271                         9      139, 249
```

INDEXES

```
    10    249
    12    126, 139, 155, 175, 190,
          219, 248
    13    107
    14    155
    15-19 209
    17-21 107
    17    139, 251
    18    107, 175
    19    139, 155, 175, 209, 219,
          248
 6: 1-23  248
    1-11  65
    1,2   254
    2-4   157
    3-5   193, 249
    3     76, 128, 140, 178, 210
    4     128, 140, 178, 221, 224
    5     178
    6-22  253
    6     178, 210, 248
    8     178, 210
    9     139
    10    139, 178
    11    178, 193
    13    219
    14    176
    19,20 190
    22    155, 210
    23    155, 175, 178, 190, 219
 7: 1-4   183
    2     157, 198
    3     198
    14-25 248
    15    190
    17    219
    18    190, 219
    19    190
    20    219
    21,22 176, 219
    23    219
 8: 1-18  248
    1-4   60
    1-3   247
    1     190, 192
    2     191
    3     175, 177, 189
    4     177
    6     175, 191
    7     175, 220
    9-11  126, 247
    9     127, 140
    11    73, 189, 190
    13-14 140
    14 ff. 59, 126, 127, 155,
          176, 192, 246, 247, 248
    15    196, 246, 247
    16    61, 127, 140, 177, 193,
          208, 247
    17    177, 193, 221
    19-23 73
    19 ff. 199
    19    251
    23    184

    26-28 60
    26    140, 193, 228, 247
    27    140, 247
    28-39 249
    29-39 248
    29    248
    30    139
    34    139, 191, 227, 247
    35    192
    37    192
    38-39 73, 191
  9—10   62
 9: 1-3  272
    5    139, 174, 189
    22,23 141
10: 2-4  59
    3    155
    4    63, 175, 247
    9    107, 181, 196, 212, 249
    10   181, 196, 212, 249
    11   107
    12-15 249
    13-15 252
    13   62, 107, 249
    15   156
    17   107, 175, 191, 218
11: 5-7  249
    26-36 249
    26   62
    33-36 207
    33,34 175, 189
    36   218
12:      254
    1-12 253
    1-8  67
    1    65, 69, 177, 192, 210
    2    267
    3-8  275
    3    191
    4-8  141
    5    129, 155, 156, 193
    6-11 265
    6    193
    7    156
    8    156, 227
    9,10 68
    15   212
    18,19 254
13:      254
    1-7  72, 129, 183, 214, 228,
         254
    1    198
    2    157, 198
    3    157, 198, 214
    4    157, 198
    5-7  198
    5    157, 265
    7    265
    11-14 249
14:      254
    4-13 108
    5    197
    8    198
    9    126

    10-12 215
    10   141, 251
    12   141, 176, 219
    17   61
    19   70, 254
    23   193, 219
15: 4-16 188
    4    137, 246
    6    156, 218
    7    64
    14   156
    25,26 188
    27   227
16: 1,2  131, 141, 142
    5    222
    17   132, 212
    18   212
    25,26 246
    27   137, 174, 189

1 Corinthians
 1: 1    249
    2    67, 108, 141, 155, 222,
         249, 250
    7,8  184, 214
    10-17 253
    10   207
    18-31 252
    18   62, 249
    21-31 248
    21   175, 268
    23   269
    27   211
    30   60, 107, 127, 139, 177,
         210, 247, 249
    31   127, 139
    33   193
    40   193
 2: 2    247
    4    173, 196, 209, 275
    5    173, 209, 227
    10   139, 218, 247
    11   174, 247
    12   139, 219, 247
    13   173, 193, 196, 247
    14   60, 175, 177, 209, 247
 3: 1-9  142
    3    190
    5-15 253
    5-8  130
    5-7  209
    5    191
    9    70, 212
    11-13 212
    16   127, 140, 174, 192, 208,
         247, 250
    17   174
    22 ff. 61
 4: 1-4  253
    1    130, 180, 212
    2    180, 212
    5    251
    13   190
 5:      131, 132
```

1-13 156
1 228
2 143
3-13 181, 213
4-5 250
5 68
6 43
7 143, 228
8 228
9-13 141, 143
9-10 254
10 267
11 194, 196, 225
12 225
13 68, 194, 196, 225
17 221
6: 1-7 254
9 ff. 71
11 140, 192, 226
16-19 197
19 71, 140, 192, 249, 253
20 177, 249, 253
7: 157
2-39 213
2-5 197
7 71
9 198
10-16 197
10 183
11 183
15 227
17 250
20-24 254
27 183
39 182, 226, 227
8: 4 61, 137, 174
6 137, 174, 189, 218, 246, 247
9: 6 130
7-14 130
11-14 132
13-14 250
14 227
16 108
19-23 272, 273
10: 11 137
13 228
14 194
16 66, 68, 128, 140, 157, 179, 194, 210, 250
17 128, 140, 157, 179, 211
19-21 194
21 179, 210, 250
23 to 11:1 254
11: 16 141
17-29 194
23-29 66, 128, 140, 250
23-28 179
23-25 58, 194
23 218
24,25 157, 194, 224
26 157, 194, 211, 214
27-30 211
27-29 194

28 224
12: 67, 250, 253
1-11 69
3-11 247
3 190, 275
4-31 275
4-10 156
7 193
8-10 193
11 140, 174, 193
12-31 141
12-17 211
12 60
13 65, 129, 140, 178, 179, 193, 194
14-18 156
18-27 211
25 193
27 156
28 127
29 127, 193
30 193
31 193
13: 1,2 196
14 218
14: 67
1 193
3 194
4 222
5 141, 222
11 207
12 141
19 141
26-40 141
26 156, 207
29 127, 194
30 127
33 181, 212
37 126, 173, 188
40 194, 195, 212
15: 1-8 247
1-3 209
3 139, 190, 269
4 139, 190, 208, 269
10 249
12 128
14-22 58
16-20 184
19 248
20-24 141
20 73, 128
21 248
22 199, 248
23 184, 199
24-28 247, 249, 251
25 139, 141
26 176, 199
28 75, 189, 199
35,36 198, 251
37-38 251
42-58 128
42-49 75
42-44 139, 198
42 184, 229

43 184
51 109, 158
52 109, 158, 214, 229
53 184, 198, 214, 229
54 176, 198
55 176
56 73
58 73
16: 1-19 211
1-4 67, 253
1 127, 180, 181, 197, 211, 213, 227, 251
2 129, 180, 181, 194, 197, 213, 225, 251
3 127, 131
19 211, 222

2 Corinthians
1: 1 155
19 218
20 62
21 179, 193, 210
22 140, 193, 210
24 130
2: 1-11 132, 143
5-8 196
6-8 131, 181, 213
17 274
3: 62
3 208, 219
17 174, 189, 207, 219
18 155, 174, 226, 270, 275
4: 2 274
3 274
4 274
5 64, 269, 273
7 267
5: 1-4 199
5 140
10 109, 126, 141, 184, 215, 219, 229, 251
11 269
14 126, 178
15 126
17-21 58
17-20 249
18-20 196
18 155, 220
19 64, 126, 139, 155, 247
20 155, 247, 269
21 139, 155, 175, 176, 190, 208, 209, 247
6: 1-10 60
3,4 270
14 194, 197, 214, 227
15 214
16-18 194
16 180, 211
17 180, 211, 226
7: 7 177, 192, 210
10 176, 191
8: 253
1 211
4 262

INDEXES

18-24	141
18	130
19	127, 130, 131
23,24	127, 131
9:	253
6-8	180, 212
6	227
7	227, 266
15	196
10: 3-5	274
11: 2	108
3	138
7-10	130
14	138
28	261
12: 15	253
13: 13	126, 137, 140, 174, 189, 207

Galatians
1: 6-12 126, 137
   6-10 153
   6-9 268, 274
   8 173, 212
   9 212
   11 188, 218
   12 188
   22 222
2: 69
   16 155, 192
   20 60, 191, 249
3: 2 65
   10 155, 209
   13 107, 175, 249
   24 177
   26-28 140, 254
   26 107, 175
   27 128, 178, 193, 210
   28 156
4: 4-6 139, 155
   4 57, 107, 126, 139, 175, 177, 189, 190, 209, 247
   5 107, 177, 190, 209, 247
   6 140, 189, 190, 246, 247
   7 192
   26 195
5: 1 60, 254
   5 140
   6 191, 212
   11 275
   13 254
   16 127, 140
   18 127, 140
   19 197
   20 197
   22-25 191, 249
   22 127, 140, 193, 208, 210, 221, 275
   23 193, 208, 221, 275
   24 210
   25 140
6: 1 68, 194, 196, 265
   2 71, 265
   6 132, 212

10 194
12 275
14 270
15 177, 210, 249
17 270

Ephesians
1: 1 155
   3 ff. 64
   4-23 249
   5 192
   7-14 139
   7 107, 176, 208, 220, 249
   9,10 270
   11 267
   13 127, 140, 179, 193, 210, 218, 248
   14 127, 140, 193, 248
   17 108, 268
   18 108, 139, 268
   19 139
   20 247, 268
   21 268
   22 108, 156, 179, 195, 211, 221, 222, 250
   23 108, 156, 179, 195, 211, 221, 222, 250
2: 1-22 248
   1-10 249
   1-5 209
   1-3 209, 219
   1 155, 175
   2 138, 208
   3 175
   5-8 139, 209
   8-22 249
   8 107, 127, 155, 177, 209, 220
   9 107, 220
   10 221, 264
   11-13 192
   13 57
   14 70
   15 156
   18 207
   19 192
   19-22 180, 195, 211, 250
   20-22 108, 193
   20 155
3: 1-11 249, 252
   2,3,4,5 188
   8-11 250
   9-11 270
   10 268
   11 247
   16 140, 190, 192, 208
   18 156, 268
   19 140, 156, 222
   21 250
4: 1-16 253
   1-6 69
   1 211
   3-16 211
   3-6 67, 68, 207

3 177, 271
4-8 126
4-7 141
4 108, 156, 271
5 108, 140, 178, 210
6 174, 207, 218, 246
7-10 247
8 176
11-16 67, 141, 142, 249, 252
11 127, 156, 193, 273
12-15 156
12 193, 222, 262, 267, 273
13 93, 260
15-25 108
15-65 177, 195, 212
16 156, 195, 260
17-19 190
22 ff. 10
28 264
30 140, 174, 193, 248
5: 2 139
   3-5 197
   3 222
   8 210
   9 127
   11 196
   18 140, 248
   19 194, 196
   20 194, 196, 225
   21 181, 212
   22-32 250
   22-25 197
   22 214
   23-29 132
   23 214, 222
   24 194
   25 71
   28-33 197
6: 4 107, 265
   5-9 254
   9 70
   11 195, 274
   12 138, 195, 274
   13-18 274
   17 140, 207
   18 140, 196
   19 196
   23 155
   24 197

Philippians
1: 1 127, 129, 130, 131, 142, 212, 223, 250
   5 156, 271
   6 228
   15-18 153
   21 198
   23 198
   27 154, 270, 271
2: 211
   1 ff. 68
   1 193, 207
   5-11 58, 247

5-7 273
6-11 107
6-8 139
6 209
7 189, 190, 207, 209
8 126, 175, 190, 209
9-11 268
10,11 214
12 192, 249
13 192, 226, 249
3: 2 156
12 192
13,14 259
16 207
20 184, 199, 214, 251, 254
21 184, 199, 229, 251
24 141
4: 2 196
6 196, 225
7 192
8 182, 198, 252
9 198
10-19 253
13 176
14-16 132
15 180, 271
16-18 227
21 176

Colossians
1: 5 251
9-22 249
12-14 249
12 196
13-22 247
13 59, 64, 176, 251
14 155, 176, 190, 208
15 189, 246
16 137, 154, 189, 198, 208
17 208
18 141, 180, 212, 222, 250
19 139
20 155
21 248
22 226, 248
23 226
27,28 273
2: 2 156
3 139, 252
5 181, 212
8 252
9-15 65
9 126, 139, 175, 189, 247, 252
10 126, 198
11 193
12-14 210
12 128, 140, 178, 193, 250
13 155, 175, 178
14 155, 190
15 61, 176
16 108, 182, 197, 213, 251
17 108, 182, 197, 213
19 211

3: 1-4 209
1 ff. 65, 249
4 184, 199, 214, 251
5-10 210
9-11 248
9 221
10 221
11 156
12-17 254
16 156, 251
17 182, 261
18,19 197
20 65
24 275
4: 12 226
15 222
17 130, 142

1 Thessalonians
1: 5 196
6-8 271
8 252
9 65, 73, 75
10 139, 176, 229
2: 13 173, 188
3: 5 208
12 254
13 126, 139
4: 1 192
3 177, 192, 226, 263
7 177, 192, 210, 226
13-18 72, 184
14-18 128, 247, 251
14 141
15-17 139
16 109, 158, 215, 229
17 109, 158, 199, 215
5: 1 ff. 251
2 158
4-10 158
11-23 211
12-14 130
12 127, 132, 142, 195
13 132, 142, 195
14 194, 212
16-18 60
17 196
19-21 193
19 140, 248, 275
20 207
23 139, 249
24 249

2 Thessalonians
1: 5-10 141
6-12 128
6-10 109
7 ff. 251, 268
8 138, 184, 268
9 59, 126, 138, 184, 268
11 197, 226
2: 251
13 139, 140, 155, 190, 192, 249

14 139, 140, 249
15 189
3: 1 197
6-15 132
6 143, 189, 196, 213, 225
9 30
10-13 189
10 264
13-15 143
14 189, 196
15 196
5: 14,15 195
17 177

1 Timothy
1: 1-4 275
3-7 252
3 142
4 142
17 137, 174, 189, 207, 246
19,20 68, 132, 181, 196, 213
2: 1-4 157, 265
1-3 183, 214, 228
1 ff. 64, 72
1 129, 198, 225, 254
2 129, 198, 254
4 74, 176, 220
5 107, 126, 139, 155, 158, 174, 175, 189, 191, 207, 208, 225, 227, 247, 268
6 155, 247, 268
3: 67
1-15 250
1-12 156
1-7 127, 142, 180, 223
1-6 130
2-13 195
8-13 131, 223
8-10 180, 212
11 180
14 141
15 108, 141, 263
16 107, 139, 141, 175, 247, 248
4: 1-3 197
1 248
4 ff. 61
12-16 67, 130, 142
13-16 127
14 130, 141, 193, 195, 212, 223, 250
16 195
5: 17-22 67, 130
17-21 142
17-19 195
17 130, 132, 212
18 30, 132, 212, 227
19 223
22 195, 212
6: 3-5 132, 142, 212, 213
11-14 142
12 181, 195, 212
14 251

INDEXES

```
         15   189
         16   189

2 Timothy
  1:  6   130
     10   176
     12   191, 249
     13   218
     14   248
  2:  2   67, 127, 130, 142
     15   180, 212, 252
     19-21  270
     24   195
     25   195, 196
     26   196
  3:  1-5  132
     14-17  252
     14   188
     15-17  137, 154, 246
     15   188, 206
     16   63, 126, 173, 188, 206,
          218, 248, 268
     17   189, 206, 260
  4:  1   126, 139, 142, 251
     2   142, 180, 212
     5   142, 180, 212, 252
     8   109, 251

Titus
  1:  2   189
     5-9  130, 142, 156, 195, 212,
          223
     5   127, 212, 273
     6-9  180
     9   273
     10  196
     11  196, 220
     13  196
     16  196
  2:  5   220
     7   156
     8   156
     11  191
     11-14  249
     13  184, 247, 251
     14  176, 247
  3:  1   129, 183, 198, 214, 228,
          265
     2   198
     3-7  139
     4-7  192
     5   65, 128, 208
     8-11  141
     8   191, 196
     10  132, 181, 196, 213, 225
     11  132, 181, 196, 213
     13  227

Philemon  254

Hebrews
  1:  1-3  247
     1   57, 63, 154, 173, 246
```

```
     2-6  126
     2   139, 154, 173, 189, 246
     3   176, 189, 209
     5   139
     6   139
     8 ff.  174
     9   178
  2:  1-3  249, 252
     9-17  107
     9   139, 155, 209
     14  139, 175, 176, 199, 209
     15  176
     17  139, 189
     18  189
  3:  4   207
     7,8  193
     12,13  196
  4:  2   191
     12  176, 188, 209, 246
     13  175
     14  158, 176, 178, 181, 209,
          247
     15  126, 139, 175, 197, 247
     16  197
  5:  8   175, 249
     9   107, 175, 249
     12 to 6:3  252
  7:  12  108
     14-28  247
     25  227
     25,26  139, 209
     28  139
  8:  1   176, 209
     6-13  62
     7   227
  9:  8   248
     12-15  107, 247
     12  175
     13-15  209
     14  139, 175, 190, 248
     15-24  227
     22  155, 175
     24-28  247, 249
     24  139, 191
     26  175
     27  184, 198, 219, 251
     28  175, 184, 214, 251, 276
  10: 5,6  175
     10-14  155
     10  139
     11  155
     12-14  175
     12  191
     14  190
     22  178, 197
     23  178
     24  141, 143, 195
     25  141, 143, 180, 196, 213,
          265
     36  259
     37  214
     39  192
  11: 1 to 12:8  249
     1   191, 193
```

```
     2   193
     3   61, 189, 191, 208
     5   191
     6   191, 197, 246
     7   191
     10  251
     14  249
     16  251
     27  191
     39 to 12:2  252
  12: 2   139, 247
     5-7  192
     9   189, 246
     11  192
     12-17  127
     14  70, 177, 198, 254, 265
     18  195
     22  155, 195
     23  155, 195, 221
     24  227
     28  251
  13: 1-3  71, 275
     4   157, 197, 214
     7   142, 195
     8   247
     12  226
     16  194
     17  127, 142, 180, 195
     18  142
     20,21  226

James
  1:  5   197, 252
     6,7  197
     12  192
     13-15  190
     15  219
     17  137
     18  107, 155, 177, 191, 210
     22-25  60
     27  194, 197, 227, 254, 272
  2:  1-9  272
     8   254
     14-26  249
     14-16  269
     14  127
     18  127
     19-22  191
     20  270
     25  127, 191
     26  191
  3:  1   142, 180, 212
     9   269
     17  252
  4:  1,2  254
     3   197
     8   196
     12  254
     17  219
  5:  7   184
     8   184, 251
     12  183
     16  197
     19,20  68, 196
```

1 Peter
1: 1-12   70
    1   108, 192
    2-23   249
    2-5   250
    2   127, 140, 192, 218, 226
    3   107
    4   184
    5   155, 184, 227
    7-9   184
    8   191
    9   191, 192
    10-12   206
    10,11   137
    12   218
    13   250
    14-16   195
    14   192
    15   137, 177, 192, 210
    16   137, 177, 210, 226
    17-21   190
    17   246
    18   155, 157, 253
    19   139, 155, 157, 253
    20   139, 175
    22   127, 180, 191, 195, 212
    23   107, 127, 155, 177, 188,
        191, 210, 220
    25   188, 246
2: 1-10   141
    1-3   195
    1,2   127, 192
    4-10   250, 251, 252
    5-10   67
    5   179, 192, 211, 223
    9   64, 196, 223
    11,12   127, 195
    12-17   254
    13-17   129, 214
    13   182, 183, 198, 214
    14   183, 214
    16   198
    17   183, 198
    21-25   247
    22   175
    24   190
3: 1,2   197
    7   197
    11-17   254
    12   197
    15   69, 196
    18-20   198
    18   139, 190
    19   190
    21   65, 76, 128, 140, 157,
        178, 210, 224
    22   227, 247
4: 7   197
    10   68, 156, 193
    11   193, 207
    12-19   70, 254
    13   251
    14   174, 189
5: 1-5   127, 142

    1-4   127, 156, 250
    1-3   130, 195
    3   22
    4   199, 215
    5   132, 181, 212
    8   208

2 Peter
1: 15-21   188
    16   184
    19-21   63, 137, 246
    19   173
    20   173
    21   154, 173, 206, 248, 268
2: 4-9   141
    4   138, 209, 229
    9   227, 229
    13   17, 228
    17   229
3: 2   188
    3,4   199
    7 ff.   251
    8-12   199
    9   176, 191, 268
    10-13   128
    13   72, 199, 276
    14   199
    15   137, 188, 199
    16   137, 188
    18   264

1 John
1: 1 ff.   63
    5   137
    6 to 2:11   249
    7-9   247, 250
    7   177, 226
    8   73, 177, 219
    9   59, 139, 177, 191
2: 1   139, 176, 191, 208, 209,
        227
    2   107, 139, 155, 190, 209,
        220
    3-5   196
    4   212
    18-26   274
    19   250
    20   140, 193
    23   174
    24   218
    27   140, 193
    28   184, 214, 251
3: 1   192
    2   73, 139, 192, 247, 250,
        252
    3   176
    4-9   127
    4   126
    6   138
    7   219
    8   176
    9,10   195
    11   212
    16-18   212

    21,22   197
    23   218
4: 1-3   274
    1   193, 194, 195, 207
    6   207
    8   137, 154
    10   209
    13   140, 193, 248
    14   247
    15   196, 218, 247
    16   58, 137, 154
5: 6   248
    7   174, 207, 218, 246, 248
    9   247
    11,12   107, 155, 176
    14   192, 197
    16   219
    20   137, 174, 189, 207

2 John
    6   212, 227
    7-9   247
    8,9   194
    9-11   132
    10,11   143

3 John
    5-8   141
    8-10   156

Jude
    3   207, 268
    6   109, 138, 141, 209
    7   109, 141
    14   158, 215, 252
    15   215
    20   140, 156
    22,23   196
    24   155, 227
    25   189

Revelation
1: 3   215
    4,5,   207
    6   223, 251
    7   126, 128, 139, 158, 198,
        199, 229
    8   139, 214
    9   251
    10   108, 129, 181, 213, 225,
        248, 251
    13-16   247
    18   252
2:    250
    2   156
    7   180
    14   132
    20   132
3: 11   214, 215, 252
    20   249
4: 6   207
    8   174, 207
    9   189
    10   189

INDEXES

	11 126, 207	19:	11-14 158	21:	251
5:	9-14 247		15-19 158		1 199
	9 156		16 214, 247		1 to 22:5 249
	10 156, 184, 251		20 209		1-5 74, 276
6:	9,10 228	20:	1 to 22:13 252		2 195, 250
7:	9 195, 228		1-3 209		3 230, 250
	14 195, 228		2 175		4 73, 199
10:	6 208		4-6 141		7 230
11:	15 251		4 158, 184		8 141, 198, 230
12:	9 138, 208		5 158		9-27 75
	10 209, 247		7-15 158	22:	1,2 75
	11 247		10-15 138, 184		3-5 74, 230
13:	72		10 199, 209		7 215
	8 247		11 to 21:8 73		11 260
14:	10 230		11-15 109, 141, 155, 199		12 215
	11 184, 230		12 229		15 198
	13 198		13 229		17 248, 252
15:	4 154, 189		14 73		18 126, 207
	11 209		15 126, 230		19 207
18:	21-24 73		18 173		20 208, 215

Index 2: Names

Adorian, Constantin 216
Alexandre, Manuel 121
Alf, Gottfried 171
American Baptists 95, 118, 122
American Baptist Missionary Union 94
Anabaptists 19, 22, 185, 200, 216
Andru, H. 124
Anglican Church 31

Baptists, Conservative 121
    General 32, 41
    Particular 32, 41
    New Connection 33, 34
    Southern 21, 78, 95, 116, 118, 119, 121, 145, 203, 235, 236, 243, 244, 245
Baptist World Alliance 18, 26, 49, 97, 116, 152, 186, 203, 235
Bassett, T. M. 47
Bereans 37
Bethlen, Gabor Duke 185
Bichkov, A. 154
Bickel, P. 55
Blocher, Arthur 135
Bousios, Marcus 145
Brethren 22, 48, 56, 153
British Council of Churches 33
British and Foreign Bible Society 152, 185, 200, 202, 217, 231
British Missionary Society 115
Buchow 56
Buhler, F. M. 136
Bunaciu, I. 218
Burns, N. 145

Carey, W. 33
Carlo, Alberto 115
Carson, Alexander 48
Claas, Gerhard 17, 57
Clark, Edward 115
Clifford, John 33
Clough, John 55
Cocar, Rodica T. 218
Cocorda, O. 116
Congregational Church 33
Cromwell 37, 48

Damann, Rolf 57
David, R. 42
Darby, J. N. 48, 82
Deliakov, I. 150
Deminger, Sigfrid 104
Doycheff, P. 231
Dubarry, R. 135

Eidberg, Peder A. 96, 256
European Baptist Convention 235, 245
European Baptist Federation 26, 49, 97, 235
Evangelical Alliance 34
Evangelical Association of French Speaking Baptist Churches 135

Evans, T. 41

Feisser, Johannes E. 81, 82
Fischer, Andreas 185
Forsell, D. 99
Free Church Council 33
Fuller, Andrew 33, 44, 48

Gerzsenyi, László 199
Gheorgita, Nicolae 230
Glasites 37
Guyot, Georges 135, 136

Hacker, Franz 57
Haldane Brothers 37, 48, 53, 122
Hall, Robert 33
Hansson, O. B. 95
Hatcher, W. L. 121
Heikel, Henric 110
Hejdenberg, P. F. 99
Helwys, Thomas 31
Hirnböck, August 57
Hoffman, J. 136
Hopper, J. D. 204
Horn, J. 84
Hübert, Gottfried 95
Huguenots 93
Hussites 200
Hylleberg, B. 94
Hymander, John 105

Ivanov-Klyshnikov, V. V. 149

Jacob, Luthrop Jessey 32
James I 31
Jews 118, 172
John, Rhys M. 43
Jones, Joseph 120
Joseph II 79, 200

Kahle, Wilhelm 154
Kalweit, M. K. 149, 150
Karev, Alexandre 153, 166
Kargel, Johann 149, 153, 164
Kircun, Aleksander Jr. 173, 184
Kiss, Emil 188, 199
Kisszebeni, John 185
Kloekers, H. Z. 84
Klundt, J. 231
Knapp, William 118
Knappe, A. 200
Köbner, Julius 54, 56, 81, 82, 93, 94, 100, 153, 161
Koester, Arnold 79, 80
Kornya, Mihaly 186, 217
Kothavnori, Anneli 109
Krinchkov, G. K. 168

Lagergren, David 100
Lajo, J. 217
Landel, W. Kemme 115

INDEXES

Lange, Martin 80
Lehmann, Gottfried W. 54, 162
Lehmann, Josef 55
Lehotsky, Ruth 215
Lewis, T. 44
Liebig, August 202, 216
Liefde, de Jan 82
Luckey, H. 56
Lumpkin, W. L. 14, 19, 36, 76
Lund, E. 118
Lundberg, Esaias 105
Luther, Martin 185

MacGothlin, W. J. 14, 21, 23
MacLaren, A. 18, 33
MacLean, A. 43
Mac Rae, A. 39
Machado, Eduardo 121
Macher, Johann 188, 199
Maier, Friedrich 77
Maria Theresia 185, 216
Marjaren, Antti 106, 109
Mauricio, Antonio 120
Meeris, A. 200
Meister, Claus 57
Mennonites 22, 31, 82, 152, 153
Methodism 43, 53
Meyer, Heinrich 185, 186, 202, 217
Miles, J. 41
Millard, Edward 79
Möllersvärd, C. J. 110
Moody, D. L. 153
Moore, John Allen 203
Mønster, Peter Christian 93, 94
Murray, D. 39

Neui, Peter J. 84
Nicolaus II 151
Nilsson, F. O. 99
Niskanen, Markku 106
Novak, Antal 185, 186
Novotny, Henry 201

Olin, Leif 111
Oliveira, J. J. de 120
Oncken, J. G. 16, 19, 23, 53, 54, 77, 79, 93, 99, 150-153, 160, 202, 216
Ongman, John 103
Ortie, S. 204
Orthodox Church 110, 145, 149, 203, 217, 231

Paschetto, E. L. 116
Pashkov, V. A. 151
Pavlov, V. G. 149, 150, 152, 165
Payne, E. A. 34, 35, 36, 278
Pego, Abel and Isabel 121
Pentecostals 56, 103, 152, 153
Petrick, P. E. 231
Piasecki, Marcin 184
Pobjedonoszev, K. P. 151
Pohl, Adolf 57
Powell, V. 41
Presbyterians 32
Prochanov, I. S. 151, 152, 153, 163
Prokofiev, A. F. 168

Pyt, Henri 122

Quakers 41

Ramseyer, A. 124
Rausenbusch, E. 55
Rebane, Ants 154
Reformed Church 20, 77, 81, 86, 203
Reiling, Jannes 87, 89
Reiling, Roelof 81
Religion in Communist Dominated Areas 266
Richards, W. 43
Robinson, R. 43
Roman Catholicism 77, 79, 86, 115, 118, 171, 172, 200, 202
Ross, Ulrike 215
Rossi, M. 116
Rostan, Casimir 122
Rottmayer, J. 185
Rudén, E. 102
Rymker, Frederik L. 95

Saillens, R. 135
Sauer, Erich 56
Sawatsky, W. 154, 170
Scharschmidt, K. 185, 216
Scheve, Albert 54
Scheve, Eduard 55
Schoorens, Angela and Lieven 136
Schroeder, G. W. 99
Schröter, Kristof 185
Schütz, Eduard 57
Sears, Barnas 53
Sinclair, W. 37
Smith, Tor 111
Smyth, John 31
Sousa, Teixera de 120
Spurgeon, Charles, 22, 34, 55, 120
Steeves, P. D. 154, 170
Steely, John 75
Stundists 150

Taborg, Franz 202
Tasca, Radu 216
Taylor, G. B. 115
Taylor, Zacharia C. 120
Thomas, J. 41
Thomas, W. 42
Toth, Mihaly 186
Tsymbal, E. 150
Turoci, Josip 203

Underhill, E. B. 14
Üxküll, von W. R. A. 151

Vacek, Vinco 203
Vincent 135
Vins, Georgi P. 168, 170
Vogel, Maria 158
Voronin, N. I. 149, 150

Wagner, Günter 57
Waldenses 115
Waldgrave, G. A. W. 151
Wall, James 115

Wiberg, Anders 99, 100, 106
Wieser, Emmanual 80
Willard, Erasmus 124
Williams, James 215
Willmarth, Isaac 122
World Council of Churches 33, 39, 86

Woyka, J. 185

Young, Kate and Reginald 120

Zhidkov, 1. I. 167